Irish O'Malley

... & the Ozark Mountain Boys

By R. D. Morgan

NEW
FORUMS
Stillwater, Oklahoma
U.S.A.

This book may be ordered in bulk quantities at discount from New Forums Press, Inc., P.O. Box 876, Stillwater, OK 74076 [Federal I.D. No. 73 1123239]. Printed in the United States of America.

International Standard Book Number 10: 1-58107-211-2
International Standard Book Number 10: 978-1-581072-11-2

On the Cover

Top: Wanted poster for Blackie Doyle; *Bottom Left:* Irish O'Malley; *Bottom:* Walter O'Malley.

Contents

All photos are from the author's private collection unless noted.

Introduction

The Irish O'Malley Gang represented the final install-
ment of America's great 1930s depression-era "Super Gangs"
following in the footsteps of both the John Dillinger and "Ma"
Barker/Karpis Gangs. The final version of the outlaw band
was the result of the merging of two separate and unique criminal enterprises, one deriving from a rural environment, the
second urban in nature. Their story involved a small cadre of
hard-nosed underworld hoodlums joined by an army of thrill-
starved gangster molls and criminal associates, which eventually evolved into a loosely-knit organization. It's members
drifted across the Midwest committing a national headline
grabbing kidnapping and several brutal murders as well as
looting a dozen banks.

Law enforcement dubbed the lawless band the most highly
disciplined and efficient of the day. Their bank raids were well-
planned and conducted in precise clockwork fashion. Not until the final months of the group's existence did investigators,
including J. Edger Hoover's vaunted G-Men, connect the dots
and conclude a single group initially dubbed "The Midwest
Bank Robbers" was behind the epidemic of bank heists. On
realizing this fact, Hoover's boys began tracking the group
like the hound and the hare. But, track them they did and with
deadly efficiency.

During the gang's heyday its members operated in a shadowy paranoid community of desperate souls, seeking sanctuary in run down inner-city flophouses, the homes of sympathetic friends and relatives or isolated rural tourist courts, existing on roadhouse slop and rarely sleeping in the same bed two nights in a row. If captured many turned informant under brutal questioning techniques while some went down in a blood-soaked blaze of glory.

Members of this evil brotherhood were either hard luck characters forced off the farm by the agriculture crash, crowded by tough times into the illegal liquor business before finally swapping the plow for a six-gun, while others were big city ethnic slum dwellers trained from childhood to circumvent the law, guided by a ruthless street-wise philosophy of survival by any means at hand. Nearly all were ex-cons, doing time in various gladiator-styled youth reformatories before graduating to the tax-funded school of crime, the state penitentiary. In the end, not a single member or associate of the group escaped justice. Although some paid for their sins with their lives, many were sent to Alcatraz, the gulag of American prisons.

This thrilling narrative is presented in straightforward chronological order. The story is a complex one involving a host of characters and a myriad of events stretching across many states over a lengthy period. Unlike the other major organized criminal groups of the 1930s, the O'Malley Gang had a habit of coming together to commit a major robbery, then split to the four winds after the heist was complete. The members would then, singularly or in groups of two or three, fan out and commit lesser crimes before once again connecting with their lawless brethren in order to pull off another substantial hijacking.

Since I've tried to report on and each and every one of the gang's deprivations, both big and small, as well as give a biographical sketch of all the many members of the O'Malley combination, the reader must remain attentive throughout this account in order to grasp the scope and magnitude of the many crimes and activities of distinct American criminal phenomena.

Acknowledgments

A big to thanks to Brian Beerman, Al Grooms, George Franklin, James Knight, Robert Bates, John Strange, Jared Barker, Richard Jones, Nancy McDaniel, Raymond Overall, Rick "Maddog" Mattix, George Miller, Elliott Gordon, Robert Winters, Michael Webb, Marisa Boone, Pam Tippet, Mike Koch, Lenora Space, Joe Moore, Calvin Sheets, Mary Pease, Audrae Turner Mathis, Mary Turner and the late Ken Butler for sharing information concerning the O'Malley Gang. I also wish to express my gratitude to all those descendents of "Dapper Dan" Heady, Robert 'Major' Taylor, Roy Mogridge, Jack Miller, Virgil 'Red' Melton, and Marsh Corgan who shared information, family stories, photos, and documents with a nosy and sometimes bothersome writer in his efforts to track down the story.

About the Author

R. D. Morgan is the author of six non-fiction books dealing with early day Oklahoma lawmen and outlaws. He has also written numerous articles for Oklahoma newspapers and historical magazines on the subject.

Morgan spent his childhood in the East Texas oil patch country and his teen years living in a small Iowa farming community. Upon graduation from high school, he knocked around a year or so working construction before entering the U.S. Army where he served as a law enforcement officer. After his military career, he attended the College of the Ozarks before being employed as an electrician and maintenance supervisor for many years in Missouri and Arkansas. On retirement, he moved to Oklahoma to fulfill his lifelong desire to commit his energies full-time into writing and researching depression era American history. Morgan developed a passion for the subject as a teenager listening to his Grandfathers tales of life and culture in Middle America during the 1920s and 1930s. Morgan and his wife Naomi currently reside in Haskell, Oklahoma.

Dedicated to the memory of Rick Mattix and Bill Guy, pioneer Oklahoma newspaperman.

"Write me another one of them shoot-em-ups."

Chapter 1
The Birth of a Criminal Enterprise

According to various prison and other criminal records Walter Riley, alias "Irish" O'Malley, was born in St. Louis, Missouri, on October 31, 1898, of Irish parentage and poor economic circumstances. His folks separated when he was a toddler, pawning him off on foster parents named Holland who gave him their name. By all accounts Walter lived a typical childhood for the times. His foster father, William Holland, an emigrant from Great Britain, was a brickyard foreman and a decent provider. After completing the ninth grade the lad dropped out of school finding employment as an apprentice clerk for the giant Swift Meat Packing Company.

In a burst of patriotic fever, Walter enlisted as a private in Co. B 136th Infantry Missouri National Guard at St. Louis in 1916. The unit was mobilized the following year shortly after America declared war on Germany. On Christmas Eve 1917, the youth, suffering from a case of holiday blues, deserted his post while standing guard. Within weeks of his departure, Walter arrived in Toronto where he joined the Canadian Army under a false name and eventually made his way overseas where he claimed he saw action on the European killing fields. After returning to the states, Walter turned himself into the military authorities at Jefferson Barracks where he was tossed in the brig on a charge of desertion and given a Bad Conduct discharge on October 26, 1919.

Upon receiving his less than honorable discharge, O'Malley garnered employment at an area resort located in nearby Venice, Illinois, as a desk clerk. However, in an obvious case of "You can't keep them down on the farm once they've seen Gay Paree," the young veteran promptly tired of the mundane tasks assigned a clerk and began casting about for a career offering a bit more excitement and higher wages. His efforts in self-betterment led him directly into the field of marketing illicit spirits or in plain English; he became a "Bootlegger."

Ever since the passage of the Volstead Act in 1919, which outlawed the sale of alcoholic beverages on America's shores, there was a decent living to be made from the illegal sale of liquor. If a young entrepreneur had enough sand in his craw to enable him to put up with the bad hours, frequent arrests, and competitor's roughhouse ways, which might include dodging a bullet every now and again or being given a one-way ride to oblivion, he might just be a success....By all indications, Walter was up to the task.

As for his home life, it appears once he shed his uniform Walter made a stab at domestication, marrying a local gal in mid 1920. Apparently the pair was unable to work out the inevitable do's and don't of married life and with Walter working such odd hours while using the couples happy home as a warehouse for his "goods," the woman of the house filed and was

"Irish" O'Malley

granted a divorce in early 1923 on grounds of incompatibility. In regards to other family connections, it seems the youth's only contact with relatives after reaching adulthood was an occasional visit with his married foster sister living in Nameoki, Illinois, where she operated a small cafe.

Walter O'Malley

Over the next decade, Walter, now going by the alias of "Irish" O'Malley, evolved into an incorrigible degenerate career criminal. His illicit actions led to his being arrested and incarcerated several times on charges of violation of the Volstead Act, larceny, and auto theft. During this time frame he apparently made his headquarters in East St. Louis, Illinois, running liquor to destinations as far away as Kansas City for a massive bootlegging operation ran by the notorious Shelton brothers, Earl, Carl, and Bernie.

Records indicate Walter was also heavily involved with various members of the notorious "Egan's Rats Gang" of St. Louis during the early 1920s. Headquartered in the city's Irish dominated slums, the "Rats" were originally organized just after the turn of the century by saloon operator Thomas Egan to provide political muscle for State Senator Tom Kinney. On election day Egan's crew practiced strong-arm techniques, ballot box stuffing and the destruction of polling sites by fire-bombing. Over time the group moved beyond political shenanigans evolving into a tightly structured gangland enterprise involved in such illicit activities as gambling, bootlegging, murder-for-hire and armed robbery.

In the early twenties, the group was caught up in a lengthy feud with a rival mob dubbed the "Hogan Gang" in which numerous individuals were slain on both sides. Although the 'Rats' were broken as an organized gangland powerhouse by the late 1920s, former members continued to operate in the St. Louis underworld for decades to come.

Most certainly O'Malley's time with Egan's Rats assisted him greatly in his efforts to hone his criminal skills.

On June 20, 1921, Walter and five others robbed American Railway Express Company Messenger Alvin Powell of a payroll shipment consisting of $17,423.65 in Granite City, Illinois. The day after the heist, police arrested O'Malley, Clem Forrestal, Robert Riley, and James Traynor at Traynor's apartment in Granite City charging all three with the messenger job as well as the recent hijacking of a local diamond merchant named Edward Fox of $5,000 in precious stones. While all four men were reportedly armed with automatic pistols when arrested, none offered resistance. According to police reports, investigators uncovered several sticks of dynamite, a vast array of burglar and safe blowing tools, as well as two sawed-off shotguns during their search of the residence.

Walter O'Malley soon made bail and pulled a disappearing act. A warrant was quickly issued for his arrest for bond jumping. Both Forrestal and Traynor were eventually convicted of the Granite City heist and sentenced to lengthy terms at the state penitentiary at Joliet. Other suspects in the case were George "Mickey" O'Malley (*Claimed to be a relative of Walter O'Malley), as well as George "Maddog" Aye.

Panama, Illinois, Late 1921

On the morning of December 12, two large sedans filled with six white and two black men came to a halt in front of the State Bank of Panama located about fifty miles northeast of St. Louis. While a single individual remained at the wheel of each rig, two men entered the financial institution as two others took up positions at the front door. The third pair, armed with shotguns, strolled to an adjoining pool hall to keep watch on the patrons in order to assure that no one interfered in their pressing business. According to Banker E. A. Murray, one of the men (*Later identified as "Irish" O'Malley) approached him requesting change for a twenty-dollar bill. Murray added, "As I turned toward the cash drawer he and a second individual drew automatic pistols from their pockets and ordered me to lie on the floor. Then two others suddenly entered the lobby and began gathering all the money in sight."

The bandits harvested some $19,000 in cash along with $12,000 in negotiable bonds before departing. Just as the hijackers were exiting the bank heading for the getaway cars, an overly curious local resident identified as Jack Williams, boldly approached the scene on foot. Suddenly, one of the robbers, mistaking him for an officer, turned and shot him in the mouth for his troubles. Luckily, the missile merely provided Williams some free dental work as well as slicing off his upper lip instead of delivering a deadly blow.

The robbers made a clean getaway. The investigation into the heist was stymied until detectives arrested an unnamed suspect who spilled the beans on his comrades in crime. The individual named Walter O'Malley as being one of the hijackers. He further charged Bond County Sheriff John W. Wilson along with Constable Ben Battleson as being in on the heist providing protection for a $1200 cut of the proceeds. State cops promptly picked up both officers, provoking a rather embarrassing incident for all involved. To his great consternation, Battleson was apprehended on a Sunday morning while attending church. He was callously dragged off the front pew and down the aisle of the church kicking and screaming by three burley troopers.

Several days after the Panama robbery, five men using a Haynes automobile for transportation, hijacked the State Bank of Iuka, Illinois, for $15,000 in cash and liberty bonds. The bandits abandoned their getaway car at the edge of town taking to the woods on foot. A fifty-man posse, accompanied by bloodhounds, promptly converged on the area where the thieves had entered the timber. Although the posse searched through the night, they failed to track down their quarry.

The authorities suspected Walter O'Malley as being one of the escaping Iuka robbery suspects.

On January 28, 1922, O'Malley was arrested in Sarpy County, Nebraska, on a charge of vagrancy and extradited back to Illinois to face the music. Although Walter had been officially charged with a plethora of crimes, the authorities decided their strongest case against him concerned the hijacking of the Panama bank.

A week after his capture, O'Malley, and his co-defendants, ex-lawmen Wilson and Battleson, pled not guilty in open court and chose a trial by a jury. On the morning of April 29, after deliberating a mere forty minutes, the jury found all three guilty of armed robbery. The following day Walter was sentenced to a term of one to twenty years imprisonment at the Southern Illinois Penitentiary located in Menard, hard on the banks of the Mississippi River.

Shortly after his arrival at the facility as convict # 5461, Walter was overcome by a severe case of jailhouse fever and swiftly transferred down the road to the Chester State Hospital for the Criminally Insane where he was diagnosed with dementia praecox. Walter was described by prison documents as White, Catholic, 5'7", 150 lbs, medium build, chestnut hair, hazel colored eyes, a jutting jaw, with two bullet scars in the fleshy part of his left leg between the foot and the knee. He was also depicted as high-strung and cunning with an IQ of 117. Another report characterized him as cool and collected but rather restless in nature, agreeable at times but likely desperate when cornered. Later statements made to a prison psychiatrist show him to be an unrepentant soul who stated, "I've only robbed rich men and insurance companies who can stand the loss."

Meanwhile, back in the free world, the final chapter concerning the Granite City robbery was being written. In the early morning hours of July 22, 1922, a posse, acting on a tip, raided James Traynor's Granite City apartment, located at the Newman Hotel on Nineteenth and "C" Streets, which was occupied by his wife, Bernice, and several roughly dressed individuals. The man of the house was absent from the premises currently serving a ten-year sentence for the aforementioned heist. The officers were met by a wall of gunfire. In the ensuing melee, Deputy Sheriff Patrick Nalty was fatally wounded taking four slugs to the torso while City Policeman Ross Johnson barely survived three bullets to the chest and arms.

At the conclusion of a running gun battle, which spilled into the street in front of the hotel, three gunmen escaped the scene in a Marmon automobile. A "Be On the Lookout" bulletin was swiftly issued to area police departments concerning the fleeing gunsels. St. Louis authorities quickly posted officers armed with riot shotguns on the Missouri side of all three bridges spanning the Mississippi River.

An hour and a half after the gunfight, a party of St. Louis detectives arrested three subjects identified as George Ayers, "Mickey" O'Malley, and James 'Sticky' Hennessey sitting in a parked bullet-riddled Marmon, which fit the description of the vehicle used in the Illinois shootout. Fortunately for prosecutors, a theatre employee named C. C. Cravens had witnessed the Newman Hotel shootout and aftermath from his position in front of the box-office. Cravens bravely stood up in open court and positively identified both Ayers and O'Malley as two of the gunman involved in the deadly gunbattle. Owing greatly to Craven's testimony, Mickey O'Malley and Ayers were eventually convicted and sentenced to life for the murder of Deputy Nalty. Hennessey, who was a full-fledged member of Egan's Rats, was held for his suspected participation in the July 10 robbery of the Tri-State Bank in Madison, Illinois. Mrs. Traynor was charged with harboring but later acquitted. Even though the two cop-killers, Ayers and O'Malley, were implicated in the Granite City heist, the prosecutor declined to pursue the matter since the pair was already under life sentences. Incidentally, just days after giving his damning testimony in the case against the two cop-killers, eyewitness C. C. Craven was dragged into a dark alley, robbed and severely beaten by a pair of thugs who cursed him for testifying against their pals.

A year into "Irish" O'Malley's incarceration at the mental institution he and forty other inmates busted out of the facility, armed with knives and clubs, stabbing one guard and severely pummeling two others in the process. Other casualties in the event were Dr. Frank Stubblefield, the medical superintendent, who suffered a fractured arm and a Negro patient named William Jackson who was stabbed to death by a fellow inmate.

According to witnesses, O'Malley was the ringleader of the mass exodus. Authorities suspected he had gained possession of a long bladed knife through his ex-wife, who had visited him the day before the breakout. The majority of the inmates, including O'Malley, were captured in a wooded area located near the hospital a few hours into the insurrection.

According to prison records, Walter spent nearly half of his remaining time at the facility held in solitary confinement due to his being branded a constant source of inmate unrest and presenting a severe security risk to hospital staff. Officers further described him as an "Incorrigible misfit with severe criminal tendencies." When not locked in a windowless 8'X 8' soundproof cell, it seems he spent his time reading classic books checked out from the prison library in an effort to improve his vocabulary.

Over time O'Malley evolved into a pseudo-intellectual, fancying himself a bit of a swell, a cut above the masses, assuming the personality and mannerisms of the "Gatsby" character from F. Scott Fitzgerald's classic tale concerning a mysterious sophisticated rumrunner living on a plush Long Island estate. For the remainder of his life, the neurotic outlaw would play this fantasy to the hilt.

On November 18, 1929, he was paroled into the custody of Granite City barkeep George Hanlon.

While O'Malley had entered the penitentiary at the height of the "Roaring Twenties," a time of flappers, flag-pole sitters, speakeasies, unseemly Wall Street profits , and the advent of the Jazz age, the good times were about to come to a screeching halt. Just five days before O'Malley's release from incarceration, the New York Stock Market crashed. The event, known as "Black Tuesday," marked the loss of $30 billion by investors. The nation's economy would soon become a basket case. Over the next few years, unemployment would hit 30% in many parts of the country. The era would be dubbed, "The Great Depression," and the decade, "The Dirty Thirties." The hard times were accompanied by a series of severe droughts, which caused the soil of Midwest farms to dry up and blow away. The western sections of Kansas, Oklahoma, Texas, and the Dakotas would be christened "The Dust Bowl."

According to government figures, the most alarming statistic to rise measurably during the coming decade, excepting the unemployment rate, was the crime rate. While the average citizen simply sat back and endured the economic hardships, tightening their belts and doing without luxuries, there soon appeared a certain class of persons living in America's underbelly that reacted to the crisis in an opposing manner. They turned to crime. "Irish" O'Malley was certainly among the latter.

After his release from prison, Walter lived several months with his foster sister in Nameoki, Illinois, while making weekly visits to St. Louis where he placed himself under a doctor's care due to a hereditary heart valve impairment, which would plague him the rest of his days. He also made several stabs at collecting a Veteran's pension concerning his disability but failed to qualify for compensation due to his bad conduct discharge from the service. Failing that, the wily thug took his act on the road spending the next few years casting about the Midwest operating con games.

On one occasion, O'Malley was arrested in Hastings, Nebraska, and charged with larceny. Soon afterwards he was apprehended in the capital city of Lincoln where the authorities there described him as a bunco-artist. In 1931, he spent the summer tending bar for his pal Henry Murdock, the owner of the notorious Mounds Club located in Madison, Illinois. The place simply reeked with sin offering it's patrons a collage of services including high-stakes gambling, ladies-for-hire and illicit liquor the drink.

Kansas City, Missouri - January 1932

After a few months of serving watered down bathtub gin to the patrons at the Mounds Club, O'Malley relocated to Kansas City ingraining himself into the city's underworld, making his headquarters at the Sportsman's Club, which was ran by a mobbed-up narcotics trafficker dubbed "Needles" LaCapra.

Walter also spent considerable time pitching dice and playing the pasteboards at either Nell Howard's Club located on 15th Street or Abe Spillman's Place on Troost Avenue, as well as Johnny Baker's Oasis Club, and the Armour Inn, a gangland connected establishment situated in the industrial West Bottoms.

At the time of O'Malley's arrival in Kansas City the town was firmly under the firm guiding hand of political "Boss" Tom Pendergast. Little of any importance took place in the city of nearly 400,000 without the blessing of Pendergast, whether it be a street paving job, the hiring of a beat cop, or the letting of profitable city construction contracts. Over the years, the Pendergast machine had also established its long tentacles into the local underworld, becoming political allies with mob boss Johnny Lazia, who provided muscle at election time and terrorized the machine's political enemies into submission.

While folks in the surrounding areas suffered terribly from the effects of the ongoing economic depression, Kansas City somehow managed to keep its head above water. When the three mainstays of town's economy, meatpacking, railroads, and flourmills began to falter, the Pendergast machine managed to soften the blow somewhat for a multitude of Kansas City citizens by employing tens of thousands of residents in ongoing public construction projects…. Need a job, running low on groceries, coal to keep your family warm in the winter? See the "Boss." His benevolent hand stretched out to anyone and everyone as long as they remembered his name come election time.

Simply said, under the Pendergast machine, "Tom's Town" was considered wide-open. The police department was filled from the bottom up with Pendergast appointments. Fugitives were provided sanctuary within the confines of the city limits, for a price. It was said whatever crime existed in the area was either condoned by "Boss Tom" or efficiently rubbed out.

Even during prohibition, hundreds of bars, each supplied with a bevy of slot machines and serving illegal liquor, operated unimpeded in full view throughout the city under the protection of the machine. Brothels and gambling houses also operated openly as long as they rendered unto Caesar. When the sun went down the booze flowed like water, the swinging sounds of Kansas City Jazz spilled into the streets from countless chic nightclubs like the Pla-Mor Ballroom and the El Torrean Club featuring trendy musical acts like the Count Basie and Duke Ellington Orchestras. For a seasoned, arch-criminal like O'Malley, well schooled in the tradition of underworld graft, the big berg acted as an ideal base of operations as well as a sanctuary from the law.

After making his appearance in Kansas City, another of one of O'Malley's many hangouts was a seedy roadhouse named the Schlitz Club located in nearby St. Joseph, a town most notably known as the site where badman Jesse James was plugged in the back by the, "The dirty little coward who shot Mr. Howard." (Bob Ford). The joint was managed by Lulu Hickey and her second husband. It offered every transgression in the book from prostitution, cheap booze, and a crap game in the back room....Walter must have felt right at home.

The formidable Mrs. Hickey was locally known as the Granddame of the St. Jo underworld. She was described as stoutly built, equipped with shocking red flowing hair, pierc-

Clarence Sparger

ing sky-blue eyes, and forever wearing thick coke-bottle glasses. She had an only son from her first marriage named Clarence Leroy Vaughn. In young Clarence, O'Malley would discover a kindred soul and obedient criminal associate .

Recognized in gangland and police circles under his alias, "Bonnie" Sparger (*Sometimes spelled Spargur), Clarence was physically tall, rangy, and intellectually dull. His most noticeable physical peculiarity was his protruding Adams apple that bobbed up and down like a pinball when excited. He was a dedicated lifelong criminal, having been in trouble with the law since he was in three-cornered pants, arrested a dozen or more times on charges of burglary, larceny, and highway robbery.

Although Clarence sported a world-class police record, he matched that record with an uncanny ability to wiggle out of a tight spot. It was said his staying out of jail had less to do with luck and more to do with the fact his mother had serious connections with the local powers to be. In fact, her first cousin was married to St. Jo's chief of police, Charles Enos. Apparently, numerous area politicians and law enforcement officers made liberal use of Lulu's roadhouse in order to garner their supply of illicit spirits and be serviced by her girls. Others owed the establishment hefty gambling debts thus putting them in hock to the chunky damsel.

Sparger's first arrest as an adult came in 1923 when he faced a charge of burglary. The charges were eventually dropped. The following year the youth was locked up on a charge dropped. The following year the youth was locked up on a charge of petty larceny. Again charges were dropped. Three charge of burglarizing a store in Mt. Moriah for $1500 worth of merchandise. On November 29, 1924 he was held for burglary of a general store in rural Barnard for $2500 in goods. On both occasions the hood was able to gain his freedom through a cash bond. The following year Clarence was sentenced to a six-month hitch to be served in the Buchanan County Jail for grand larceny.

Although Clarence married seventeen-year-old Juanita Noah in 1926, marital bliss didn't slow down his criminal tendencies a bit. In early 1928, Sparger along with two of his crime partners, Ted Rogers and Louis Miller, were arrested in a massive police sweep in response to the bloody robbery of the bank of Lamar, Colorado, where four innocent victims were slaughtered during the actual heist and immediate aftermath. The trio was later released when it was ascertained the notorious Fleagle brothers, Jake and Ralph, were responsible the heist.

In June 1928 the misdirected lad was picked-up for suspicion of robbing a Kansas City clothing store at gunpoint. He was questioned and released. A few months later Sparger was charged and tried for highway robbery but a jury failed to convict him. Another highway robbery charge was lodged against him in early 1929 but the chief witness not only failed to show up at the trial but permanently vanished from the face of the earth. The lead investigator in the case expressed the opinion Sparger and his pals had taken the man on a one-way-ride straight to the Pearly Gates.

On the morning of August 28, 1929, the spindly hood along with twenty-three-year-old Charles Burke was arrested and held for their suspected participation in the robbery of several area financial institutions including the Traders Bank of St. Joseph as well as the Quindaro Bank of Kansas City, Kansas. According to detectives the duo was believed to have also been involved in the hijacking of a dozen filling stations in the past few months as well. Although the pair was vigorously questioned authorities were eventually forced to release them due to lack of evidence.

Sparger's luck finally ran out in 1930 when he and George Neff were arrested on the streets of downtown KC for being in possession of a stolen vehicle. When officers searched the car, they discovered $850 in Liberty bonds, which had been stolen in a recent hold-up taking place in Beatrice, Nebraska. Although the pair was held and questioned concerning their suspected participation in the Nebraska heist, neither was officially charged with the crime.

Missouri officials were not so forgiving; they charged and eventually convicted Clarence of Grand Larceny (Auto theft) and sentenced him to three years at the Missouri State Penitentiary in Jefferson City. Paroled in November 1, 1932, Sparger made a bee-line back to St. Jo where he made the acquaintance of Walter O'Malley at his mother's gin-joint. The duo formed a partnership and traveled to East St. Louis, Illinois, where they spent several months knocking off various illegal high-stakes poker games. Their roommate, criminal ac-

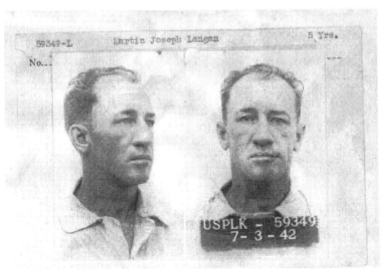

John Langan

complice and likely sex-toy at the time was Vivian Chase, a well-known gangster moll.

In mid-March 1933, the pair, feeling things were getting a bit dicey in the East St. Louis area, returned to St Jo where they split company, Sparger quickly joined up with fellow area mobster Johnny Langan pulling off a few nighttime burglaries in the Kansas City area. Unlike Sparger, Langan, described as a tough "Mick" equipped with an overly aggressive personality, had a relatively short police record, which included several juvenile crimes, a couple of liquor violations during the 1920s, an incident involving an assault and an arrest in 1930 for suspicion of auto theft. Born and raised in Kansas City, Kansas, Langan was the son of a successful butcher of Irish descent. After graduating from high school he attended a two year business course. His business training led to his being hired as a clerk at the Drovers Bank in Kansas City, a job he held for several years until establishing his own downtown café and candy confectionary. In the latter 1920s the budding young businessman became entangled in the area bootlegging trade. Naturally his illegal liquor activities led to his involvement with numerous unsavory individuals.

In 1930 Langan sold his business and took a job working days pressing pants at a local dry-cleaning establishment while employed evenings as a bouncer at various Kansas City nightclubs where he soon garnered a reputation as an expert "Cooler" due to his expertise with a blackjack and brass-knucks. The same year he married Margaret Cooper. The couple was soon blessed with the birth of a son. In 1931-32 Langan was twice picked up and questioned on suspicion of burglary.

As of late Langan had gotten into the odd habit of not going anywhere without his prize English Bulldog sitting next to him in the front seat of the car. A hunting enthusiast and self-admitted gun-nut, the youthful hoodlum was also known as a crack shot especially with his weapon of choice, a Government Model 1911 Colt .45 semi-automatic pistol. Although he maintained the appearance of a happily married man Langan had a reputation as a notorious womanizer. FBI reports state the thug was observed visiting various Kansas City whorehouses while simultaneously engaged in an adulterous affair with a woman he kept in a Springfield, Missouri, apartment.

In early April 1933, Clarence Sparger and his wife were out making the rounds of local speakeasies with another couple when he was involved in a drunken altercation with a hoodlum named Virgil Dixon, which resulted in his receiving three .45 caliber rounds to the torso. When his wife demanded the gunman cease firing the shooter turned to her stating, "Well, I'll give you some too, sister," before putting a round through her left breast. Miraculously, both victims survived. The assailant escaped on foot into the night. When interviewed by police at the hospital Sparger refused to make an official statement, saying, "I'll handle this myself."

Investigators suspected the shooting had its roots in the inequitable splitting of the proceeds from a recent armed robbery. Sparger spent the next few months recuperating from his wounds. In December he and Johnny Langan were arrested on a charge of shamelessly burglarizing the coffers of the First Presbyterian Church of Kansas City, Kansas, of nearly $800. Both men posted a $2000 security but immediately jumped bond fleeing to parts unknown. Warrants were issued in Wyandotte County for both men's arrest for failure to appear.

After Sparger and O'Malley went their separate ways O'Malley became involved with a notorious Kansas City burglary/hijacking/gambling ring whose membership included such gangland luminaries as Dave Sherman and Lloyd 'Blackie" Doyle, alias "Little Charlie." The group made it's headquarters at the "Three Little Pigs" saloon, located just outside the Kansas City municipal limits. The honky-tonk featured sawdust and blood covered floors, painted ladies for hire, gambling and a swift bump on the head for sore losers.

Sherman, whose parents were Orthodox Jews , was raised in a small KC shul surrounded by black slums located just north of the downtown area. His father, Peter, was a street peddler who had emigrated to America from Romania in 1902. Young Dave grew up surrounded by poverty, disadvantaged and uneducated. He quit school in the 5th grade opting for a career as a petty criminal running with a pack of juvenile delinquents shoplifting and committing a host of minor burglaries as well as strong-arm heists.

After serving time at the Boonville Boys Reformatory, he stepped up to the major leagues, was convicted of armed robbery in 1922 and sentenced to five years at the Missouri State Penitentiary in Jefferson City. He was described by officials there as " Yiddish, height 5' 10", swarthy in complexion, with black hair and gray eyes." After his release in 1925 he evolved into a professional nighttime burglar or "Yeggman" as they were known in those days. Over the next few years, he was arrested and detained in such diverse locations as Tulsa, Oklahoma, and Seattle, Washington, for suspicion of burglary before being arrested in Los Angeles in 1928 on a similar charge. On that occasion he was convicted and sentenced to one to fifteen years at Folsom prison.

Sherman's partner, Blackie Doyle, was also a career criminal, rumored to have long been associated with the Egan's Rats in St. Louis. Little is known of his childhood or youth except he oftentimes told his associates he was born and raised in Kansas City. It was rumored he had known David Sherman since the pair were teens hustling on the mean streets.

According to FBI reports, Doyle was picked-up in St. Louis in 1926 for suspicion of robbery. The charge was eventually dismissed for lack of evidence. He was arrested in mid-1932 in Clayton, Missouri, for possession of liquor and turned over to St. Louis authorities on a charge of kidnapping and robbery. Once again, the charges were dropped and the hoodlum released from custody. In December of '32, the hooligan was nabbed in Overland, Missouri, for violating the town vagrancy law.

The owner of the Three Little Pigs saloon, Russell "Spike" Lane, born in Dewitt County Illinois on February 9, 1900, was a professional safe blower and drug addict with serious connections to Kansas City mob boss Johnny Lazia. He spent his leisure hours operating his gin-joint, which was rumored to be under the protection of the "Pendergast" machine.

Lane was the descendant of a prominent Illinois pioneer family whose members included a co-founder of the town of Lane. Another ancestor was one of the first sheriff's of Dewitt County. Russell's father operated a series of cafes in Clinton, Illinois, as well as in several mining camps in Colorado before finally coming to roost in Kansas City around 1918. Like his Grandfather and an older brother, "Spike" spoke with a stammer, often getting a bit tongue-tied when excited. Lane was also a long-time associate of David Sherman.

On April 3, 1933, six men and a woman successfully looted the First National Bank of Leavenworth, Kansas, of $5000. A few hours after the heist, the bandits, riding in two automobiles, ran into a roadblock located just outside of Kansas City, Kansas, manned by a half-dozen Wyandotte County deputies and local officers sporting automatic weapons. A gunfight ensued in which one of the robbers, Louis Shorter, was killed, his body filled with fourteen heavy caliber slugs. Four of his companions, Charles Muller, Joe Caruso, Joe Porello, and Tony Loscalzo were all wounded and captured. The unidentified woman driver and a sixth man sped away from the scene in the second car successfully evading the blockade with the loot in hand.

In the days following the failed, blood-soaked heist an underworld informant came forward telling Department of Justice agents the names of the missing pair. Furthermore the snitch claimed Irish O'Malley had planned the heist and both O'Malley and a man named Doyle were supposed to participate in the robbery but had pulled out at the last moment.

Just days after the bloody Leavenworth bank heist O'Malley and 'Blackie' Doyle suddenly moved their operations back to the St. Louis area. For the next few months, the duo ran a gambling operation in the basement of the New Drovers Hotel located in downtown East St. Louis as well as participating in several burglaries with thirty-nine-year-old professional safecracker Percy M. Fitzgerald, alias "The Dice Box Kid."

According to the authorities the "Kid" had been arrested thirty-eight times since 1913. In 1925, he was sentenced to a five-year hitch for burglary in Tennessee. Shortly after his parole, he was nabbed for grand theft in Madison County, Illinois, and placed in the county jail to await trial. Fitzgerald promptly escaped from the facility by picking the lock on the cell door but the slippery thief was nabbed by the cops a few months later in Washington DC, in possession of burglar tools. When it became known the hoodlum had received the rubber-hose treatment during interrogation a sympathetic judge allowed him to post bail. Never one to look a gift horse in the mouth, the thug quickly departed the area. Naturally, he failed to give the court the courtesy of posting a change of address.

In early 1933 Fitzgerald drifted to St. Louis where the local cops suspected him of committing several burglaries. His most recent apprehension occurred in June of 1933 when he was held for suspicion of burglary in Edwardsville, Illinois. Due to a paperwork snafu

Vivian Chase

the brigand was released from custody without posting bond even though he was actively wanted in several locals. Fitzgerald's wife, "Big Lou", operated a whorehouse in nearby Madison.

For companionship, O'Malley linked up with thirty-year-old Norma Vaughn, alias Grace Noland, a divorcee and the manager of a cheap underworld connected boarding house located at 92A Clair Avenue in East St. Louis, Illinois. Norma had been arrested several times in the past for operating a "Bawdy" house. Also registered at the hotel at the time was Mrs. Vaughn's friend, Grace Hickey, whose real name was Vivian Chase.

Ms. Chase, an on again off again player in the life of Irish O'Malley and his ex-roomie, could best be described as a dedicated thrill-seeker with a history of associating with some of the country's most dangerous criminals. She arrived on the scene in March, rooming with Pearl Loge, a common street corner prostitute soon to be in the employee of Norma Vaughn.

Any attempt to discover Ms. Chase's roots amount to a murky affair. Throughout her short violent life, Vivian took great pains to hide her background, age, and birthplace from the authorities as well as her criminal companions. Some researchers suggest she was born Vivian Davis in Nebraska around 1905 and raised in and around Springfield, Missouri.

What is known is that sometime around 1921, young Vivian married or least shacked up with an ex-con named George Chase. Seems her lover was a bank robber by trade and according to which police report you believe he was either killed by the cops during a bank heist or died in a car wreck in Los Angeles a few years after the pair had taken their nuptials.

According to Kansas City Chief of Detectives Thomas Higgins, after her husband's death ,Vivian, evolved into a full-blown alcoholic. Impoverished and homeless she began working the streets, being picked-up several times in the "West

Bottoms" district on charges of petty larceny and prostitution. Long the meat packing center for the Midwest, the bottoms was an overcrowded, smelly, mud-soaked area crowded by a half-dozen giant slaughter houses as well as the Kansas City stockyards. The area around the plants was jam-packed with saloons, pool halls, and houses of ill-repute, their proprietors lying in wait to take their fair share of the meat-packer's wages.

One investigator described Vivian as, "Mannish in appearance, with her hair always tightly bobbed. Not pretty, but well built and tough as nails." Another said she was "Kinda horsey-looking." US Department of Justice records from 1933 describe Ms Chase as, age 24, weight 115 lbs., height 5'6", hair-brown, eyes- gray, completion-fair.

In 1925, Vivian hooked up with handsome Joplin born ex-con Charley Mayes (Alias Pighead Hardman). Mayes, along with his long-time crime partner, Lee Flournoy, were actively engaged at the time running illegal hooch from isolated stills located in the Ozark hinterlands to various liquor concerns such as the Osage Oil Patch located in Northeast Oklahoma, Omaha's liquor cartel, or the Kansas City "Bottoms," at the behest of Joplin based Whiskey Baron William "King" Creekmore. The pair was also connected to the "Tri-State Theft Ring," which operated throughout the massive Oklahoma-Kansas-Missouri mining district. Early in the pair's criminal career they fell under the influence of Joplin crime figure Stephen Decatur "Kate" Melton. According to FBI records, "Melton is believed to be a major crook having contacts with organized crime throughout the country."

On August 9, 1925, Flournoy, Mayes, and Vivian along with John Clark were arrested by Springfield, Missouri, detectives on vagrancy charges. While Mayes, Vivian, and Clark were released the following morning after spending the night in lockup, Flournoy was extradited to Nebraska to face charges stemming from his suspected participation in a 1923 Omaha bank robbery.

Amazingly, on his arrival in Nebraska Lee was allowed to gain his freedom by posting bond, the funds provided by "Kate" Melton. On October 5, Charlie Mayes turned up at a Joplin hospital sporting a bullet lodged in his guts requesting medical treatment. Apparently, he and John Clark had gotten involved in a gunfight in Lawrence, Kansas, the previous night with several individuals who were attempting to hijack the load of whiskey they were transporting.

While Clark was killed in the melee Mayes was somehow able to escape the scene and make his way back to Joplin where he sought medical assistance. After his release from the hospital into the custody of the local laws, Mayes was sent packing back to Kansas City, Kansas, where he was wanted for shooting a motorcycle cop in the jaw during a traffic stop that took place in April. As was his habit, he was released from custody upon posting bail (Provided by Kate Melton). In early 1926, Flournoy, Mayes, and their wives were arrested in Wichita, Kansas, for drunk and disorderly conduct. They were each fined fifty dollars and sent on their merry way.

On May 27, 1926, Mayes, Flournoy, and Lyman Ford, who had previously been convicted of looting the Bank of Quapaw, Oklahoma, for $2000 back in 1915, robbed the Montgomery County National Bank of Cherryvale, Kansas, for $66,000 in cash and negotiable bonds. Ford was soon captured in El Paso, Texas, by federal agents. When questioned, he dropped a dime on his comrades. Warrants were promptly issued for the arrest of Mayes and Flournoy for suspicion of bank robbery.

Turns out, the bank heist was an inside job engineered by Bank President George Robertson with the aide of Chief Cashier Clarence Howard.

While their fellow conspirators were all rounded up and placed in jail, Mayes and Flournoy remained fugitives, taking refuge in the Oklahoma mining community of Picher where Mayes and Chase made themselves to home at a local boarding house posing as man and wife while Flournoy stayed at a friends home located in nearby Cardin.

In the early morning hours of June 9, 1926, Flournoy and Mayes, in the company of Ms. Chase, got liquored up and attempted to hooray the town. Unfortunately for them, they ran smack into lawman William "Billy" Schmulbach, a double

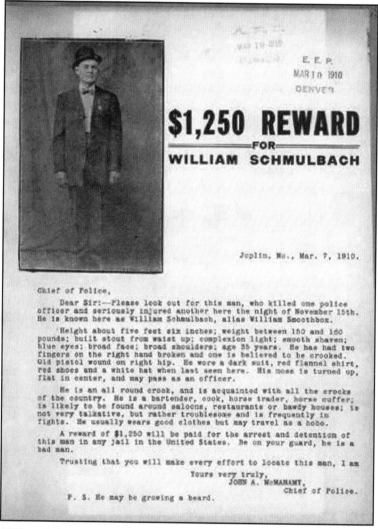

William Schmulbach – lawman later turned outlaw.

tough hombre and slayer of five men in his bloody career as a law enforcement officer. Schmulbach and his companion, Ottawa County Deputy Sheriff M. L. Woolsey, caught up with the hell raisers in the act of shooting out the town's streetlights and the windows of various businesses. When the officers demanded the trio cease their foolishness, Flournoy pulled a pistol and fired on the lawmen before speeding away into the dark countryside.

For the next five miles the two sides engaged in a high-speed running gunbattle until the officers ran out of bullets just outside of the tiny mining community of Zincville and were forced to return to the police station to rearm themselves with a Winchester rifle, a sawed-off shotgun, and ammunition.

Around 3 am the two cops encountered the misfits on the streets of downtown Picher changing the right rear tire on their Buick, which had been punctured by gunfire in the earlier firefight. A deadly gun-duel ensued ending with the deaths of both Flournoy and Mayes and the wounding of Officer Grover McCleary who upon arriving at the scene was mistaken as an enemy combatant by the ever-deadly Mr. Schmulbach who responded to his unexpected presence by shooting him in square in the chest, the round piercing both lungs. While Mayes died instantly from a bullet to the heart, Flournoy survived only moments before expiring due to a rifle slug entering his left side traveling through his midsection before exiting and entering his right arm.

A hysterical and heavily inebriated Vivian Chase was pulled out from behind the wheel of the car and charged with a multitude of sins including conspiring to rob the Cherryvale bank and harboring fugitives from the law. Chase, who gave her name as Gracie Adams at the time, was held in the Ottawa County Jail in Miami, Oklahoma where she sat mum refusing to answer questions from either the press or police investigators. According to several other female prisoners being held at the jail at the time, Vivian even refused to communicate with the other inmates choosing to simply sit silently in her cell with a perpetual scowl on the face.

The bullet-riddled bodies of her spouse and his pal were hauled back to Joplin for burial. Vivian was not allowed to attend her husband's last rites. Instead, she was extradited to Kansas to tried by a jury of her peers. Somehow, she was acquitted and freed. Apparently, she and Lee Flournoy's grieving widow, also charged with harboring, paid for their defense with proceeds from the hot bank bonds that had been sold to a Kansas City fence named Joe Ham. The transaction had been arranged by "Kate" Melton. The third victim of the shootout, Deputy Grover McCleary, would eventually recover from his wounds.

It appears after her trial Vivian laid low working the Kansas City streets for a couple of years prior to hooking up with a Kansas hood identified as Luther Jordan. The pair spent their honeymoon hijacking gas stations in the Kansas City area in the company of a third subject named Earl McDowell. On April 9, 1932, the happy couple along with McDowell and Enos Weakly knocked off the National Bank and Trust Co. of North Kansas City, Kansas, for $2000. A month later, the quartet robbed a bank in Waldo, Kansas. On June 5, officers discovered the body of McDowell dumped in a ditch in Wyandotte County Kansas suffering from a severe case of lead poisoning. Rumor has it, Lee Jordan plugged McDowell after he began paying too much attention to Miss Chase's comely figure.

On June 7, the two lovebirds were arrested at a seedy apartment in Kansas City and charged with bank robbery. Four months later Chase sawed the steel bars of her jail cell in Liberty, Missouri, with a smuggled hacksaw blade and using a rope made of bed sheets crawled to freedom.

After her escape Chase fled to St Jo, Missouri, where she worked as a hostess at Lulu Hickey's joint before relocating to Omaha, Nebraska. There she 'pulled tricks' and pushed shots of watered down bourbon at various local speakeasies and gin-joints as a "B" Girl. According to recently released FBI reports it seems Chase moved to the East St. Louis area around December 1932 where she shared a bed with Clarence Sparger, Irish O'Malley or both for several months before the men returned to Kansas City after perpetrating a slew of robberies.

Next time we hear of Vivian she was living at Norma Vaughn's boarding house in East St. Louis working the grift and gambling circuit with Vaughn's lover, Irish O'Malley. Vivian would soon fall head over heels in love with the slippery con man and the pair would make music heard all the way to the office of the Director of the FBI in faraway Washington DC.

Tiring of their penny ante profits, O'Malley, inspired by the recent wave of nationally famous kidnappings, came up with the idea of trying his hand at the newly fashionable snatch racket.

Chapter 2
The Luer Kidnapping

The Year of our Lord 1933 is remembered as not just the cruelest year of the ongoing worldwide economic depression but the very apex of the great Midwest Crime Wave. Class warfare broke out throughout rural middle America when a legion of poor dirt farmers and small town residents reacted to losing their farms, homes and savings by either foreclosure or total bank collapse by cheering on bank robbers as well as actively assisting desperate personalities such as "Pretty Boy" Floyd and John Dillinger. The likes of Bonnie and Clyde, Wilbur Underhill, and a hundred others ranged across the land pillaging and plundering the nation's financial institutions. During this time the term "Evil Banker" came into vogue. However, the crime of bank robbery was soon overshadowed in the press by an even more high profile and sinister transgression, kidnapping.

Ever since the abduction and murder of the Lindbergh baby Americans in general along with newsmen were both fascinated and distressed by this audacious crime. The more noted snatches taking place in 1933 were those of Charles Boettcher II in Denver for $60,000 and that of Minnesota beer baron William Hamm, nabbed by the Barker-Karpis Gang and held until $100,000 was paid. Oklahoma oilman Charles Urschel was grabbed off his porch by members of the 'Machine Gun' Kelly Gang. In the case of Urschel a record $200,000 ransom was forked over by his family.

Although the crime of kidnapping paid big dividends and made blazing headlines it was actually a very risky enterprise. The kidnappers were vulnerable on at least four occasions. Once, when the snatch was made, a second time when contact was made, a third when the ransom was paid and a fourth when they spent the often times marked loot. In the end, very few kidnappers got away scot-free.

Feeling the heat from public opinion congress enacted the Patterson Act (Little Lindbergh Law) on June 22, 1933, making it a federal offense to transport a kidnap victim across state lines. The law provided a maximum sentence of life imprisonment. The Cochran Act, enacted the previous year, had

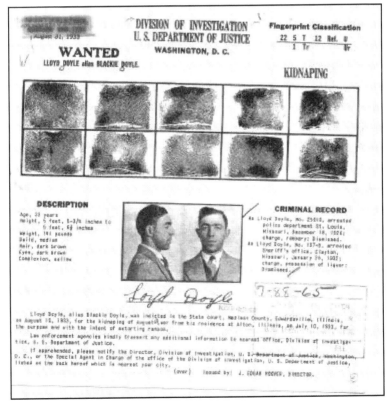

Wanted poster for Blackie Doyle.

made the use of US mails in the furtherance of a kidnapping a federal offense as well.

St Louis, Missouri

In late June 1933 Irish O'Malley and "Blackie" Doyle, were joined by Clarence Sparger. After spending two months lying on his back recuperating at St. Jo's Methodist Hospital Clarence figured he was on the mend and needed to get back into the game. The trio began casting about for a suitable victim in the St. Louis-East St. Louis area. Soon joined by Percy Fitzgerald, who had just made bond on a burglary charge, the quartet decided on St. Louis bookie "Mulepole" Fritz but later nixed the idea for some unknown reason. They also considered snatching the ten-year-old son of a Granite City banker but that deal fell through as well.

They then began shadowing one of the wealthy Olin brothers, the owners of an Alton, Illinois, munitions manufacturing firm (Winchester), in hopes of grabbing him at an opportune moment. To their great disappointment, just as they were about to consummate the plan their victim suddenly departed town on a lengthy vacation.

Frustrated by their lack of success the kidnappers visited the East Alton, Illinois, home of a matronly fifty year-old gray-haired sleazy underworld linked real-estate broker and boot-

Perry Fitzgerald

legging queen named Lillian Chessen in hopes she could turn them on to a decent setup. Mrs. Chessen and her husband, Charles, a bartender by trade, could best be described as a pair of shady malcontents who had been arrested on numerous occasions in the past for such crimes as larceny, bootlegging, conspiracy to defraud, and most recently, forging the name of a rich cousin on a financial instrument. The scheming old lady came up with the name of August Luer, a wealthy retired seventy-seven-year-old entrepreneur living in a lavish mansion in nearby Alton as a likely mark, claiming "He is your next best bet." Adding, " The cops will probably put the blame on his son-in-law. The old man disowned him for some reason." Luer owned several meatpacking plants in the area as well as

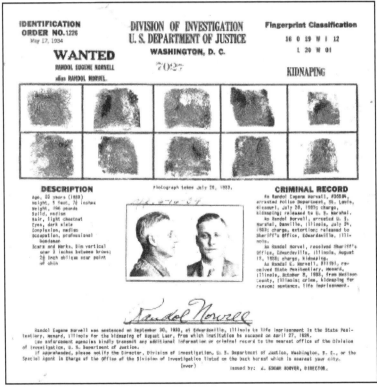

Randol Norvel – FBI wanted poster.

the Alton Banking and Trust Company. Norvell and O'Malley spent the next few nights scouting out the Luer residence located at 759 Washington Street.

Around this time, "Bonnie" Sparger pulled out of the deal deciding to return to St. Jo. While his motives for crawfishing on the job is unknown, rumor has it, Sparger, unfamiliar with the snatch racket, chose to stay with more familiar territory, pulling armed robberies in Kansas. Seeking a replacement for Sparger, the conspirators turned to Fitzgerald's bondsman, thirty-three-year-old Randol Eugene Norvell. The blonde haired blue-eyed handsome ex-steel worker turned professional gambler, bookie, bootlegger, and owner of an East St. Louis laundry was put in charge of supplying transportation for the snatch. For the past year, Norvell had bankrolled a crap game located in the basement of an area hotel in concert with Irish O'Malley, who acted as overseer for the illegal operation.

August Luer

Others brought into the affair were Madison, Illinois, grocer and bootlegger Christ Gitcho and an illegal alien from Austria named Mike Musiala, who rented a small farm located just north of East St. Louis. He and Fitzgerald often used the farm as a drop off point in their illegal liquor operations. Musiala also had a second job, working nights at a St. Louis steel mill. He was instructed by the kidnappers to find a safe place on his farm to keep the victim secure until the ransom was paid. According to a statement made by Norvell after his arrest,

"O'Malley did not want to transport Luer into St. Louis due to his belief the St. Louis bridges would be watched in the aftermath of the kidnapping."

Several days before the actual snatch, Norvell and O'Malley drove to Musiala's place to inspect the accommodations. They were shown a small tool shed that contained an even smaller cave or underground dugout that was oftentimes used as a whiskey cache. According to the Austrian, while on the property O'Malley paced back and forth in front of the shed talking to himself incoherently, carrying a pistol in his right hand, waving it about "like a walking cane."

Although the gang originally planned to pull off the snatch the first week of July they were forced to postpone their plans when Blackie Doyle was arrested on the evening of July 3 by St Louis Police detectives for suspicion of being somehow involved in the botched blood-soaked Leavenworth bank heist. The thug was held for questioning for three days before being released due to the prosecutor's inability to gather enough evidence to charge him with complicity in the robbery.

The snatch job was postponed a second time when Fitzgerald announced the date would interfere with is plans to burglarize a safe located in a St. Louis warehouse.

On the evening of July 10, 1933, a car occupied by O'Malley, Vivian Chase, and "Dice Box" Fitzgerald arrived at the residence of Randol Norvell. The trio hopped into Norvell's Pontiac Sedan speeding to a destination ten miles north. According to statements made later to police by Norvell, Fitzgerald sat next to him in the front seat, nervously fiddling with a pistol while Miss Chase and O'Malley positioned themselves in the rear.

At approximately 9:15 pm, Norvell eased his car onto Washington Street in the Mississippi River community of Alton, Illinois, braking just short of the Luer mansion letting his three occupants out. Norvell drove around the road's bend through the main gate before parking the rig a short distance from the residence while his cohorts approached the front of the house on foot. Chase and O'Malley strolled up to the main entrance while Fitzgerald took up a position in the driveway. When Vivian Chase rang the doorbell Mrs. Luer opened the door a crack, inquiring if she could be of assistance. The sharply dressed Chase replied she was looking for the home of Henry Busse, a local banker. Mrs. Luer responded that Mr. Busse lived nearby to which Chase inquired if she could use the phone. Mrs.Luer unwittingly invited the pair inside the hallway. When shown the location of the telephone Chase reacted by grabbing the cord and quickly cutting it with a pair of scissors. In the meantime, O'Malley pushed Helen Luer aside rushing into the parlor where Mr. Luer sat in an easy chair dressed in his pajamas and silk evening slippers listening to the 'Amos and Andy' show on the radio. Suddenly, O'Malley grabbed the old gentleman and wrestled him to the floor applying a heavy bandage over his mouth, which he secured with adhesive tape. Meanwhile, Mrs. Luer dashed into the room and

Musiala farm where Luer was kept.

began screaming. Hearing the woman's cries Fitzgerald scooted into the house where he grabbed the hysterical woman with both hands violently flinging her across the room so forcefully she struck her head on a mantelpiece causing a bloody gash.

Once the noise died down, O'Malley and his paramour manhandled the old gentleman out the front door into the driveway shoving him into the backseat of the waiting car. O'Malley promptly crammed him into the floorboard and roughly fitted a blindfolded over his eyes.

Luer would later tell investigators, "The man who had snatched me sat with his knees jammed into my back and prior to his blindfolding me, I noticed him repeatedly clutch his chest with a look of pain on his face. He seemed to be the leader of the bunch." Adding, "Their female companion spoke in a husky voice and wore a rather pungent perfume."

In the meantime, Mrs. Luer, regaining her senses, sprang

Building were Luer was kept.

to her feet, rushed out the front door of the mansion and down the street to her son's house shreiking, "Help, Carl!" Hearing his mother's screams, Carl Luer and his wife hurried into the road in time to observe the Pontiac exit the area. Initially Carl suspected his dad had suffered a heart attack since the old gentleman had a history of severe coronary heart disease. Young Mr. Luer instructed his mother to calm down, "The doctors will take care of things" to which Mrs. Luer replied, "No Carl, They have stolen Papa!"

Across the street, the neighbors, alarmed by Mrs. Luer's blood-curdling cries, ventured out onto their well-kept lawns in time to hear one of the kidnappers tell their victim to "Shut up or I'll knock your G-d damn head off!"

Observing the kidnap car speed past his position, young John Bass, visiting a friend who lived nearby, rushed into the road and leaped upon the running board of a passing vehicle being driven by Merle Manley, ordering the driver to, "Follow that car!" After motoring about seven blocks, the driver, fearful for his safety, pulled off the road refusing to follow the rig any further. Bass did mange to ascertain the suspect's rig sported Illinois plates ending with the digits 288.

After departing the Luer estate, the kidnap car roared along about eighty miles-per-hour until it reached the home of O'Malley's sister in Nameoki where the hijackers switched to Norma Vaughn's late model Plymouth, which had been previously stashed at that location. Norvell later stated they took the stolen license plate off his car throwing it in an isolated pond. The kidnappers then motored to Madison, Illinois, where they physically manhandled Luer into the basement of Gitcho's business located at 604 State Street. An hour later Gitcho became frightened when he heard a commotion outside and insisted the gang immediately move Luer to their preplanned hideout at the farm of Mike Musiala. "Blackie" Doyle and Fitzgerald were appointed his keepers.

The place where Luer was forced to spend the next 123

hours, shoeless (he had lost his slippers during the scuffle at the mansion) and scantily clothed, was actually an old underground cellar located in Musiala's back yard, accessible by a trap door and a homemade wooden ladder. Luer later described it as seven or eight feet long by four feet wide and three and a half feet high. He also claimed, "I had no blanket but was supplied with a pillowcase filled with grass. It was hard to breathe in that hole. At first I lay on the hard ground until they provided me a seat cushion from a car."

For the next few days, Luer endured a hell on earth. He was kept bound and gagged except when being fed an endless series of dry ham sandwiches along with an occasional peeled orange and allowed a cup of well water every few hours. He was spoken to only when the kidnappers ordered him to sign a series of ransom notes. Apparently, the old man constantly complained of his heart condition and digestive difficulties. So much so in fact Norvell later testified he made so many trips to the local drug store in order to purchase medicines for their victim he feared the proprietor would suspect him as one of the kidnappers since the radio and news reports had reported the fact Luer was in ill health and needed various medications for his complaints. Perry Fitzgerald would tell investigators, "When it came to feeding him he was mighty damn particular and constantly complained about his bowels and such."

Back at the Luer mansion, Carl Luer immediately reported the kidnapping to the local authorities who in turn contacted the FBI. Local police rushed to the scene of the crime throwing a cordon of security around the residence. Once the news services caught wind of the crime, newspapers across the country reported the kidnapping with florid headlines. An army of reporters, including film crews from "Movie-Tone News," as well as radio announcers and technicians quickly arrived at the mansion turning the atmosphere into a veritable three-ring circus. The Alton city council reacted to the news by calling an emergency meeting, which resulted in the chamber issuing a condemnation of the kidnapper's actions and approving a $250 cash reward for the capture of the guilty parties.

Sitting in his oversized Washington DC office, FBI Chief J. Edger Hoover was a bit overwhelmed on receiving news of another high-profile kidnapping case. His agency was currently besieged by several extensive ongoing investigations. Agents were already spread thin following up multiple leads concerning the June 15th kidnapping of St. Paul Beer Baron William Hamm. Hoover was determined to catch the culprits and he was not a patient man. Also on his plate was the intense nationwide inquiry into the June 17th deaths of four law enforcement officers, including FBI Agent Raymond Caffrey, by a group of machinegun wielding assassins on the steps of Kansas City's Union Station depot. The officers were slain while in the process of transporting a recently captured felon to Leavenworth Penitentiary. Within hours of receiving news of the officers' deaths, Hoover, in an attempt to use the deadly incident as an enticement to push congress into increasing the agency's powers, publicly announced the bureau was officially declaring, "War on crime." Speculating a quick conclusion to the Luer snatch might yield the flurry of positive headlines the bureau dearly sought at the moment, the Director pulled no punches, ordering all spare agents stationed in the Midwest along with whatever resources were needed, to proceed to St. Louis to, in his words, "Crack the case!"

The day following the kidnapping a small army of FBI agents arrived at the mansion. While bureau technicians arranged for a tap on the phones, along with taking fingerprints and tire impressions from the scene, other agents fanned out across the St. Louis area following leads.

That afternoon the Luer family received a ransom note in the mail demanding $100,000 in small bills be forked over in order to insure the safe return of the victim. Problem was, the correspondence was characterized by the authorities as practically unreadable and lacking in specifics such as how or where the ransom was to be paid. Postal officials were immediately contacted in an effort to discover the exact origin of the letter, which was postmarked special delivery, St. Louis, Missouri. One lucid detail contained in the note was the demand that the Luer family insert the words, "John, come home. Mother is ill. Have dad write. Funds low" in the personal column of the *St. Louis Globe* if they were willing to deal with the kidnappers. The family immediately complied with the bizarre command.

The following day, a second note, postmarked Jefferson City, Missouri, arrived at the home of Carl Luer. Once again, the note was written in an incoherent manner. In an attempt to clear up the confusion the Luer family appointed Lawrence Keller, a trust officer of Luer's Alton Banking and Trust Company as well as Orville Catt, the manager of one of Luer's meat packing plants, to act as middlemen with the kidnappers. The pair dictated a note for publication in the *St. Louis Globe, Alton Evening Telegraph,* and the *East St. Louis Journal* stating, " On behalf of Mrs. Luer we have been requested to ask the kidnappers to grant Mr. Luer permission to directly communicate with his wife......Your instructions have been confusing and complicated. We urge that you act immediately by issuing new instructions that are more concise and contact the man named in order to affect a speedy release....... We must insist that the new instructions include specimens of Mr. Luer's handwriting and his signature. We will try to meet any reasonable demands." Mr. Catt informed reporters, "The reason we demand a signature is the fact no jewelry, watch, or document will satisfy us he is still alive and well. Possessions can be taken from a body but not a signature."

The family then set about raising some $60,000 in cash with full intentions of paying at least most of the ransom. The following morning Lawrence Keller received a brief phone call from "Irish" O' Malley directing him to "Go to the Highland Park city limit sign and you will find another note under a rock."

Agents rushed to the location discovering the note as promised. The communication was signed by August Luer. It was a rambling three-page set of instructions, which again made little or no sense. Although federal agents poured over the written demands with a fine-tooth comb, nothing could be discerned from the scrawl nor were any fingerprints detected.

A description of the kidnappers was broadcast on area radio stations and printed in newspapers across the nation. Law enforcement organizations located within a hundred mile radius of Alton was put on high alert. Federal investigators concluded that at least one of the kidnappers was likely a local man due to the gang's familiarity with the mansion and area roads.

In the days following the kidnapping Mrs. Luer took to the radio airwaves and made numerous statements expressing deep concern over he husband's health, begged his captors to make sure he had his heart medicine available. Back in the nation's capital, J. Edger Hoover publicly blustered, "I am determined to stamp out this epidemic of kidnapping once and for all." When questioned why the FBI was called into the case, Hoover snarled, "These kidnappers often times travel from jurisdiction to jurisdiction thus imposing a heavy burden on local police." US District Attorney Louis Bruer was quoted as saying, "This kidnapping wave is a symptom of the current revolution in crime characterized by the displacement of lone wolves with highly structured organizations and a shocking number of women engaging in crime."

Three days after the kidnapping a decomposing body was found lying facedown in a shallow creek located just off a dirt road seven miles east of nearby Edwardsville, Illinois. The corpse was characterized by investigators as having a large jagged shotgun wound to the back and side of the head as well as another smaller wound to the jaw.

On receiving the news of the discovery, a horde of G-Men rushed to the scene accompanied by great excitement in the media who suggested the victim was poor Mr. Luer. After a brief investigation, the body was identified as twenty-eight-year-old Nelson Voss, a local rural mail carrier.

The Luer family, holding their collective breaths, let out a large sigh of relief when the identification was made. According to press reports, seventy-five-year-old Helen Luer had since composed herself and perched like a faithful sentinel, took up a position on the mansion's front porch sitting in a wicker rocking chair patiently waiting for word of her husband. The stoic lady became the family bedrock and inspiration to those around her who had been emotionally falling to pieces since the kidnapping.

On the night of July 15, Fitzgerald and Doyle, fearful that the elderly gentleman might expire due to his bad heart and upset over the complications involved in the fruitless ransom negotiations, ordered Luer up the little stairs of the underground lair and after re-securing his blindfold placed him in a car. The kidnappers then woke Musiala, who was asleep on the farmhouse porch, instructing him to fill in the hole. According to the Austrian, he first checked to make sure the hole was empty before throwing a few shove loads of dirt into the culler's entrance before thinking, "The hell with it" and going back to sleep.

After driving their victim in circles for several hours his captors released him on a deserted road located near the Collinsville water works. According to Luer, he was informed by his captors to wait twenty minutes before walking east to a red and blue sign where he could call for assistance. One of the kidnappers added, "Old man, if we had known you were in such bad shape we would not of bothered you."

Moments after his captors raced away, Luer took off his blinders and strolled two miles to Grace Miller's Country Club Roadhouse. He was met at the door by the proprietor, who upon observing his unshaven face and disheveled clothes, took him for a bum looking for a handout. After convincing the skeptical hostess of his identity, Luer was allowed inside the gin-joint where he promptly placed a phone call to his son Carl.

Within minutes the county sheriff and a deputy arrived at the club where they greeted an unkempt but composed August Luer calmly drinking a cup of coffee and visiting with the club's manager. On his arrival home, the old man burst into tears on greeting his wife, telling her, "I'm OK momma." Although Luer claimed he was not badly mistreated by the kidnappers, his very appearance suggested he certainly had not been treated in the manner he was accustomed.

When questioned by the feds, Luer stated, "I was held in a cellar somewhere in the country. It was very quite except for the crowing of a few roosters and I drank heavy mineraled well water. I never got a good look at any of the kidnappers." After being interrogated, Mr. Luer was bathed, fed, and checked out by a physician before being put to bed at his son's home.

Right to left: Mike Musiala, Mrs. Musiala, Pearl Loge, Lillian Chessen and Mr. Chessen.

Armed guards were posted around the residence and local police blocked the street in front of the house so the old fellow could get some sleep.

Meanwhile, back at the location where Luer had been released a hundred man posse made up of local and federal officers spent the remainder of the evening and late into the next morning searching every house, barn, tool shed, and chicken coup located within a three mile radius. Madison County Sheriff Peter Fitzgerald took to the airwaves instructing the public to report any suspicious activity.

The following day an employee of the Luer Packing Company identified as Dr. Meyer discovered a signed note in a bottle lying in his yard that demanded $16,000 from the victim's family threatening to harm family members if their conditions were not met. The note ordered Luer neighbor and employee, Frank Piskorsky, to place a sign in his yard stating, "For Sale-Cash Only" if the family agreed to continued negotiations. This belated demand was evidently a desperate effort engineered by Lillian Chessen and Norvell in an attempt to profit something from the failed enterprise.

The big break in the case came on the morning of July 18 when Patrolman George Miller of the Madison Police Department suddenly realized he had not seen Percy Fitzgerald around his usual haunts for over a week. Since the description of the individual who slugged Mrs. Luer fit the yeggmen to the tee, he went to police headquarters, pulled out the crook's mug shot and motored to Alton where he showed the photo to Mrs. Luer who immediately identified the man as the person who assaulted her in the early stages of the snatch.

An all points bulletin was put out for the arrest of Fitzgerald and within hours the subject was in custody. After a vigorous all night grilling under a spotlight in the back room of the station house the balding thug spilled the beans telling investigators, "Alright, you got me! I'm right for the job." He then proceeded to tell the entire story of the kidnapping, naming the Chessens, O'Malley, Chase, Norvell, Gitcho, 'Blackie' Doyle and Musiala as the subjects involved in the crime. He further explained; "We had hopes of snatching the old man on the night of July 8 but turned back when we realized he had visitors at the house. We then put off the job until the evening of the 10th since I had plans to blow a safe in Granite City on July 9th." One of Fitzgerald's inquisitors would tell reporters," Boy, he was a tough nut to crack."

In a series of lightning-like dawn raids conducted by a bevy of federal, state, and local officers many of the suspects in the case were rapidly rounded up.

Norvell was arrested at his home. He followed Fitzgerald's lead making a lengthy self-serving confession stating O'Malley, whom he claimed he greatly feared, had visited his home within the past hour borrowing fifty bucks for use in skipping town. He added: " I was forced into this affair. O'Malley threatened to kill me if I did not assist him and the others in the kidnapping." The slippery malcontent also stated, "O'Malley was furious the boys had released Luer prematurely without collecting any dough."

Christ Gitcho was also arrested as was Mike Musiala and his wife, Anna. All three quickly joined the choir informing on their co-conspirators hoping to gain favor with the authorities. Information concerning the arrests was withheld from the public for several days in order prevent the at-large suspects from turning rabbit.

The morning following the raids officials escorted Luer and his wife to the Musiala farm where he identified his place of imprisonment. After peering down into the tiny crawlspace he calmly proclaimed, "Yea, that's it." Upon surveying the cave, which had been partially filled in by the kidnappers, a local cop stated, "The place wasn't fit to keep a dog in."

Over the next few days, hundreds of curious citizens visited the little cellar causing major traffic jams in the area. According to local news reports a pair of enterprising youths roped off the area and began charging a dime a pop to view the crime scene.

A "Be-On-The Lookout" bulletin was issued to area police departments concerning Walter O'Malley and his girlfriend Vivian Chase as well as "Blackie" Doyle, who had apparently kept watch over Mr. Luer for part of his captivity. Although Norvell furnished the authorities with the exact location of O'Malley and Chase's living quarters at Norma Vaughn's boarding house in East St. Louis, when the laws raided the establishment on the morning of July 20, there was no sign of the duo. Norma Vaughn and Pearl Loge were both hustled to St. Louis police headquarters for interrogation. According to investigators, when arrested, Ms Vaughn had a fully packed suitcase resting at the foot of her bed.

When questioned, Vaughn informed detectives that on the night of the kidnapping (July 10). Vivian, known to her only as Grace Noland, left the boarding house in the afternoon returning around 10 P.M. "So drunk she could hardly stand up, her dress, a brown and white striped affair, was covered in blood." Adding, "Norma sent the dress to the dry cleaners the next morning. In the early morning hours of the 11th, she packed a single bag and hastily departed…A few days later I received a call from Paul "Red" Hunter (an area bootlegger) saying he would send someone for her other things. Around dawn a cabdriver picked up her stuff, which included a pair of pistols." Vaughn further claimed Walter departed her place on the afternoon of July 10, driving her Plymouth and "I haven't seen him since" adding "I don't know Jack about no kidnapping."

When federal agents interviewed James Leezy, the operator of the taxicab stand located in front of Vaughn's establishment, he told investigators he picked up a lady matching Vivian's description around 1 AM the morning in question transporting her to the nearby Lomay Hotel. An examination of the hotel's register noted Grace Adams, no address listed, staying in Room #10 on July 11 and 12.

Miss Loge turned out to be a very cooperative witness, a virtual fountain of information. She knew where the bodies were buried, so to speak, and prosecutors were able to convince her to turn states witness and be placed into protective custody. When asked if she was acquainted with O'Malley she stated, "Yea, he's a bum. Never works, just sits around the place all the time allowing Norma to keep him." Her further testimony contradicted that of Ms. Vaughn's. She claimed, "I left East St. Louis to visit my ailing father in Wayne City on July 7 and returned on July 13. The following night I let Walter into the boarding house at 3 A.M. the morning of July 14. He left the following afternoon and that evening Norma and me went to a show. When we returned home we found a note from Walter on Norma's dresser stating 'Why didn't you wait?' On July 17, Walter phoned Norma with instructions to meet him somewhere. She packed a bag of his clothes and left with a gentleman and a blonde-headed woman in a Chevy Sedan. She returned the following morning, informing me at the time, 'The laws are looking for Walter and he is probably going to hide out in Tulsa, Oklahoma, where he has friends.'" When asked if she had ever observed Randal Norvell visiting the boarding house, she replied, "Ya, he came by every once in a while to see Walter. They ran a dice game downtown somewhere."

When shown a series of mug shots of known area female criminal types she picked out a photo of Vivian Chase from the stack. When asked to describe Miss Chase she stated, "Her hair is different now, she wears it in a boyish bob. She's thin and her hair is black with a few steaks of gray in it. She is drunk practically all the time. The only mail she received was from Detroit, addressed to a Norma Dalton."

Fugitive warrants were issued for O'Malley, Chase, and Doyle charging them with kidnapping for ransom and illegal use of the mails. Several of Fitzgerald's acquaintances were also arrested in the raids including fellow yeggmen Paul Douglas. The day after being interviewed by detectives Norma Vaughn was arrested for bearing false witness with interrogators. Upon being looked over by Mrs. Luer Norma was partially identified as the woman who entered her home with the kidnappers. The dress Vivian was wearing on the night of the crime was retrieved from the Spick and Span Dry Cleaners and positively identified as the dress worn by the female kidnapper. The garment was transported to St. Louis Police headquarters and examined under a ultra-violet ray. No bloodstains or spots could be discerned from the test. Norma Vaughn again vehemently denied any knowledge of the crime. Mrs. Luer later recanted her identification of Ms. Vaughn and she was released from custody, at least for the time being.

On the afternoon of August 4, six FBI agents accompanied by three St. Louis Police Officers raided the home of Lillian Chessen at 143 Ridge Street, East Alton, Illinois. Madam was not in residence at the time. After searching the premises the posse turned out the lights and settled down to wait for the couples return. At dusk, the hunted pair motored into the driveway and were immediately arrested as they entered the garage. The portly criminal mistress reacted to her arrest by saying, "What's the big idea? You got no right to pinch us, were just a pair of Honest Johns!" Under questioning Lillian Chessen finally broke down and in the process contradicted Norvell's statement claiming it was Norvell who was angry over the premature release of the prisoner not O'Malley, stating, "When Randol found out Fitzgerald and Doyle had let the old man go he began screaming, 'I'm going to kill those two shitbirds!"

During the investigation, Special Agent John Brennan ascertained from the telephone company that at least a dozen calls had been made from Norvell's residence to that of the Chessens from July 10-20, 1933. Six more calls were made to Norma Vaughn's apartment during the same time frame.

Soon afterwards, FBI agents raided "Red" Hunter's home

in nearby French Village. The subject was transported to St. Louis police headquarters where he initially denied knowing any of the subjects involved in the case. He later changed his mind telling investigators, "I have been manufacturing home-made beer at my place for eight or ten years. I supply booze to numerous saloons and boarding houses in East St. Louis including Norma Vaughn's place. I've known her for several years." Adding, "On the evening of July 13, Blackie Doyle came to my home in the company of a woman (later identified as Vivian Chase) asking if she could stay there for awhile. A few days later Walter had me arrange to pick up her clothes from Norma's rooming house. An hour or so before you fellows arrived she took off walking down the highway toward French Village in order to buy some makeup. She did not return in time to enjoy the festivities."

It was later discovered that on her way back to the Hunter residence Ms Chase witnessed the raid from a distance. Evidently, she walked back to town and was seen boarding an afternoon bus bound for Springfield, Illinois.

Hunter agreed to play ball with the authorities and do some inquiring as to the whereabouts of Walter O'Malley and the other kidnappers. He also informed investigators Randol Norvell had a two-story hunting cabin located on the Gasconade River near Hooker, Missouri, where he often visited when he wanted to get away from the pressures of big city life.

The following morning a dozen federal agents swooped down on Norvell's cabin in hopes of cornering the fugitives. Unfortunately, only a elderly caretaker was in residence. When shown mug shots of O'Malley and "Blackie" Doyle he admitted they had visited the cabin in the company of Norvell on several occasions, but stated, "Neither have been here in months."

The cabin and surrounding area was vigorously searched but nothing of any importance was found. A second round of "All Points Bulletins" were issued throughout the Midwest to over a three hundred law enforcement agencies asking for help in discovering the whereabouts of O'Malley, Doyle, and Chase. Over the next few weeks FBI agent's raided dozens of gambling dens, houses of ill repute, saloons, and private homes belonging to acquaintances of the fugitives in the St. Louis area but on each occasion, drew a blank. The trio seemed to have been swallowed up into the bowls of the earth.

After a great deal of debate, the state of Illinois decided to try the defendants in state instead of federal court since the crime of kidnapping under Illinois law was deemed a capital offense while federal kidnapping statutes were germane only when the victim was transported across state lines. Apparently the only federal law that was broken in the affair was the illegal use of the mails in the commission of a crime, which provided punishment of a mere five years incarceration and a $20,000 fine.

In a succession of jury trials, all six suspects were ultimately found guilty of either kidnapping or accessory to the fact. Although Assistant Illinois States Attorney John McGinnis initially demanded the death penalty for all the defendants, he later withdrew his stipulation and requested life sentences from the jury.

In the end, fifty-year-old Lillian Chessen, suspected by the authorities of writing the kidnap notes including the belated $16,000 demand, was sentenced to life imprisonment while her husband was given a five-year sentence. According to reports, Mrs. Chessen calmly sat through her sentencing wearing a silk polka dot dress with a perplexing smile pasted on her face.

"The Dice Box Kid" was also given life, as was Randol Norvell. The blond Adonis again protested his innocence testifying he was forced to participate in the crime by O'Malley under threat of death while his wife and two small children sat quietly dripping tears in the front row of the courtroom. Christ Gitcho was given a five-year sentence while Mike Musiala received twenty years. Musiala's wife, Anna, and Fitzgerald's partner, Paul Douglas, were eventually freed from custody.

The only member of the Luer family to speak to the press during the trial was Mrs. Floyd Jenkins, a niece, who told reporters; "They ought to string them up! I'm in favor of something that will put the fear of G-d in 'em."

On the second day of the trials, Norma Vaughn suddenly reappeared on the scene pounding on the door of her ex-roomer, Pearl Loge, who was scheduled to testify against the defendants the following day. After issuing a few dire threats against the petite witness, Norma stomped out of the residence right into the arms of a plain-clothes detective stationed just outside the door where he was in the act of taking his shift providing protection for the prosecutions key witness. Vaughn was jailed and charged by a federal grand jury with intimidating a federal witness. She pled guilty to the charge and was sentenced to serve three months in the slammer and fined $200. Fortunately for her, the charge of conspiracy to commit kidnapping was dropped. Within a month of her release from prison, Norma purchased a two-story residence located next to the Madison, Illinois, rail yards and promptly turned the place into a four-star whorehouse. It was rumored the venture was secretly financed by her boyfriend, Irish O'Malley, as an expression of his gratitude for her loyalty and silence.

Chapter 3
A Gathering of Rouges

While their crime-partners were receiving their come-uppance back in St. Louis, "Irish" O'Malley, in the company of Vivian Chase and Blackie Doyle, made a beeline back to their haunts in Kansas City. The trio quickly re-connected with Clarence Sparger, Dave Sherman, Johnny Langan, and Spike Lane, becoming involved in a lengthy crime spree burglarizing various jewelry and department stores as well as a host of other business located in St Joseph, Kansas City, and Omaha, Nebraska.

In due time, Walter O'Malley began casting about for another big score and possibly a change in zip-code. It appears he had little luck until he was introduced to recently paroled Daniel Turner Heady, an acquaintance of Clarence Sparger, the two being cellmates in the antiquated Missouri State pen for several months in the fall of 1932. Known in underworld circles as "Dapper Dan," Heady was a classic hard-case and a four-time looser spending more time behind bars than in front of them during his lifetime.

Born in 1905, Heady was the direct descendant of a prominent family of pioneers to the area of Southwest Missouri. At the age of ten Dan's father relocated his family to Picher, Oklahoma, located in the massive Tri-State lead and zinc-mining district. John Heady took a job in the mines but before long his lungs began to fail due to working in the poorly ventilated underground shafts.

In 1919, the family moved to Wichita, Kansas, seeking a healthier work environment. Tragically, within a year John Heady suddenly died at the age of forty-eight. Dan's mother quickly buried her husband, gathered up her offspring and scampered back to the bosom of her family in Springfield. She rented a small home on the city's north side, finding work as a seamstress for a boarding school.

Shortly after arriving in Springfield Dan quit school and went to work delivering newspapers. In his spare time Dan began hanging around a pool hall located just north of the downtown square. Before long he fell in with a youth gang and began committing thefts and burglaries. Soon enough his luck ran out when he was arrested for stealing a bicycle. The lad was sent to the Boonville School for Boys, a rough over-crowded reformatory for juvenile delinquents. After his release from Boonville, a local gambler hired him as a racetrack

Dapper Dan Heady

jockey. His newfound employment afforded the youth the opportunity to travel to such exotic locations as Cuba, Canada, Florida, and upstate New York competing in high stakes horse racing events.

By 1923, Dan, now grown to 5'6" and 130 lbs, had outgrown the physical requirements for a jockey. He took a job as a head-knocker for the railroad during the nationwide rail strike. Soon after the strike was settled the youth was laid off work and returned to Springfield. Failing to find employment and lacking funds, he and a partner were nabbed in the act of stealing a vacuum sweeper valued at $50 from a private residence. The youth pled guilty to theft and was sentenced to three years at the Missouri state pen for his indiscretion. Before he was transferred to the big house Heady escaped from the Greene County Jail, stealing a car off the street in order to make his getaway. After enjoying just a few hours of freedom he was recaptured and finally made the trip to Jefferson City.

On the evening of March 6, 1925, a recently paroled Heady and a pal drove up to a Springfield filling station located at the intersection of Nichols and Broadway in a Ford Roadster. When the pair, armed with automatic pistols, confronted the proprietor, Leroy Best, demanding he put his hands in the air and cough-up the cash from the register, Best drew a revolver and began trading shots with his tormenters. Surprised by their victim's stiff resistance, the hooligans retreated to the roadster and attempted to take flight. Best reacted by riddling the getaway vehicle, smashing the front windshield and flattening a rear tire as well as wounding one of the hijackers. Both bandits bailed out of the car fleeing on foot.

Later that night police received a tip indicating a man suffering from a gunshot wound had requested an ambulance at a residence located at 316 Boonville Avenue. The wounded man was taken into custody on his arrival at Springfield Baptist Hospital. As soon as he was able to speak the injured suspect admitted he was one of the filling station bandits. He named his partner as Dan Heady.

Heady was promptly picked up at his mother's residence located at 743 North Campbell Avenue and charged with armed robbery. This time the thug refused to plead guilty instead choosing to take his chances with a jury.

Although Heady attempted to set up an alibi for the night of the crime using the testimony of a girlfriend, the jury failed to buy his story and the badman was convicted and sentenced to a five-year term at the Missouri State Penitentiary.

Upon his release from the joint Heady settled in St. Louis where he and an accomplice perpetrated another armed robbery. Once again, his bad luck ran true and he was arrested and sent back to the pen. Paroled a few years later he returned to his anti-social behavior hijacking a gas station. In due time he was apprehended and dispatched to the state slammer for a fourth time where he stayed put until his May 1934 release.

In the weeks following his parole from prison, Heady took time out to visit his mother in Springfield before journeying to Kansas City to look up his old cellmate, "Bonnie" Sparger. His bunkie in turn introduced the hoodlum to Irish O'Malley.

Shortly after the pair linked up, Heady and O'Malley traveled to Claremore, Oklahoma, on a gambling junket. Another

Leonard Short and Dewey Gilmore

purpose for the trip seems to have been the laundering of some freshly counterfeited money O'Malley was attempting to pass for the Lazia organization, for a price of course.

On the pair's return to Kansas City they stopped in Springfield where Heady introduced his new sidekick to several of his underworld contacts in the area. Among those contacts was local gangland middleman, "Kate" Melton and his brainy associate, Leonard "Shock" Short, the head of an oversized band of burglars and bootleggers dubbed "The Ozark Mountain Boys."

At this fateful meeting, the stage was set for the coupling of the urbanized Irish O'Malley Gang with the countrified Ozark Mountain Boys. This rare merging of a rural and urban criminal enterprise would eventually go down in history as one of the strangest yet most efficient "Supergangs" of the depression-era. Only "Ma" Barker's colossal Barker-Karpis Gang would best it in size and scope.

Oddly, while the FBI as well as the press consistently named O'Malley as being the group's generalissimo, it is more likely he shared power and influence with both Leonard Short and Dan Heady in the day to day operations of the organization.

Chapter 4
Six Daring Bandits Inc.

George Leonard Short, the chief operating officer of the Ozark Mountain Boys was known to family and friends throughout his short life as either Leonard or "Shock." Short was born on February 3, 1894, in the small Ozark Mountain village of Galena, Missouri, which was located near the Missouri-Arkansas border in Stone County. Dissected by both the ever-flooding James and White Rivers, the rugged, hilly and sparsely populated county was originally settled by immigrants hailing from Kentucky and Tennessee. Initially part of Taney County, the much fought over region was part of the so-called "Burt District" during the Civil War, so named due to the fact not one single standing structure survived the torch applied by free ranging bloodthirsty bushwhackers supporting both the northern and southern causes. By wars end the area was a nearly depopulated, citizens having fled the area in fear for their lives to Springfield, one-step ahead of the opposing combatants.

After resettlement, the mainstay of the economy was farming and lumbering. Folks raised cotton and corn in the river bottoms and tomatoes on the deforested hillsides. During the 1920's thru the end of World War II, tomato canning was the chief industry in the area. Many ambitious individuals made their fortunes at the rate of one tomato-two cups of water. The raising of cattle and stewarding free-ranging hogs added to the agricultural mix.

Leonard was the son of Jack Short, a decent hard working area pioneer and successful businessman. According to family lore, Jack's mother, a feisty hill-woman, had killed a bushwhacker during the Civil War with an ax in defense of her husband. Jack was at different times the owner of a hardware business and a tomato canning plant as well as the town's Post Master.

Leonard's younger brother, Dewey, was a long-serving US Congressman for Missouri's 14th District. A die-hard Republican and a true populist as well as an ordained minister, he was first elected to the house in 1928 under the pretext of being a genuine, "Common Man of the Hills." Dubbed the "Orator of the Ozarks" by many, Dewey soon garnered the reputation of being the finest public speaker to ever sprout from the backwater hills. In 1930, he was defeated for re-election and threw his hat in the ring for a senate seat. Once again he went down in defeat. Both losses were likely due to his stand on prohibition. Although he was a licensed preacher, schooled at the Boston Collage of Theology, it seems Dewey liked to take a nip now and again and was what they called in those days a "Wet," standing firm against national prohibition.... Except for a shared fondness of spirits and similar magnetic personalities it appears the brothers were polar opposites.

According to most accounts, the enigmatic Leonard experienced a normal childhood. His family was well off by hill standards and being a member of the "First Family" of Galena, Leonard assuredly lacked little in his upbringing relating to material items, proper shelter, education, and nourishment. After graduating from Galena High School he worked at his father's store.

Soon after America became involved in the Great War, Leonard traveled to the Kansas City Recruit Depot where he enlisted in the US Navy. The young man took his training at Great Lakes Training Station in Illinois before being assigned to the Philadelphia Naval Yard, eventually attaining the rating of Storekeeper 3rd Class.

Upon his discharge from service in late November 1918

he returned home, married and become involved in the real estate and land abstract business. Short was afforded many rare opportunities in life such as the time he journeyed with Dewey on a political fact finding mission to Mexico where the pair spent an evening sitting in a cantina discussing politics and drinking Tequila with the bandit Poncho Villa. On their return north, they were met by the famed poet Edger Lee Masters who had arrived in Galena for a visit.

By the latter 1920s Leonard appeared to have it all, a successful business, a loving wife and a good reputation. He was also known for his kindness to children. It was said that on many a Saturday morning Leonard would slap a $20 bill on the ticket counter of the local theatre demanding every kid get in free for the rest of the day. At other times he would stroll into a drug store, buying every child in attendance an ice crème cone. It was also told that at the height of his career in outlawry and in the depths of the Great Depression, Short purchased a sack of groceries for more poor hill families than could be remembered.

However, behind that veil of legitimacy and generosity lurked a dedicated hooligan and true black sheep who shortly after prohibition was declared involved himself in the bootlegging trade. It appears the likable rouge evolved into a slick bunco-artist with a restless spirit and an attraction to risk taking and larceny. Some folks claimed the balding rotund bandit spent his entire adult life attempting to best his politician-brother's success by amassing wealth by any means possible.

By the early 1930s Short had added the title of "Sports Promoter" to his growing repertoire. Initially he began his professional career in the "Sportin" life by arranging backwoods cock-fighting events throughout the region.

He began arranging and bankrolling high stakes poker games in area hotels before spreading his wings to include the promotion of garish wrestling matches held at Springfield's Shrine Mosque. The matches, which brought out as many as

3500 screaming fans on an average Saturday night, featured such acts as "Sherry the Leg-breaker" vs "Big Bertha" in an eye gouging hair pulling spectacle or "Red" Berry "The Fighting Kansan" taking on "Brutus the Strongman." On one occasion, six midgets entered the ring unceremoniously beating "Jimmy the Ox" to a pulp with brass-knucks. It was a common occurrence for fistfights to break out amongst the frenzied spectators. The events, in which Short oftentimes acted as the master of ceremonies, were blood-filled earthy extravaganzas, the gaudier the better, appealing to the common man of the day.

After a week of backbreaking labor hardworking farmers living in isolated hollers in the nearby mountains laid down their plow lines, dressed up in a pair of clean bib-overalls and filed out of their log or rough sawmill cedar slab constructed dogtrot cabins in droves heading to town to enjoy the show while nipping on a pint of potent homemade corn-liquor.

Within a year of Short's taking over the wrestling events at the facility the powers-that-be placed him under investigation for selling several thousand counterfeit tickets as well as peddling whiskey to the frothing crowd on numerous occasions.

In order to repair his failing reputation Short organized a boxing exhibition to benefit the widows and families of six law enforcement officers slain in a recent raid on a farmhouse located just west of Springfield. The event, perpetrated by a pair of brothers named Young, represented the worst recorded police massacre in American history.

"Shock" Short's chief henchman and flunkey in his many enterprises was an out of work drug addict and alcoholic named Dewey Gilmore. Raised on a farm situated near the small community of Willard, located just west of Springfield, Gilmore quit school at the age of fifteen spending the next four years laboring on the farm from sun to sun, paid at the daily rate of three squares and a bunk. At age of twenty, he bolted from the plow and harness, drifting into Oklahoma's Osage oilfields where he worked as a roughneck until he was severely burned in an oil-rig explosion, which resulted in his becoming addicted to pain-killing opiates. He later claimed he took to the booze in order to kick his drug habit.

In 1918, Gilmore relocated back to Springfield where he wed a local gal who bore him a pair of daughters. Over the next few years Dewey worked as a pipefitter on various pipelines in a three state area. He did make an effort to settle down although it appears his heart wasn't really into a life of domestication. Predictably, as his drinking problem grew worse he was unable to hold a job and consequently he took to street hustling. After enduring her husband's excesses for most of a decade, Gilmore's wife finally gathered up the couple's daughters and exited the scene leaving Dewey to his own devises.

After his divorce Gilmore took up with an attractive blonde-haired blue-eyed twenty-year- old Dorothy Rose Young. The happy couple took up residence in a rundown apartment house on Booneville Street located on Springfield's seedy north side. By this time, Dewey had evolved into a full-blown alco-

Dewey Gilmore

holic, surviving by running errands for local gambling Czar/ Bootleg King, Leonard Short. From all indications Dewey often-times displayed a dog-like devotion to the pudgy con-man, unquestioningly doing his bidding, reminding those in attendance of master and servant.

By the end of prohibition in mid-1933, Short's illegal booze operation had peaked in size, employing several dozen individuals.

One of those was fellow Stone County native, Virgil "Red" Melton. Born in 1908, Melton was raised in comfortable circumstances in the small Ozark Mountain village of Ponce De Leon, located just a few miles northeast of Galena. His father was a prominent pioneer physician, twice married to women who bore him sixteen children of which Virgil was the youngest. "Red," described by prison records as six feet tall and weighing one-hundred and eighty pounds with a shock of flaming red hair, came from the second hatching. Apparently, the good doctor built two homes on his property. The children of his first wife lived in one while he, his second wife and her children lived in the other.

Legend has it Virgil began his career in crime at the age of ten helping a brother operate a crudely fashioned illegal moonshine still located deep in the isolated cedar-covered hills of Stone County. At the time, there was countless stills in service throughout the district producing thousands of gallons of a potent product locally dubbed "Old Skull-Pop" or "Panther Piss."

Red was later hired by Leonard Short as a truck driver, transporting unlawful liquor from Stone County to its ultimate destination in the urban centers located in Springfield, Kansas City, Omaha, and Joplin where an army of thirsty consumers impatiently awaited its arrival.

It appears Virgil initially made Short's acquaintance through one of his older half-brothers, either Epp, a rural mail-carrier and part-time moonshiner or Stephen, nicknamed, "Kate", a Short associate described by the authorities as "An underworld character suspected of operating a large-scale fencing operation as well as a being involved in the Joplin bootlegging trade."

As previously mentioned, "Kate" was also an acquaintance of Irish O'Malley's sweetheart, Vivian Chase, through her slain husband, Charley Mayes.

Somewhere along the line, Red formed a relationship with Arkansas native Fred Reese, another of Short's booze handlers. The pair soon became running buddies. Reese, described as a hulking, thuggish fellow with an IQ listed as near-moron was born in the Ozark Mountain community of Salem, Arkansas, in 1896 to poor circumstances. He and his three siblings were left fatherless when his dad died just days before Fred's birth. His mother remarried a moderately successful but cash-poor honest farmer named Carlile in 1897.

Fred quit school in the third grade in order to work on the farm, there being a more pressing need in those days for strong-backed lads to slop the hogs, milk the cows, and pick corn then study the three R's. The family moved to another rent farm located near the tiny Oregon County Missouri settlement of Koshkonong around 1912. While still in his teens Fred departed the bosom of his family drifting into the border communities located along the Missouri-Arkansas hinterlands living as a tramp stealing most anything of value for his daily bread when not employed as a day-laborer for various area

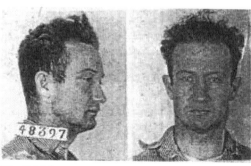

Virgil Melton   *Joe Morgan*

farmers. His fall from grace appears to have been tied to his love of strong drink.

Around 1914 Reese was shot in the ass during a drunken altercation. Although he would walk the rest of his life with a slight limp, the physical disability failed to deter or disqualify him from joining the US Army in September 1918. Pvt. Reese was honorably discharged from service at Camp Donavan, Oklahoma, as a member of Co. D 140th Infantry shortly after completing his training due to the cessation of hostilities. Upon his release from the military Reese remained in the Oklahoma oil patch district running dice games, committing strong-arm robberies, and peddling moonshine for several years.

Reese was married in Enid to Myrtle Whitaker in 1919. The couple was soon blessed with the birth of a daughter. Apparently the couple's relationship was no bed of roses, the little woman filed for divorce in 1924 claiming abandonment.

The following year Fred was picked up in Newkirk for suspicion of robbery but eventually released after questioning. Soon afterwards he was apprehended on the downtown streets of Tulsa, casually sitting in a Ford Model "T" loaded down with a truck load of carefully bottled "White Lightning." Curb service no doubt. Just days after making bond on the liquor charge the big man was involved in a knife fight in which he sliced a man into bloody ribbons. Although he was initially charged with assault-with-intent-to-kill, the charges were dropped the following

Fred Reese

day when it was determined his part in the altercation was purely an act of self-defense.

The oversized ruffian married a second time to a Springfield, Missouri, telephone operator in 1926. After taking his nuptials Reese traveled with his new bride to Kansas City where he became a familiar police character. After being rousted by the cops several times on charges of 'investigation' and 'vagrancy' he got the message and took his show on the road drifting to the opposite side of the state. In mid-1931 he was picked up in St. Louis under the alias of Fred Carlile (*his stepfather's last name) and being charged with operating as a "gambler and con- man."

In 1932 Reese relocated to Springfield, Missouri. Due to his depraved nature he was naturally a welcome addition to the Short organization. Over the next year or two, when not employed by Mr. Short, he and Red Melton worked the mountainous byways of Stone and Taney Counties, swindling the hayseeds out of their property when not outright stealing livestock and farm equipment.

A Reese descendant tells a story dating from this period concerning the time Fred approached a Koshkonong car dealer informing him he needed to borrow an automobile off his lot for a brief but hurried trip to Oklahoma. Reese further told the dealer he would return the rig intact in three days time. The proprietor, fearing bodily harm if he denied the thug the use of the car, hesitantly agreed to the proposition knowing full well he was likely to lose a new vehicle. Amazingly, the outlaw returned the car on time in pristine condition.

Another of Short's more junior partners was twenty-two year-old Homer Hight. Homer was raised by an uncle near the isolated crossroads settlement of Bradleyville, located about fifty miles south of Springfield. The hilly little berg was noted for its fast running pristine steams, commercial cedar mills and moonshine stills. Homer's running partner in the hills was his angelic-faced cousin, Elmer "Coody" Johnson. Over time the pair built up a reputation for showing up at the "Y," a crossroads that represented the settlements main gathering place, or local barn dances with a belly full of "wildcat" whiskey, engaging in the vulgar art of fisticuffs, county style.

In the mid-1920s, while Homer was still in his mid-teens, his uncle uprooted the family relocating to a small farmstead located on the south side of Springfield near the National Cemetery. Homer promptly dropped out of school. By all indications the lad arrived in town a spirited but harmless sod desperately seeking a release from typical depression-era farm life, which offered little more excitement than being permanently attached to a plow line looking up a mule's ass from dawn to dusk.

Shortly after his arrival in the big city he fell in with a group of street toughs operating on the city's north side. In due time he was jailed on a liquor charge in which he pled guilty as charged, serving a short stint in the county calaboose. Around this time both he and his cousin "Coody" somehow managed to fall under the spell of "Shock" Short.

Others involved with the balding bandit's illicit enterprise was Joe Morgan and Frank Simmons. Morgan, alias " Dago Joe", was a three-time loser hailing from Chicago. He had recently escaped from a cellblock at the Tennessee State Penitentiary where he was serving a ten-year sentence for burglary, via a three-hundred-foot hand dug tunnel. Records show he had previously done time in both the Missouri and Kansas state prisons. Morgan, along with fellow Chicago import Paul "Blackie" Bagby, arrived in Springfield after spending several months drifting across the Midwest pulling stickups.

Frank Simmons, an Eastern Oklahoma product, had a reputation of being tough as nails. It was rumored that he had acted as a wheelman on several Oklahoma bank jobs before making his appearance in the Springfield area.

Attaching himself to Joe Morgan soon after his arrival in town was twenty-year-old Dorsal "Moose" Upshaw, an over-

Congressman Dewey Short

Elmer Coody Johnson

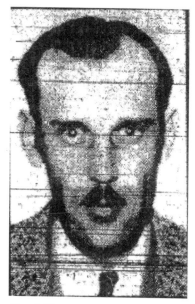

Frank Simmons

Homer Haight

sized street urchin with a juvenile record that included a host of penny-ante purse snatching and shoplifting charges as well as a nighttime burglary arrest. Raised on a farm in the mountainous regions of rural Douglas County, Moose's family relocated to Springfield when farm prices hit rock bottom due to the ongoing economic depression. By 1930 Upshaw's daddy was serving time at the Greene County Jail and Moose, unemployed and without prospects, soon turned to a life of crime. He had served at least one term at the boys reformatory in Boonville.

Additional charter members of Short's organization included Kansas City native Otto Jackson (alias Big Johnny Lasco), and a rough and tumble hillbilly named Bob Johnson and his ex-con sidekick, Buster Cooper. Floyd Maples and Ralph Wilson, both restless sons of Stone County sharecroppers, joined the group through their association with the Melton boys.

Also affiliated with the group was Springfield natives, Clifford Wilcockson alias, 'Sleepy" Lawrence, Floyd Hosman, and ex- star collage football jock George Calvin along with "Kentucky Slim" Rutherford, a rough customer hailing from parts unknown, who according to news reports possessed a shameless craving for violence.

Lanky Joplin born ex-lead miner, Floyd "Slim" Henderson, Galena, Kansas, native Art Austin, and "Scarface" Johnny Dillon, a vicious gunsel afflicted with a seemingly incurable case of the clap, drifted in and out of the organization at various times.

Knowing the Volstead Act (Prohibition) was about to be repealed, Short realized he would soon be left with a well organized sales and transportation department but without a product. Reacting to this fact he began guiding his group of daring-dos to greener pastures. Short's minions began a campaign of burglary, armed robbery, and wholesale theft not seen in the area since the invasion of Lane's Jayhawkers taking place shortly after the outbreak of the War Between the States.

Galena, Missouri - Summer of 1932

The first bank robbery accredited to Short's bunch occurred in Leonard's home town of Galena. According to investigators, on the evening of August 18, 1932, Short met with "Kentucky Slim" Rutherford, Ernest Teagarden and Galena farmer Haywood Scott in the backroom of his Springfield office. While his accomplices were given their marching orders Short remained in the background since he was well known at the victim bank.

On the evening of August 26 the three hoodlums motored in a freshly stolen car to the Galena residence of bank cashier Troy Stone where they made a forced entry. After holding their victim hostage for twelve hours at the point of a gun the trio escorted Stone to the financial institution located on the Galena courthouse square where he opened the vault giving the men $1700 in cash and coin. The trio then successfully fled town while their victim hightailed it to the nearby sheriff's office to report the crime.

A week after the heist, officers of the Highway Patrol, acting on a tip received from Stone County Sheriff Seth Tuttle, raided Teagarden's farm in rural Bolivar capturing the three thieves along with the getaway car which was hidden in a barn located behind the house. That evening, a posse led by Springfield Detective "Boots" Miller took Leonard into custody. All four men were charged with bank robbery. In short order, Short made bond and was set free. Amazingly, robbery charges would eventually be dropped against the quartet by Circuit Court Judge Robert Gideon. The lead prosecutor reacted by publicly labeling the case, "A perfect example of legal chicanery perpetrated by a pack of high-dollar hyenas operating under the title of defense attorney."

Ash Grove, Missouri - Mid-1933

The next major crime connected to the Short combination appears to have been the looting of the Bank of Ash Grove, Missouri, located twelve miles west of Springfield.

According to eyewitnesses, at high noon January 12,[th] a Ford Sedan containing three individuals parked in front of the bank. While two bandits entered the financial institution, a third remained at the wheel of the running getaway car. Once inside the building, which was manned by the bank's chief cashier J. H. Perryman and Assistant Cashier Nora Anglum, one of the men approached the cashier requesting change for a five-dollar bill. While the teller was busy making change, a second person began flashing a pistol while announcing a robbery was under progress and with a twinkle in his eye bragged he was "Pretty Boy" Floyd. Shortly after the robbery had gotten underway the third robber leaped from the car following a customer named Perry Titus into the bank. Observing the festivities Titus attempted to exit the scene but was ordered to "Sit down and shut up!"

Unable to open the safe, one of the hijackers forced Perryman to do so at the point of a gun. After gathering up roughly $3000 in mostly folding money, the robber claiming to be Floyd complained, "That's not all the money, where's the rest?" Informed there was no more the disappointed trio departed the business leaving town in a cloud of dust.

Since it was court day in the county seat community and most of the areas lawmen were tied up at the court house there was no organized pursuit of the thieves although three bystanders observing the goings on did jump into a car and follow the hijackers for a couple of miles firing several rounds at the fleeing getaway car with a deer rifle. The vigilantes abandoned the chase when the bandits broke out the rear window of their car unleashing a hot volley of lead in their direction.

The night of the robbery the bandit's heavily burned get-away car was discovered abandoned just south of town. The rig turned out to have been recently stolen from a garage in nearby Richland. The authorities immediately but erroneously laid the hold-up on the shoulders of the Floyd Gang.

The bank had been previously robbed in 1931 by eighteen-year-old Roy Ledbetter, an Ash Grove native. Ledbetter was sentenced to a five year prison term for his demonstration of poor behavior but released after serving just a year of his sentence. Soon after his release from prison, which was just days after the Ash Grove heist, Ledbetter began a close association with Leonard Short through his connection with Dewey Gilmore.

A few months after the Ash Grove hijacking an ex-carnival sideshow 'Strongman' identified as Roland "Corkscrew" Haley was arrested and charged with the crime. Haley, an alcoholic, duly confessed to the robbery and implicated Texas born drifter Jack Allen in the affair. Although neither man would divulge the name of the third individual involved in the affair, the authorities suspected Short associate Frank Simmons as being the guilty party. While Investigators naturally assumed the robbery was engineered by Leonard Short, they lacked enough concrete evidence to charge him with collusion.

In the meantime, Dewey Gilmore and his brother Floyd, a Willard High School track-star turned hoodlum, became involved in several area holdups beginning with the armed hijacking of a Springfield man named W.C. Johnson for $184.

The pair later robbed Walker's Greystone filling station located ten miles west of Springfield on Route 66. In that case, Dewey casually held a sawed-off shotgun to Mr. Walker's head while his baby brother rifled the cash register of approximately $40 in mostly silver. The robbers also stole a slot machine from the station's back room. Dewey was later arrested and charged with the crime. Walker positively identified him as the man holding the scattergun. Officers also located the stolen slot machine at the home of Dewey's ex-mother-in-law. The outlaw was charged with armed robbery and warehoused in the Greene County Jail awaiting trial. Floyd was also captured and charged with both the Johnson and Walker hijackings. He would eventually receive an invitation to a ten-year vacation behind the walls of the Missouri State Penitentiary at Jefferson City.

On May 9, Short associate Frank Simmons and Henry "Doc" Williams along with "Blackie" Bagby hijacked the Bank of Bourbon, Missouri, for $1600. The trio was also suspected of pulling off the recent robbery of a bank in Camden, Arkansas. Although Williams and Bagby were soon captured in Illinois, Simmons remained at large. Leonard Short was suspected of setting up the Bourbon bank job.

Springfield, Missouri - October 17, 1933

At the very hour relief officials were passing out 12,000 pounds of surplus pork on the steps of the Springfield's Greene County courthouse to the poor at the rate of six pounds per family of four, across town, Frank Simmons, Joe Morgan and Homer Hight kidnapped youthful money courier George William Bush, an employee of the Model Bakery, relieving him of some $1800 he was in the act of delivering in a brown paper bag to a local bank. It appears the red-haired twenty-year-old Bush had just departed the bakery, located at the corner of Robberson Avenue and Elm Street, where he had picked up the weekly receipts when Simmons ambled up to the lad as he was about to enter his car, pointing a pistol in his face.

After being forced to place his hands over his eyes by an individual he later described as middle-aged, "swarthy," and dressed in a blue suit and tan fedora, the pimply-faced lad was forced into the backseat of a mud-splattered blue Chevy Sedan sporting Oklahoma plates, which was occupied by a driver with a third individual sharing the front seat. The getaway car was driven to a vacant lot some blocks away where Bush was relieved of the loot and released with orders not to move an inch for five minutes.

A half hour after the heist, Patrolman Frank Pike observed Frank Simmons and Leonard Short calmly sitting in a muddy vehicle with Oklahoma plates parked in front of the Union Bus Depot. The vehicle matched the description of the one used in the bakery heist. When Pike approached the pair, they sped off in an easterly direction. The following day Simmons was taken into custody at his Campbell Avenue apartment.

Short was picked up a few hours later while he was eating lunch at a trendy café located on the public square. Upon his arrest the feisty hoodlum verbally lashed out at the arresting officers saying, "I'm getting pretty sick of this idea I'm implicated in all the crime around here!" Adding, "The imagination of my enemies has cost me many a dollar and sleepless night."

Back at the station house young Mr. Bush was able to identify Simmons as the man who accosted him but was unable to identify Short as either the getaway car's driver or passenger saying, "My eyes were covered and he hid his face from me during the ride."

When questioned, Short stated he had met Simmons at the Metropolitan Hotel the morning of the robbery but the pair was never near the Model Bakery. The outlaw was released after being interrogated for over twenty hours.

Homer Hight, who was immediately suspected to have been the third man in the robbery, was arrested in Taney County a few weeks after the incident for suspicion of robbing a Forsyth grocery store. Upon questioning the youth admitted his role in both the store heist and the Model Bakery job. He also implicated Joe Morgan as well as Simmons as assisting him in the bakery heist. Furthermore, the lad insisted Leonard Short had masterminded the job. Hight eventually pled guilty to the bakery robbery and was duly sentenced to a term of five years at Jeff City.

Short was once again picked up for questioning. Both Simmons and Short later posted a cash bond and returned to their wicked ways while Morgan remained at large.

On the evening of October 24, 1933, Joe Morgan wed blonde, petite twenty-year-old Jesse Sage at a private residence located on Pine Street in Springfield. The following afternoon Morgan and "Moose" Upshaw celebrated the happy occasion by sticking-up young store-clerk Lester Payne at gunpoint for $200 in small bills. Before exiting the store Morgan asked the clerk, "Is that all of it? Kinda slim." To which Payne replied, "Hell fellow, don't you know there is a depression going on?"

At approximately 10 o'clock on the evening of November 1st, the nefarious pair was driving past Springfield's St. Johns Hospital in a stolen vehicle when they observed Dr. E. M. Fessenden entering his Ford Coach. Fearing the authorities may be on the lookout for the car they were currently driving, the pair parked and approached the physician, guns drawn. The doctor, noticing the menacing duo, immediately threw up his hands declaring, "You've got the wrong guy." "No we don't. Get in the back seat pal," responded Morgan with a grin.

The hijackers drove the doc to an isolated spot in the country where they booted him out after relieving him of an expensive wristwatch, four dollars in cash, and his doctor's bag filled with drugs. Fessenden walked to a nearby farmhouse and phoned the authorities.

After discarding their hostage the two hooligans motored back to town where they held-up filling station attendant E. H. Godfrey for seven dollars in change and a tank of gas. As they prepared to depart the scene, a pair of businessmen on their way to Jackson, Mississippi, pulled into the station for fuel. The thieves decided to abandon the doctor's rig and kidnapped the unsuspecting pair along with their car at gunpoint. After robbing the salesmen of fifteen dollars, they were released at the Hickory Hills Golf Club before the hoodlums drove into the night.

The following morning an enraged Chief of Police Paul Frey responded to the pair's mini-crime wave by telling a police reporter; "We have got to get the men responsible for plundering this town. Over the past year not a night has gone by without a robbery within the city limits." When asked who he thought was responsible for the recent crime wave. He stated; "There is no doubt in my mind, Leonard Short and his band of henchmen are behind many of these crimes and we will bring them to justice."

Just days later Morgan and Upshaw were arrested and charged with both the store robbery and the Fessenden kidnapping. Morgan was also charged with the Model Bakery messenger heist. At his preliminary hearing, Morgan's recently acquired wife informed reporters on the court house steps, "I think the law has put a bum rap on my man. Joe is a sweet fellow when you get to know him."

The outlaw immediately sent word to Leonard Short to bail him out of the can or else. When bail was not forthcoming Morgan reacted to the rejection by informing investigators of Short's part in the bakery job. Within days of Morgan's Mea Culpa, Short and Frank Simmons were rearrested and officially charged with the bakery heist. Short again bailed out but refused to post bond for his partner. Simmons, angered by his pal's selfish ways joined the crowd dropping a dime on Mr. Short.

At approximately 8:00 on the evening of November 23, Joe Morgan was calmly sitting on his steel bunk in the Greene County Jail when Jailor George Harp stopped by, offering him the daily newspaper. Morgan thanked the jailor before causally rolling onto his back to read the paper. His bunkmate, Glenn Hill, a recently captured escapee from the Kansas State Penitentiary, lazily glanced at Morgan before falling to sleep.

While making his midnight rounds, Jailor George Mitchell noticed Morgan's bunk was empty. A closer inspection revealed two bars on the cell house window had been sawed in two producing a hole barely large enough for a man to crawl through. A general alarm was sounded and the premises searched but to no avail. When questioned, Morgan's doe-eyed bunkie informed lawmen, "I was as surprised as you to see him missing. I never heard a thing."

The fugitive's freedom was short-lived. He was captured a week after his escape at the home of a relative in East St. Louis, Illinois, and promptly returned to Springfield by rail to face trial. A short investigation revealed that Moose Upshaw's father had smuggled a straight razor, hack-saw blade and a screw driver to his son on visiting day. Apparently the youth had turned over the contraband to his senior partner who used them to bust out of the aging jail.

On December 14, with his weeping bride looking on, Morgan appeared in district court handcuffed to Ora Upshaw, (Dorsal's daddy), who was charged with aiding and abetting in Morgan's jail delivery. Joe Morgan was sentenced to a twenty-year hitch at the Missouri pen for the grocery store heist. The following day Dorsal Upshaw was given a dose of the same judicial medicine.

In the waning days of November, Dewey Gilmore finally went to court for the Greystone filling station robbery. After a short trial the thug was convicted and sentenced to a twelve-year hitch at the Missouri state pen. He immediately appealed the sentence. Gilmore's sister put up a $5000 appeal bond (using property owned in Osage Co. Oklahoma) causing the outlaws temporary release from custody.

Billings, Missouri - December 24, 1933

A cold blustery pre-dawn wind greeted the red Ford V8 Sedan as the driver maneuvered the rig into a dark alley located behind the Bank of Billings, Missouri, a small town located just southwest of Springfield. While Short mobsters J. W. Baggett and George Calvin stayed in the car, Red Melton and Dewey Gilmore, dressed in dark clothing, ran through the shadows edging up to the side of the bank building where they used a crowbar to force open a window. The pair then slid into the opening and armed with automatic pistols took up positions in wait for the soon to arrive bankers while their companions remained in the parked Ford.

At roughly 8 o'clock Cashier A. J. Howard entered the bank and was confronted by the pair who forced him to open the vault. Meanwhile, Tom White, a local filling station operator, strolled through the bank's main door and was taken hostage as well.

While the bank robbery was in progress a road contractor named Charles Barrett and his son Burl, innocently approached the parked getaway car thinking the occupants were a pair of transportation officers they had arranged to meet that morning. When they attempted to start a conversation they were met with cold blank stares.

Back in the bank, the bandits remained until the inner vault, which was on a time lock set for 8:15, was opened and after gathering up $1099 they tied up the hostages before joining Baggett and Calvin in the red Ford.

Charles Barrett and son, still trying to pass the time of day with the individuals sitting in the getaway car, looked up and to their surprise noticed the two bandits shuffling toward the car holding guns and carrying a burlap bag full of loot. Unnerved by the sight of the approaching outlaws and finally realizing what the men were up to, the amazed road workers raised their hands skyward and slowly backed away from the bandits with great care. After observing the robber's departure the Barrett's ran into a nearby business giving the alarm. Witnesses picked out the rouges gallery photos of Melton, Gilmore, Baggett and Calvin identifying the quartet as the robbers. Leonard Short was once again suspected of engineering the job.

Reeds Springs, Missouri - January 4, 1934

Cashier C. D. Jenkins of the Shepard of the Hills Bank of Reeds Springs, Missouri, approached his place of business on foot as he had every morning for years. Suddenly, he got the feeling that something was amiss. Something about the bank's side window looked a bit out of place. He also observed a strange car containing a pair of unsavory-looking types parked about a hundred yards down the street. Ever since the bank had been robbed the previous year he had been very careful when opening the financial institution and much more observant of his surroundings when on the job.

Jenkins decided to play it safe. Instead of going on to the bank, he entered a local grocery store, placing a call to Constable Dale Davis voicing his suspicions. The Constable gathered up a small but heavily armed posse, which included two employees of the store, the banker, and a man named Arthur Tilden.

The five men warily approached the parked car, guns at ready and began questioning the occupants, who stated they were merely on a pleasure trip. When Davis searched the car, he discovered four pistols hidden under the seats and a batch of nitroglycerin and blasting caps in the trunk. "Funny stuff to be hauling on a pleasure trip" the lawman commented.

The occupants of the car were later identified as George Layton and Guy Majors, a couple of Springfield thugs with lengthy police records. Davis left the store proprietor along with Tilden to watch the pair while he and the banker, accompanied by Almon Gracey, moved toward the bank. The cashier unlocked the bank's front door. While everything appeared normal in the lobby the back room was in disarray. Spotting a shadow in the rear Davis called out a warning, ordering whoever was in there to, "Come out with your hands up."

Hearing nothing but silence he fired a round from his shotgun into the dark room. The explosion was answered by the report of a lone shot, the round bouncing harmlessly off a wall. The posse reacted by unleashing several more shotgun blasts and a half-dozen pistol rounds toward the gun flash. As soon as the shooting died down a man shouted his surrender.

Presently two individuals walked out of the rear, hands in the air. One of the men, later identified as George Crossman, was wounded, being struck by buckshot in one shoulder and a pistol round to the other while the other individual, identified as Red Melton, was unharmed. All four suspects were transported to the Stone County Jail in nearby Galena.

An investigation of the culprits uncovered the fact George Layton had in the past been the proprietor of a Springfield ice-cream business and a taxi driver. He had as of late been mixed up in the bootlegging business with Leonard Short. The previous year he was involved in a short gun-battle with local cops as well as a brawl with a Springfield officer who knocked his front teeth down his throat with a blackjack. Layton was the brother of a noted area prizefighter. His companion, Guy Majors, was also a Springfield bootlegger and noted as a notorious police character being convicted numerous times for selling and transporting illegal spirits.

Forty-year-old George Crossman was a drifter hailing from Wyoming, who since his arrival from the west had been picked up several times by the Springfield police for investigation. He was described as a pool hall tramp and gambler. The authorities described Melton as a local Stone County burglar, cattle and hog rustler. In a move that could be characterized as just plum stupid, the authorities allowed Melton's brother, "Kate" to post a $15,000 bond in order to gain Red's freedom.

Galena, Kansas - February 24, 1934

Nearly two months after the Reeds Springs affair Red Melton and Fred Reese, probably assisted by Melton's newly acquired wife, Maxine, as well as his brother Epp, looted the

Galena, Kansas, National Bank in their usual methodical fashion. According to reports, two individuals broke into the bank at approximately 5 am under the cover of darkness by forcing their way into an unoccupied room located directly above the bank and after cutting a hole in the floor gained access to the financial institution by lowering themselves down a twenty foot rope into the bank's lobby. When janitor Charles Woods unlocked the side door he was accosted by two men armed with revolvers. After questioning the janitor as to the daily work routine he was allowed to go about his duties sweeping the floors.

At 8 o'clock Assistant Cashier T. O. Moeller entered the building. He was taken hostage, as was Bookkeeper A. H. Moorman, who was forced to open the vault. Shortly after Moorman's arrival Bookkeeper Miss Francis Coles appeared. She was promptly placed in a chair with her hands tied to her ankles while her co-workers were moved to the vault, hogtied with coarse rope and forced to lie face-down on the floor.

After restraining the employees, the hijackers left the bank using a side door entering a car parked in an adjoining alley, which was occupied by a man and a woman. The amount of dough taken by the robbers was announced as being in excess of $7000.

The day after the robbery, the authorities broadcast the hold-up was the work of the Barrow Gang (Bonnie and Clyde). Later they pointed the finger at members of the Cookson Hills Gang, who had previously robbed the bank in 1933. On that occasion the notorious Ford Bradshaw, accompanied by Charley Cotner, Clarence Eno, and others had looted the institution for several thousand dollars. The motivation for suspecting Bradshaw and company for the most recent robbery was based on the fact he, Charley Cotner, and Bradshaw's attractive moll, Stella "Boots" Moody, were seen in the Joplin area shortly after the heist. The authorities figured they were not visiting the area for their health.

Although no one was ever convicted of the second Galena robbery officials finally decided the true culprits were Red Melton and company assisted in the planning by "Shock" Short.

In March, Leonard Short went to trial for the bakery messenger robbery. Joe Morgan was transported from Jeff City to be the prosecutions chief witness. Morgan testified he had arrived in Springfield in July 1933 and made the acquaintance of Leonard Short a few months afterwards. According to the squealer, Short sought him out and recruited him for the Model Bakery job. Morgan admitted that while waiting for Short to finalize his plans he occupied himself by robbing several grocery stores, a shoe store and a theatre. He then went on to explain the details of the bakery robbery.

Short was duly convicted of the crime and sentenced to twelve years in prison. The rotund bandit chieftain immediately appealed the case to the Missouri Supreme Court. In the meantime, he was granted his freedom through appeal bond.

In due time the high court denied Short's legal appeal, revoked his bond and issued a warrant for his arrest. Instead of turning himself into the authorities the badman reacted to the news by taking a powder but not before he, Floyd Maples, Ralph Wilson, and Red Melton stole Springfield Chief of Police Paul Frey's private vehicle from his residence, driving it across the border into Oklahoma to a secluded spot on the banks of the Spring River where they set it on fire.

When questioned by Springfield Chief of Detectives Ruel Wommack, C. E. Russell, the proprietor of a country store located a mile from where the torched vehicle was discovered, claimed a carload of suspicious looking characters visited his business the day of the burning where they purchased a five-gallon can of gas. The storekeeper identified the gascan found at the crime scene as the very one the men filled at his store. When shown mug shots of Melton, Short, Maples and Wilson he stated "Ya, that's the guys." Adding, "This fellow Short appeared to be the leader of the group. He gave the others orders, handled the money and bought them and some kids hanging around the store soda pop and candy." Apparently the car burning was simply an act of revenge for certain derogatory statements Frey had made against Short during his trial.

As for Joe Morgan, on his way back to the penitentiary from testifying at Short's trial he managed to slip out of his handcuffs and when the officer's vehicle halted at a stop sign just outside the prison's gates, he leaped out and took off like a bolt, running down the road. The car's driver, Greene County Deputy Sheriff George Spencer ,reacted to the escape by calmly exiting the rig and firing three shots at the fugitive, one grazing his ribs. After falling to the pavement the prisoner meekly surrendered. Spencer told reporters, "That last shot sure took the fight out of him!"

Webb City, Missouri - May 10, 1934

Moments after the sun made it's initial appearance on the Eastern horizon, three cars motored into the aging downtown district of the Jasper County mining town of Webb City coming to a halt directly in front of the city bank located on the corner of Main and Broadway. Moments later the vehicles disgorged six individuals dressed in overalls and carrying oversized canvas bags containing burglars tools while three others remained behind the wheel of the rigs. The drivers parked one car in a nearby alley while a second automobile was positioned across the street from the bank The driver of the third vehicle then proceeded to purposely set fire to an abandoned structure located several blocks away in order to distract the attention of any curious busybodies from what was happening at the bank.

Meanwhile, the group on foot proceeded up a stairway breaking into a second story beauty shop that was located above the bank. They methodically sawed a large hole in the floor before three of the interlopers, Red Melton, Fred Reese and Floyd Henderson, shinnied down a rope through the hole into the bank director's office while the other three stayed behind in the hair salon.

At 7:30, two unsuspecting female hair-dressers, Latha Loftin and Lois Bristow, entered the shop and were taken hostage by the hoodlums. The pair was bound hand and foot with a rope and their mouths covered by adhesive tape. The ladies were informed they were, "Getting some money downstairs, so don't make no fuss."

At nearly the same time as the beauticians were being subdued, the town's fire alarm began blaring. Moments later, a pair of fire trucks loaded with emergency personal rushed to the scene of the arson.

In the meantime, janitor Tom Hill opened the bank's door and was taken captive, muffled and bound as well. Thirty minutes later, three women bookkeepers, Mary Powers, Louise McGrew, and Theresa Brewer, arrived on the scene. The frightened trio were similarly subdued. Soon afterwards, Cashier Lee Daugherty reported for work and he was given the same rough treatment.

When the time clock engaged at 8:30 opening the bank's large walk-in vault, the hijackers stuffed approximately $15,000 in paper money into a large bag before exiting the financial institution through the front door. Simultaneously, the other bandits departed their stations in the beauty salon. All six hijackers entered the two cars parked on the street while a hastily assembled crowd of townsfolk watched the goings on in morbid fascination. Witnesses observed one of the getaway cars head south out of town, while the other sped in a northerly direction.

Back in the bank, Bookkeeper Mary Powers worked a single hand free from her bonds and grasped a telephone. She rang up the local police department informing the desk sergeant there was a robbery in progress. Evidently, none of the spectators standing in the street had thought to appraise the authorities of the heist. After observing the thieves depart the area a local filling station attendant emerged from the crowd, entered the bank and freed the hostages. Other bystanders then dashed up the flight of stairs where they freed the beauty operators.

Although a large posse of officers and armed vigilantes was quickly formed and began a hot pursuit of the bold hijackers, no trace of the outlaws was uncovered. Jasper County authorities would later conclude the robbery was the work of Leonard Short's "Ozark Mountain Boys" also known to the press as, "Six Daring Bandits Inc." How some inventive journalist came up with the number six is unknown.

Those who were later identified as taking part in the bank job besides Melton, Reese and Henderson were Leonard Short, Dewey Gilmore and possibly Art Austin. The other members of the hijacking party remain unknown due to their faces being covered by handkerchiefs.

Over the next few months, the Short Gang made moonlight raids on the towns of Nixa and Ozark, Missouri. They rounded up citizens off the streets, including the town cops, tied them up with ropes, then broke into various stores, looting businesses and blowing open safes with nitro.

In the town of Ozark, Night Watchman Bill Shirkey was clubbed unmercifully then bound hand and foot to a lamp post. He was forced to watch helplessly while the gang went about their deprivations.

Missouri State Investigator O. L. Viet was assigned to look into these happenings, but little came of his efforts. He did arrest J. W. Baggett, a mysterious Arkansas ridge-runner, whom several victims identified as one of the looters. Unfortunately for the authorities, Baggett, a known associate of Leonard Short, refused to talk, thus leaving the authorities at a loss as to the whereabouts of the raiders.

Meanwhile, terrified citizens and business owners living in numerous small towns dotting the Ozark Mountains region began to wonder out loud if they would be next on the list to fall victim to the gang's rampages.

Chapter 5
Public Enemies

Although "Shock" Short may have very well been attracted to Heady and his companions counterfeiting scam, it appears his interest in any joint ventures with the O'Malley group lie mainly with the crime of bank robbery. The proof in the pudding comes from the fact Heady and O'Malley would soon enthusiastically join Short's raiders on their next stab at withdrawing copious amounts of cash from the banking industry.

Soon after the Nixa raid Short relocated his headquarters to Claremore, Oklahoma, the hometown of world famous humorist Will Rogers. The bandit took a room at the Neworth Hotel. Just days after Short's arrival Dewey Gilmore and his young bride, posing as his sister, breezed into town. While the couple initially stayed at the Neworth, they later rented a residence from Bryan Clark located at the East end of Eleventh Street. Gilmore's lady took a job as a waitress at Morton's Café. The pair was described by neighbors as quite and unassuming. While in Claremore Gilmore used the alias "Dave Grant" while Short was known to the locals as "Jimmy Johnson."

Noted as a center for illegal gambling reputably financed by the Kansas City mob, Claremore acted as a magnet for a plethora of professional gamblers. Many of those visiting the community for the purpose of indulging in the betting sports arrived from the Kansas City area by rail as part of pre-planned junkets. Although the town had a reputation of being wide-open when it came to a hodgepodge of illegal sporting events such as horse racing, cock and dog fighting, large scale crap games, the main event was high stakes poker.

The Neworth Hotel occupied the second floor of a large building located in the town's central business district. Located within walking distance was several gambling dens situated in backrooms of various pool halls, cigar, and confectionary stores as well as a number of private rooms in the nearby Sequoyah and Mason Hotels.

A horde of nightclubs and roadhouses such as the Club Claremont, The Willows, the Cotton Club, and the Tavern Inn offered legal 3.2 beer, as well as illegal whiskey, ladies of the night, and back rooms for high stakes poker.

(Fat Jack Miller from 85)

An old-timer, now in his mid-nineties, who was once "in the business" in Claremore, told this author, "Back in the old days we had a little old bar in the front of my place, but the big

money was in our gambling room located in the rear. Straight poker was the game. No dice, just poker. Naturally, we had a couple of gals from Kansas City pushing ass upstairs on the weekends."

By the early-1930s the town had taken on a bit of a trail-town aspect, alcohol fueled knifings and shootings were fairly common, gun battles occasionally spilled out into the street. It appears local law

"Fat Jack" Miller

enforcement mostly turned a blind eye when it came to the town's cottage industry.

Playing host to the gang were several native born gamblers including Earl "Wooden-foot" Clanton, owner of the notorious Route 66 Club located in nearby Miami, Oklahoma. Earl was a member of a notorious local clan, distantly related to the infamous Ike and Billy Clanton of Tombstone-OK Corral fame. His nephew's, Herman and Ed "Newt" Clanton, were both convicted bank robbers. Newt was the more famous of the two being an active member of the Cookson Hills Gang, otherwise known as the Wilbur Underhill-Ford Bradshaw Gang.

Newt began his career in crime in 1927 when he and homeboy, Robert "Major" Taylor (*who will play a role in the latter sections of this story), knocked off the bank of Bluejacket, Oklahoma. Both men were promptly captured and sentenced to terms at McAlester. Newt was given a temporary parole due to his contracting TB. He then traveled to Vian, Oklahoma, where he met up with his ex-prison cellmate, Ford Bradshaw. After marrying Bradshaw's niece, Clanton joined his crew and for the next two years was suspected of involvement in several murders and a half dozen bank robberies in four states. His criminal career ended abruptly in the early morning hours of February 4, 1934, when he, Bradshaw, and Charlie Cotner were spotted by two lawmen trying to burglarize a hardware store in downtown Chelsea. A gun battle ensued in which an officer as well as Clanton was left lying dead in the street.

Another of Short's hosts was Jackson "Fat Jack" Miller. He was born on September 7, 1896, in the Cherokee Nation, Indian Territory, modern-day Rogers County. Miller was the third of five children born to a hard working couple who farmed near the village of Verdigris.

His two brothers, Charley and Lewis, appeared to be honest citizens. One ran a blacksmith shop in Claremore while the other was a ranch hand and one-time trick-rider in a traveling wild-west show. While both his brothers served in the Great War, Jack did not due to his failing to pass the physical because of diabetes. Jack married in 1919 to what some sources claim was a hot tempered woman who never minded how he made his money as long as he kept bringing home the bacon. Not a motivation for staying on the straight and narrow.

Although it appears Miller did manage to hold a legitimate job as a novice telegraph operator for a year or two after taking his nuptials, he soon fell in with bad company. He helped operate a whiskey still at a location just west of Claremore known as Rascal Flats, employed by a man named Bill Flippen. Old-timers tell of often-times observing convoys of trucks dubbed, "The Silver Fleet," rumbling through the area on moonless nights heading to Tulsa and Oklahoma City filled with illegal hooch.

Jack's ultimate downfall seems to have been his love of dice and the pasteboards. His descendants claim, "If Jack heard there was a game somewhere, off he'd go even if he had to borrow the money to get there." Adding, "It wasn't unusual for him to disappear for days at a time." His brother, Lewis, once picked him up at the Claremore rail station and noticed he had a large satchel crammed full of money on his person.

When Miller was arrested on a larceny charge at the age of twenty-five, the authorities described him as a con-man, bootlegger, bar-room bouncer, and gambler with heavy connections to the local underworld. Descendents further describe him as henpecked, a big man but fast on his feet, even tempered, and a bit lazy.

One of his nieces commented, "He liked the finer things. Back during the depression when you couldn't get two nickels to rub together my pa had only a horse and wagon for transportation while Jack always drove a fine car. While we wore hand-me-downs his kids were always clothed in fancy duds." She added, "I was told Jack wouldn't do anything without first checking with his wife....While I don't condone his methods of obtaining money, he was a product of the times. Indian, poor, big family to provide for and no jobs to be had. He did whatever he could to get money."

Blessed with the gift of Blarney, one of Miller's nicknames was "Sugar-Lips" while another was "Fat Jack" due to his weighing over two-hundred and fifty pounds on attaining adulthood. He made a habit of carrying a sawed-off shotgun in his vehicle at all times. The scattergun, which ultimately became his weapon of choice, was always within easy reach.

The oversized hoodlum also had a reputation of being good with his fists. He beat eighteen-year-old H.A. Secrest to death in 1924 with his bare knuckles while he was employed as a bouncer at a Claremore resort. The big man was initially charged with manslaughter but eventually beat the rap.

In early 1934 Miller was indicted by the Rogers County Grand Jury on two counts of running a confidence game. On the first occasion the thug was accused of swindling Arthur Hendrix out of $533 in a bogus poker game (use of marked cards).

The second indictment concerned Miller and "Red" Autry cheating a farmer named Sol Casey out of $1500 in a "confidence" game. According to court records, on that occasion Miller and his confidant had induced the farmer to "smoke a cigarette which had been doped" before fleecing the poor sod out of his hard earned cash. Although Autry was eventually convicted in the affair, Miller's lawyer delayed the case for nearly four years until the prosecutor finally gave up and dropped the charges when the chief witness decided it would be bad for his health to persist in the matter.

Shortly after arriving in Claremore, Leonard Short began plotting the gang's next score. He was soon joined at the Neworth by Irish O'Malley and Dan Heady.

There is some evidence suggesting O'Malley was initially accompanied by his girlfriend, Vivian Chase, who evidentially stayed just a few days before exiting the scene and relocating back to Kansas City where she moved into an apartment located at 6653 Oak Street in Kansas City with an old friend named Jackie Bondurant. Ms. Bondurant (*real name Vesta Mae Collins) was noted in police files as a known gangster moll and "a woman possessing low moral standards."

Fayetteville, Arkansas - September 12, 1934

An hour before dawn a car containing Red Melton, Dan Heady, Fred Reese, and Dewey Gilmore parked in the rear of the McIlroy Bank and Trust located on the square in downtown Fayetteville, Arkansas, just a short distance from US Highway #71. While Dewey Gilmore remained at the car's wheel, Melton, Heady, and Reese bailed out bounding up a fire-escape leading to the bank's second story. Using a hammer and a crowbar the trio broke out a side window and gained entrance to the building. A second vehicle containing Art Austin, Leonard Short and Jack Miller, armed with his trusty scattergun, circled the square acting as lookouts.

At 8 o'clock, cashier A. J. Pyeatt and six other bank employees, Jasper Pyeatt, J. B. McConnell, Bertha Jones, Quinton Kendall, Mildred Jones and Col. C. F. Armistead reported for work, accessing the bank through the main entrance. The crowd of bankers was immediately met by the armed trio and lined up against a wall where they were ordered to remain in place while the bandits patiently awaited the time lock to engage opening the vault's outer door.

According to witnesses, the robbers wore gloves and their faces were covered with either ladies black nylon stockings or a handkerchief. While two of the hijackers remained in the main lobby guarding the hostages the third took a position near the front door to act as a greeter to any further interlopers.

At approximately 8:15 bond salesman J. W. Hill arrived at the financial institution, where he had arranged an early morning appointment with a loan officer. According to Hill: "I knocked on the door and no one answered so I opened the door and entered the building. I thought it strange no one appeared at the doorway but I stepped inside and suddenly the door slammed behind me. I turned halfway around and noticed a man, revolver in hand, standing behind me (*later identified as Red Melton). The lower half of his face was covered by a blue handkerchief, which kept slipping off his nose and sliding down to his chin. He wore stripped coveralls. He just stood there silently holding the pistol. At first I thought the bankers were pulling a practical joke. I half expected the man to break out in laughter." Hill added, " I asked what was going on? Is this serious business? He shifted his pistol a little before saying, 'Stand over by the wall facing me and you won't get hurt.'…After a short silence he asked my business…I replied…'I'm a bond salesman.' adding 'I have nothing of value in my case.' Actually, there was $2000 in negotiable bonds in my case." Hill went on to say, " I asked if I could sit down to which he replied, 'Hell no.' I further inquired if I could smoke. He laughed then asked if I was nervous or something? I replied, 'Yea, a smoke wouldn't do me no harm.' He then allowed me to fumble through my pockets to locate my cigarettes and a match book… I think he got a kick out of watching my nervousness."

According to witnesses, sometime during the proceedings Melton took a couple of steps into the lobby and in front of everyone brazenly unzipped his fly and took a long leisurely piss into a large potted plant positioned on the floor. He cracked a wry smile at the mortified crowd before closing his fly and returning to his position. (*years later Melton would tell a relative he, "Left those folks in Fayetteville something to remember me by.")

Once the vault's outer door sprang open at 8:30 the pair of robbers stationed in the lobby ordered J. B. McConnell to open the inner vault which was accessed by combination. After scooping up roughly $5700 in cash and coin, which was placed in three canvas bags, the seven hostages were herded into the vault.

According to Hall, before taking further action one of the pair shouted to their comrade stationed in the foyer, 'What are we going to do with that fellow?' The red-headed bandit replied, 'We'll put him in with the rest." Hill was then escorted to the vault where a tall robber (Fred Reese), his face covered with a stocking, with holes cut out at the eyes and mouth, ordered the man who had been guarding him to bring the ropes. "The fellow informed us he intended to tie us up with rope." He then asked "Who's first?" Although one of the gals stepped forward, Banker A. J. Pyeatt convinced the bandit to not tie bind them but simply shut them in the vault.

"We were then all herded into the vault and although the door was shut it was not locked." Hill went on to tell investigators, "About that time Mr. Pyeatt turned to me stating, "I bet you didn't expect a reception like this?"

After securing the hostages the bandits exited the bank through the rear door fleeing to their getaway car located in the alley. The gang then successfully made their getaway speeding back to Claremore where they split up the day's take.

Ironically, unnoticed by the bandits, located just above the vault door was a fully-loaded sawed-off shotgun hung on pegs and within arms reach of anyone who desired to make use of it.

Just moments after the hijackers departed the building bank employee, Marion Schwarz, arrived at the business. She opened the front door but noticing the bank was empty decided something was wrong and ran next door to the Collier Drug Store. Moments later, bank employees hit the alarm located in the vault summoning a legion of curious citizens.

When interviewed by detectives all the witnesses from the bank but Hill and McConnell were unable to give any worthwhile description of the robbers due to their faces being covered. A canvassing of residents living and working in the area failed to produce any witnesses to the gang's departure or description of the getaway cars.

The bank's janitor claimed he had departed the financial institution at 7:30 without noticing anything out of the ordinary (*apparently he had not spent any time cleaning the second-story offices on that particular day). A merchant policeman came forward stating he had passed by the bank at about the same time and everything looked fine.

Within twenty minutes of the heist radio station KUQA broadcast an alert from its offices located in the Washington Hotel. Police in three states reacted to the robbery by erecting roadblocks on all major highways and bridges but to no avail.

Back at the bank, officers commented to reporters on the split second timing of the heist. Fayetteville Police Chief Neal Cruse informed newsies, "These boys were not amateurs."

A single five-cent piece dropped by the hijackers was found on the floor of the bank's lobby. The coin was placed on display in the bank's front window as a souvenir.

In the aftermath of the bank heist, Red Melton and his sidekick Fred Reese departed Claremore motoring back to Missouri where they went to work attempting to pass some of O'Malley's bogus bills. Although the pair managed to scam Granby, Missouri, resident Charles Burress out of $800 of goods using play dough, the moment Burress realized he had been had he filed charges on the pair and warrants were issued.

The following day Red Melton was arrested in a police raid on his brother Epp's residence located near Cassville, Missouri. The daring bandit's $15,000 bond concerning the Reeds Springs bank job was revoked and he was transported to the Jasper County Jail in Carthage where he was charged with fraud and suspicion of bank robbery (Billings).

Just hours after Melton's arrest, Washington County Arkansas Sheriff Harley Glover arrived in Carthage with

Fayetteville bankers A. J. Pyeatt and J. B. McConnell in tow. McConnell positively identified the outlaw as one of the hijackers while Pyeatt stated the redheaded outlaw's appearance coincided with that of one of the bandits who robbed the institution but he couldn't make a positive identification. Neither of the witnesses' were able to identify a photo of Fred Reese as being one of the hijackers. Bond salesman Hill would later identify Melton as the man who tormented him in during the robbery.

Incidentally, the day after the Fayetteville robbery a bank clerk identified a mug shot of Irish O'Malley as being the same man he witnessed entering the lobby of the McIlroy bank a week before the heist requesting change for a $100 bill. He stated "The man dressed like a dandy and had a prominent jaw." He added, "The incident stuck in my mind since you don't see many $100 bills nowadays."

Just days after the Fayetteville heist, the US Congress enacted a series of sweeping anti-crime bills. One was the so-called "Dillinger Law," which made the robbery of a national bank a federal offence thus placing the full resources of the federal government behind lawmen in their pursuit of bank hijackers.

The initial test for the law came in January 1935 with the trial of Ralph Roe and Jack Lloyd for the September 10, 1934, robbery of the Farmers National Bank of Sulpher, Oklahoma. The pair was convicted in Muskogee, Oklahoma, federal court with little fanfare and sentenced to 99 years each.

Another component of the newly enacted laws was the renaming of the Department of Justice's Bureau of Investigation to the FBI. Congress also gave the bureau expanded powers in its newly announced "War on Crime," such as the right to carry and use deadly weapons and cross state lines at will. These legal maneuverings would soon lead to the downfall of nearly all the Public Enemies of the era.

Fortunately for Melton, the Billings bank was a "State"

instead of a "National" bank, thus he was charged in state circuit court located in Ozark, Missouri. Although "Red's" wife came forward at the trial testifying the two were married in Nuevo Laredo, Mexico, on the very day of the heist, even going as far as producing a dated marriage certificate. The jury convicted her husband.

The presiding judge promptly sentenced him to twelve years incarceration at the Missouri State Penitentiary in Jefferson City after publicly informing the hoodlum he was, "A stench in the nostrils of honest men and should by all rights be locked up for twice that long." The bandit immediately appealed his conviction. On October 29, 1934, the Missouri Supreme Court ordered his release from prison on a legal technicality.

Although Arkansas officials had placed a detainer on the red-headed outlaw in regards to the Fayetteville bank heist, a slip-up occurred and they were not notified of his release from custody. Melton quickly rejoined Fred Reese, who had recently sat out a weekend in a Wichita Jail on a drunk driving charge, under an assumed name. Investigators suspected Reese had spent the past few weeks ,while his pal was in stir, arranging and promoting cock-fights throughout Kansas and Missouri.

Coffeyville, Kansas - September 22, 1934-5 AM

At dawn, a few days after Red Melton's release, Ralph "Dutch" Woohlers, a US Mail contract driver employed by the Rex Transfer and Storage Co., picked up a single locked mail pouch at the Coffeyville train depot. The pouch had arrived earlier that morning on the southbound Missouri Pacific train #115.

When Woohlers pulled away from the curb he noticed a black 1933 or '34 Plymouth sedan fall in behind him. Passengers in the Plymouth included Jess Doyle as well as O'Malley associates, John Langan and Clarence Sparger. The car's driver was Jack Richards, a recent parolee from the Missouri state pen. He was given his walking papers after serving six years of a ten-year stretch for robbing a Kansas City bank. Richards had served time with both Clarence Sparger and Dan Heady at Jeff City. While incarcerated, the trio operated an alcohol still, making homemade jail-house "jungle juice." Rumor has it, Sparger ran the still while Heady and Richards acted as salesmen and muscle for the business.

When the Woohler halted the truck at a stop sign at the intersection of Twelve and Willow Streets, the Plymouth suddenly cut him off. While Richards remained at the car's wheel, the other three leaped out of the vehicle and onto the truck's running boards pointing pistols at the driver.

After stealing the mail pouch, which the hijackers had been tipped-off carried an estimated $40,000 payroll, the bandits forced Woohlers to drive a few blocks west to a vacant lot where he was manhandled from the rig into the hijacker's getaway car which proceeded to speed away from the scene heading in a southerly direction. The outlaws abandoned the postal truck on the side of the road, it's doors unlocked and motor running.

Just after crossing the Oklahoma border into South Coffeyville, the getaway car suffered a flat tire. According to Woohlers, two bandits departed the rig in order to change the tire while the others held him in place at gunpoint. After making the repairs the looters released their hostage before speeding away.

Oddly, it took Mr. Woohlers nearly an hour to report the crime. It appears instead of phoning his superiors or the police Woohlers casually strolled back to Coffeyville on foot where he hopped into his still running truck and leisurely motored back to the main post office. At 6:50 A.M., nearly two hours after the heist had occurred, the dawdling driver finally reported the crime to his bosses.

On being questioned the lackadaisical mail hack stated while he could not make out the Plymouth's license due to mud covering the plate, he felt certain he could manage to give investigators a description of three of the four bandits, claiming he never got a good look at the driver's face.

Unfortunately, for the hijackers, the postal service had recently changed the delivery schedule and the bag in question contained no cash just $6000 in non-negotiable bonds as well as a slug of private mail containing only a single five-dollar bill.

The heist proved to be a major embarrassment for such a high caliber group of desperadoes. Not only did the job fail to pay off but the theft of mails was a federal offence that would bring the FBI breathing down the perpetrators necks.

Turns out, the finger man on the job was the notorious Tommy Hill, the head of the so-called South Coffeyville Mob. Headquartered at the Casa Del Roadhouse. Hill and his associates operated an array of whorehouses, seedy pool halls, gambling dens and garish speakeasies such as Harry Sherman's Nut House, The Silver Slipper, and Harry Hicks' Night Club in the small oilfield community. Legendary Kansas lawman Joe Anderson once said about Tommy Hill, "That guy would run a crooked dice game on his own mother.....He would steal anything. I wouldn't be surprised if he once stole an elephant."

Hill's chief lieutenant was Alvin Sherwood, a one-time member of the infamous Terrill-Inman Gang. Sherwood had recently been paroled from the Oklahoma pen where he was serving a seven-year hitch for burglary. Over the years Hill had offered sanctuary and business planning to such underworld notables as "Pretty Boy" Floyd, Al Spencer, Harry Campbell, Alvin Karpis, and Ray Terrill. He was usually more reliable when it came to business.

The leader of the postal hijacking operation, Jess Doyle, was a seasoned criminal. A Tulsa native, he was convicted of auto theft in 1921 and sentenced to a thirteen-year stretch at the Oklahoma State Penitentiary at McAlester. Less than a year after his parole, he was convicted of second-degree burglary in Kansas and sentenced to five-to ten years at Lansing. Soon after gaining his freedom in mid 1932 the swarthy thug traveled to St. Paul, Minnesota, where he rejoined his boyhood pal, Freddie Barker, co-leader of the powerful "Ma" Barker-Karpis Gang.

The gang, which had began as a pack of vicious juvenile street urchins operating on the mean streets of Tulsa, had grown in size and sophistication over the years. Some of the more noted members of the combination were brothers, Fred and "Doc" Barker as well as Harry Campbell, William Weaver, Volney Davis, Larry "The Chopper" Devol, and Alvin Karpis. Although reports over the years have implicated the mother of the Barker boys as being the leader of the group, in reality, "Ma" Barker was never involved in the gang's high profile robberies.

Doyle, along with several other members of the Barker Gang, looted the Cloud County Bank of Concordia, Kansas, on July 25, 1932, for $250,000. He also assisted the gang in the April 4, 1933, robbery of the First National Bank of Fairbury, Nebraska, for $151,000 as well as the June 15, 1933, kidnapping of beer-baron William Hamm Jr.

He was evicted from the group in early January 1934 after quarrelling with the Barkers over what he clamed was an unequal division of the ransom money from the Hamm kidnapping. After leaving the Barker bunch, Doyle relocated to Kansas City with his girlfriend, Vinita Stacey (maiden name Doris Stanley), and began freelancing. Soon after arriving in the city, Doyle hooked up with Walter O'Malley's group and began assisting the slick gangster with his ongoing counterfeiting operation, among other things.

Apparently when Doyle received word from Hill concerning the planned payroll heist they decided to cut O'Malley in on the deal. Failing to find Walter, who was casting about the wilds of Oklahoma and Arkansas at the time, he hired two of his underlings in his place.

Meanwhile, "Shock" Short decided to visit his relatives in Galena, Missouri, located a little over two hundred miles west of Coffeyville. While in the area he joined with a wild-assed Oklahoma boy named Bob Johnson and his pals, Roy Ledbetter, the youthful perpetrator of the 1931 Ash Grove bank robbery, along with a convicted chicken thief by the name of Buster Cooper, engaging in the hijacking of Carthage café owner L. H. Dillard of a hoard of $800 worth of diamonds. Although the heist went off without a hitch unfortunately for the three hoodlums the affair was witnessed by several citizens. The day after the robbery Short fled back to his haunts in Claremore.

Upon receiving news of his brother's recent criminal activities, Dewey Short, currently making a run for congress as an anti-Roosevelt candidate, boldly announced Leonard was being framed by unscrupulous business competitors. His statement was promptly characterized by area law enforcement officials as pure unadulterated bullshit at best.

Leonard's difficulties had come at a bad time for Dewey. There were already rumors making their way thru the hills implying Dewey's current run for elected office was being financed by Leonard's illicit activities. As election time neared, Dewey's opponent fueled those rumors into outright public accusations. Although Short's backers feared the scandal would throw the election, in the end the smear campaign backfired. Dewey had his supporters as well as his detractors such as the editors of the powerful *Springfield News Leader*. An editorial ran under the popular *Wastebasket* column in the paper just days before the election opining the fact Dewey was not the first prominent public figure in American history to be straddled with strange relatives. They pointed out the example of actor Edwin Booth and his brother John Wilkes, the assassin of Abraham Lincoln. The editorial went on to suggest Dewey had by all appearances led an active and honest life and should not be held responsible for the actions of his notorious sibling. When it was all said and done public opinion turned in

Dewey's favor. It appears many voters not only disbelieved the ugly stories but felt sympathy for the fledgling politico. Dewy was easily elected.

In the wake of the Carthage robbery Red Melton, now joined by Fred Reese, hijacked the M. O. Cigar Co. in Joplin at gunpoint for a little spending money before departing to the Central Oklahoma oilfields. The pair visited "Red's" sister prior to pulling off a couple of filling station robberies around Seminole before re-joining Leonard Short in Claremore.

Short had plans for a big score and had put out the word he needed his personnel to assemble. What he had in mind was something rarely attempted in the past and usually with poor results, the robbery of two banks at once. The James Gang had tried this feat in Northfield, Minnesota, in 1876 to disastrous results, as had the Dalton boys in Coffeyville, Kansas, in 1892, and Henry Starr's Gang in Stroud, Oklahoma in 1915, all with similar outcomes. Only the Matt Kimes' Gang was able to successfully pull off such a bold endeavor when they simultaneously looted banks in both Covington and Beggs, Oklahoma, in the 1920s.

Russell Cooper

While scouting for recruits for his newest illicit adventure, Leonard Short made the acquaintance of Russell Land Cooper, a professional gambler and man-killer, who was visiting Claremore in order to participate in a round of high stakes poker games going on at a local billiard parlor.

The thirty-seven-year-old Cooper had a bit of a macabre past. He was one of eight children raised near the small isolated Ozark Mountain village of Rudy located twenty miles north of Ft. Smith, Arkansas.

Incidentally, Ruby was also the hometown of noted desperadoes, George and Matt Kimes. Although it is rumored Cooper was involved in at least one of the pair's numerous bank robberies, there is no evidence to back up this assertion. More than likely his only involvement with the notorious duo, excepting a boyhood prank or two, was limited to making a few liquor runs for their daddy, Cornelius Kimes, a prolific "whiskey man" in the area for many years.

In May 1918 Cooper was drafted into the US Army seeing action in France while serving with the 41st "Sunset" Division, 162nd Infantry Regiment as a machine-gunner. After his Honorable Discharge in 1919, he stayed with his parents clerking at the local bank.

Apparently, his father was a brutal man who abused his mother on occasion. Getting a belly full of his dad's outrages, Russell shot and killed him in a violent quarrel soon after his return from the war. The slaying was adjudged justifiable homicide by the authorities. For the next few years he clerked at the Ruby general store, which was managed by his mother. In the mid-1920's, he married a farm gal hailing from around Fayetteville. The couple settled in Ft. Smith where he was employed as a sales clerk.

In the latter twenties Russell brutally murdered his brother-in-law, W. G. Clayton, when Clayton apparently threatened him with a knife. After shooting his victim twice in the head and torso he cut open the stomach cavity and filled it with rocks before discarding the corpse into Frog Bayou. The body was discovered by fishermen several days later tangled up in some debris near the stream's bank.

In the aftermath of the killing Cooper fled to Tulsa but was soon captured and brought back to Arkansas where he was again charged with murder. He was eventually tried and acquitted of the slaying, it being deemed justifiable homicide.

Somewhere along the line, Cooper picked up the gaming habit and over the years evolved into a degenerate gambler. Quitting his clerking job, he spent the early 1930s gambling and engaged in the bootlegging trade. Prison records note him as a nervous, high-strung individual with an IQ of 95 and his crime-partners would one day brand him a coward, a debatable point.

It appears soon after Cooper's arrival in Claremore he made the acquaintance of Leonard Short over a brisk game of five-card stud and a shadowy partnership was formed.

Chapter 6
Two For One: The Okemah Caper

The 2200 souls living in the sleepy county seat community of Okemah, Oklahoma, found the Christmas season of 1934 a bit subdued in nature. There was little to celebrate, the blessings of the season was found wanting to say the least. Okfuskee County had fallen on hard times due to the ongoing economic depression. Farming was the area's mainstay and the price of agricultural products had hit an all-time low. Hard cash was tough to come by and many families were having a difficult time keeping food on the table. It seemed most everyone was behind on their property taxes and mortgage payments. Bank foreclosures on farms had hit an all-time high. For area residents life was evolving into a struggle for the essentials in life, a boring, backbreaking battle to survive the tough times. Area unemployment figures had soared to nearly 25%.

In the past few weeks the most exciting news coming out of Okemah was a gas explosion occurring near Hickory Ridge, injuring two men. Also news worthy was the distribution of Christmas food baskets given to the needy through the heartfelt efforts of generous local merchants and the *Okemah Daily Leader*. Problem was, there was not enough baskets to go around, the need was great while the supply was small. Some folks would just have to go hungry that Christmas.

The local post of the American Legion announced they were giving toys to disadvantaged tots and high praise was heard throughout the sleepy berg for the recent high school production at the Crystal Theatre of the musical "Cat of Nine Tails." Folks were making plans for the High School Alumni Associations annual dance to be held at St. Pauls Methodist Church.

On the freezing windswept winter's morn of December 22nd, three automobiles, a Plymouth Sedan, Ford V8, and Ford Roadster containing seven desperate men motored into Okemah's downtown district. While one vehicle parked next to the First National Bank a second pulled into an alley located directly across the street near the Okemah National Bank while the third car, manned by Irish O'Malley, began circling the downtown area acting as a lookout. Meanwhile, a fourth rig driven by "Fat Jack" Miller, armed with his trusty sawed-off shotgun, loaded with 00 buckshot, scouted the edges of town.

Okemah National Bank

With the sun peeking over the gray horizon, janitor Claude Scarborough shuffled to the side door of the Okemah National. Just as he approached the heavy door, three masked men, later identified as Leonard Short, Dewey Gilmore, and Russell Cooper, accosted him with leveled pistols. Short demanded he, "Open the door and get in and I mean fast."

In the meantime, across the street at the First National sixty-year-old bank janitor J. M. Morgan was strolling to the bank's side entrance when suddenly a car pulled in behind him. "Red" Melton and Fred Reese, both wearing masks made of ladies stockings, leaped out of the rig.

According to Morgan, "They must of known me because as soon as I crossed the street to open the side door, a car whirled in and stopped. I looked across my shoulder and two men approached and stuck a pair of .45s in my ribs, telling me to get on in. They then crowded me into the storeroom where they bound my hands with a piece of rope about as thick as a trot line." After abducting the janitor the desperadoes were joined by "Dapper" Dan Heady, who had been driving the car. The interlopers in both banks then hunkered down awaiting the arrival of other employees.

At approximately 8:00 o'clock a man attired in a light colored coat, felt hat, and black leather gloves with a handkerchief covering his face accosted Okemah National Vice President V. K. Chowning when he attempted to enter the bank. Chowning was ordered behind the counter and told to "Sit down and act natural" before being tied hand and foot and placed on the floor.

The banker, would later tell investigators, one of the robbers informed him the town was surrounded by an army of men armed with machineguns. Moments later, Bank President A. J. Martin entered the financial institution and was placed on the floor and trussed up like a hog. In due time, the bandits overpowered bank employees B. L. Rogers, J. W.

Benson, Ben Hall, George Poor, O.H. Rundles, and Mrs. S.W. Hogan in a similar fashion as they showed up for work.

While the Okemah National was being taken over by one set of bandits, the second set of robbers manning their post across the street engaged in a similar process at the First National Bank. Bank Vice President A. B. S. Bontty as well as cashiers Floyd Day, Howard Franks, and bookkeeper Nell Riley were taken hostage, bound and gagged as they entered the business. According to a statement made to the authorities by Floyd Day, "When I entered the bank a man dressed in union overalls with a cheesecloth covering his face pointed a gun at me shouting, 'Hit the floor!' I did so then began slowly crawling toward the alarm but was stopped when one of the robbers yelled, 'Get away from that buzzer.'" Day was escorted to the back room and trussed up. Bank President Bontty overheard one of the bandit's comment, "This is one setup 'Pretty Boy' Floyd missed." The banker added, "One of the men informed me they originally intended robbing all three banks in town (the third being the Citizens Bank) but at the last moment decided against it."

Both groups of bandits waited patiently for over thirty minutes in order for the vaults to go off their time clocks, the only snafu occurring when a car backfired in the street. Hearing the blast, the robbers rushed to the front windows convinced a gunfight had broken out across the street at the Okemah National. Realizing their mistake, the hijackers quickly calmed down.

Making conversation, one of the robbers informed Janitor Morgan that if there were any gunplay he would have to come with them and ride on their car's running board in order to stop a posse from shooting. Morgan replied testily, "It's too cold for anyone to ride on the outside of your car."

After harvesting $9391 from the First National and $5491 from the coffers of the Okemah National for a total take of $14,892, the courteous cool-headed hijackers loaded into their

tion involving himself in a mini-crime wave of robberies and thefts, which landed him in a Holdenville, Oklahoma, jail.

While sitting in the can, he made the acquaintance of Nix who was awaiting trail on a robbery charge. The pair broke out of the slammer, stole a car and burglarized a Choctaw, Oklahoma, hunting lodge before motoring to Tyler, Texas, where they hijacked a tavern for $100 in cash and a couple of cartons of cigarettes. When a pair of Paris, Texas, cops attempted to stop them the duo got the drop on the officers, stealing their car and abducting the lawmen. The cops were released unharmed near Antlers, Oklahoma.

On the evening of December 16, 1934, the two hoodlums robbed John Hopkins's filling station located ten miles west of Okemah. Three days later, the pair was suspected of hijacking the Haydon Store located in Northeast Okfuskee County taking ten persons hostage at gunpoint before fleeing with a carload of merchandise and six hundred pennies.

When the Okemah bank robberies occurred the laws naturally suspected the Haydon store robbers as the culprits in the affair. Two days after the double bank heists Gooch and his pal were tracked down to a residence located three miles west of Okemah where a heavily armed posse made up of federal and local lawmen confronted them. The pair opted to fight it out rather than give up peacefully. At the conclusion of the gunbattle, Nix lie dead and Gooch in chains. Gooch was taken to the Okfuskee County Jail where he was questioned by FBI Agent Frank Smith and Oklahoma Bankers Association Investigator A. B. Cooper as to the Okemah bank robberies. He denied any involvement but admitted his participation in the Haydon store job.

That evening, using information gained from Mr. Gooch, officers raided an apartment in Oklahoma City finding most of the goods stolen from the Haydon store and a cache of weapons along with ammunition.

Before his transfer to the federal detention facility in Oklahoma City, filling station owner John Hopkins strolled into the jail office approaching the prisoner. He then plunged a pistol into Gooch's gut and pulled the trigger. Fortunately, for the outlaw, the gun misfired and the attacker was subdued. Apparently, the assailant's motivation for the assault was the fact Gooch and his pal had robbed his filling station earlier that week. The man was obviously angered over his treatment by the bandits and wanted revenge.

Although the local authorities maintained the outlaw pair was somehow involved in the Okemah bank jobs, the feds did not buy the theory. Gooch was transported Oklahoma City for safekeeping. He was later tried and convicted under the newly enacted Federal Lindbergh Kidnapping Law (so named after the famous 'Baby' Lindbergh kidnapping case) for the kidnapping of the two Texas policemen. The statute had recently been revised to allow for the death penalty in such cases.

On June 19, 1936, Arthur Gooch was executed by hanging at the Oklahoma State Penitentiary in McAlester. According to reports the hanging was botched. When the trap was sprung Gooch's neck was stretched but unbroken producing a process of slow strangulation, his body twisting and turning in a grisly dance of death for a full fifteen minutes before officials were finally able to pronounce him dead.

Upon realizing they could not pin the double bank heist on the Gooch crowd, federal agents went into high gear, expanding the investigation. While the usual suspects residing in a four state area were rounded up and a legion of informants questioned and offered the moon for information concerning the robberies, they drew a blank. One theory suggested the notorious Raymond Hamilton, sometime partner of Clyde Barrow of Bonnie & Clyde fame, was the leader of the hijackers.

Investigators also speculated Ennis Fay Smiddy, who was suspected of participation in a dozen recent Oklahoma bank heists, was the chief culprit in the affair. Smiddy was captured near Addington on Christmas morning by an oversized posse made up of G-Men and local officers. Upon questioning and being viewed by witnesses lawmen quickly realized he wasn't right for the Okemah job.

The first break in the case came with the discovery of a single fingerprint found on the main counter of the Okemah National Bank. Unfortunately, through a series of mishaps and acts of pure incompetence, the print was not identified for months as belonging to none other than Dewey Gilmore.

Meanwhile, many miles to the north, O'Malley associates Johnny Langan and Spike Lane along with Jess Doyle had became involved with Blackie Doyle in a combination whiskey bootlegging/gambling enterprise ran out of Lane's Kansas City bar. It later came to light the two Doyles (no relation) were also busily engaged in fencing certain hot monies (checks, money orders, bonds, etc.) from various O'Malley Gang bank robberies.

Soon after the failed Coffeyville mail heist the group was joined by ex-Barker-Karpis gangster Volney Davis. Like Jess Doyle, Davis had been friends with the Barker brothers since childhood. He had also departed from the criminal organization in a huff. Apparently, Davis's ouster from the group came after he had quarreled with Freddie Barker over the division of spoils from the January 17, 1934, Bremer kidnapping which had yielded the group a whopping $200,000 in ransom. There was also reports indicating "Ma" Barker had accused Davis of verbally abusing her on more than one occasion. A very dangerous act considering the fact her sons, Fred and Doc, dearly loved their momma and had killed men for far less.

After parting ways with the Barkers Davis and his girlfriend, Edna "Rabbit" Murray (maiden name Martha Edna Stanley), headed to Glasgow, Montana, where he tended bar at a small tavern until being spotted by citizen who recognized his photo from a crime magazine. The pair promptly relocated to Kansas City seeking out Davis's old pal Jess Doyle.

Volney's moll, Edna Murray, was a girl with a lurid past.

By the time she started permanently sharing a bed with Davis, the comely blonde had gone through several husbands. One (her third) was "Diamond" Joe Sullivan, who met his end in the Arkansas electric chair. She then hooked up with a bootlegger named Jack Murray. Edna soon evolved into a full-time thief. According to the newspapers, her specialty was to cozy up to a victim and give him a big smooch before picking his pocket clean. Lawmen soon dubbed her the "Kissing Bandit."

Her and her latest hubbie's luck ran out in 1925 when the lovebirds were busted for highway robbery and both sentenced to twenty-five years in the Missouri state pen. Over the next few years, Edna broke out from the stony bastille a total of three times, thus her second nickname, "Rabbit." On the morning of December 13, 1932, "Rabbit" and another girl sawed the bars of their cell and fled into the snow swept countryside. After gaining her freedom she fled to Kansas City where she fell in with Volney Davis, whom she had actually known for many years. Soon afterwards, her eighteen-year-old son, Preston Paden, who had been living with his grandparents in Cardin, Oklahoma, joined the pair. Incidentally, Jess Doyle's gal, Vinita Stacy, was Edna's sister.

In September 1934 Doyle, Davis, Langan and young Preston Paden robbed an armored car near Commerce, Oklahoma, using shotguns for $1165, all in silver.

In December the quartet traveled in a car stolen off the streets of Kansas City to Drexal, Missouri. Arriving in the small town at three in the morning Davis and Langan were let out at the rear of the local bank. Paden, the car's driver, parked the rig on a nearby side-street while Doyle sat in the passenger seat armed with a high-powered rifle.

Davis and Langan made entry into the financial institution with the use of crowbars and waited for the employees to come to work. On the arrival of a single employee the thugs overcame him, forcing the man to open the vault once the time lock engaged. After harvesting $2500 in cash and coin the duo then ran from the bank pushing their hostage in front of them. The man was ordered to jump on the getaway car's running board and informed by Davis "If ya try to jump off I'll shoot ya in both kidneys." The poor fellow was shoved off the moving rig a block from the bank.

Chapter 7
All Hell Breaks Loose

On the first day of December 1934 Ozark Mountain Boys associate, William "Buster" Cooper, along with his nineteen-year-old baby brother Clinton, accompanied by Bob Johnson, robbed the weekly payroll at the Pipkin-Boyd-McNeal Packing Plant in Joplin.

They spent the next three weeks plundering their way across Kansas committing several car-jackings, looting a pair of rural general stores, and robbing a state-ran weigh station at Galena. They also ran over and killed an innocent pedestrian that got in the way of their fleeing vehicle.

Buster Cooper   *Bob Johnson*

Filled with the Christmas spirit, the hooligans then robbed a Picher, Oklahoma, grocery store owned by Mrs. H. A. Hallock. Before exiting the business, Cooper paused just long enough to viscously pistol-whip a pair of clerks. Soon afterwards, the cold-blooded thug and his companions hijacked a pair of lads outside of Picher stealing their car and forcing them to drive to Joplin where they robbed and terrorized a nightclub at gunpoint. Later that night, Buster, temporarily abandoned by his crime-partners, ejected the pair of hostages just outside of Picher. Just for kicks and giggles, the outlaw then proceeded to Quapaw, Oklahoma, (his hometown) where he looted the local bank for $300 just moments after it opened for business. Exiting the bank, he took the clerks, Mr. and Mrs. Roy Bowman, hostage releasing the pair a mile or two outside of town before driving his stolen car into a nearby sludge pond prior to departing the area on foot.

On New Years day Buster re-connected with Bob Johnson, now accompanied by Leonard Short and Floyd "Slim" Henderson, at a residence owned by Bill Burton located near Galena, Missouri. That afternoon the quartet began motoring toward the small Stone County settlement of Crane with larceny in their hearts. The fact that Short, Johnson, and Cooper were all three widely sought by the law as well as currently being under indictment for the October 1934 robbery of a Joplin diamond merchant made little difference to the trio in their quest for ill-gotten gains. Playing it safe and keeping a low profile simply wasn't in their DNA.

That night the group swept down on the town with a vengeance. While Johnson and Cooper held a crowd of citizens as well as Constable W.E. Rickman at bay, Short and Henderson, joined by Clinton Cooper, raided the Farmers Exchange and Fenton-Williams General Stores, cleaning them out of roughly $1200 in cash and merchandise. Before departing town with a truckload of plunder, the boys indulged in a little sport tying the constable to a post and flogging him to a bloody pulp.

In the aftermath of the raid the hooligans returned to the Burton place and stashed most of the goods before motoring to the town of Ozark where they burglarized the office of the county treasurer stealing $500 from his office safe before departing. Short and Henderson then retired to their separate corners to get some rest after their nocturnal labors. A highly intoxicated Bob Johnson, along with the Brothers Cooper, decided to party on into the early morning.

Around dawn, the trio, figuring they needed a second vehicle, stole one from Dr. I. W. Taylor, taking him hostage as well. After relieving the good doctor of his pocket money and medicine bag the badmen released the physician near Seneca, Missouri, located hard on the Oklahoma border. The two carloads of outlaws then motored to Picher Oklahoma, where they intended on spending the night with Cooper's sister. Before retiring, they stopped off at Tobe Rennick's Budweiser Buffet for a quick snort. Just moments after driving away from the combination bar/pool hall a flashing red light caught their attention.

Unfortunately for the trio of brigands just as they pulled away from the curb, a Constable hailing from nearby Treece, Kansas, who was prowling the area looking for a stolen car, spotted them. Thinking one of their cars appeared similar to the hot rig in question he signaled Cooper, who was in the lead position, to pull over.

Buster reacted to the officers command by stomping on the accelerator speeding to his sister's shack. Bob Johnson also hit the gas and promptly lost control of his vehicle on a sharp curve turning the car over several times. Jumping out of his rig, Johnson, bleeding from a cut on his face and armed with a sawed-off twelve-gauge shotgun loaded with buckshot, blasted the Kansas officer, riddling his torso with eight lead projectiles. The angry thug then strolled to the residence of

Claud Chambers where he forced him to help restart his damaged vehicle.

Meanwhile, a Good Samaritan called the local cops who arrived on the scene only to be confronted by Johnson and his shotgun. Getting the drop on Patrolmen Will Simmons and Mack Hocker the outlaw was engaged in disarming the pair when Patrolman Herman Brewer, accompanied by the town's mayor and Ottawa County Undersherrif William McIntosh, arrived on the scene.

After participating in a brief running gun battle with the officers, Johnson somehow managed to shake loose and flee the area on foot. Eventually he made his way to the nearby settlement of Hockerville where he stole an automobile along with its owner and headed toward Missouri, his hostage being forced to drive while the fugitive nipped on a pint of mountain dew.

In the meantime, Ottawa County Sheriff Dee Watters arrived at the site of the Picher gun-duel. After a brief pow-wow with his befuddled deputies the lawman decided to make a raid on the home of Buster Cooper's sister, figuring Johnson may be hiding out there. With darkness falling, Watters and a hastily assembled posse approached the residence located at 604 Cherokee Street. Seeing no lights or movement Watters along with Deputy Sheriff Gerald Hodge and Patrolman Brewer entered the front of the two room "shotgun" style shack while Undersheriff Bill McIntosh and Picher Police Chief Walter Young made entrance through the rear door. Failing to observe anyone in the front

Slain officer Gerald Hodge

room, Hodge stepped into the back where he came face to face with Buster Cooper, who began blazing away with a pair of .38 cal. semi-automatic pistols. Hodge dropped to the floor suffering a fatal wound to the heart while his fellow officers returned fire but were eventually forced to retreat into the yard. While fleeing the residence McIntosh was struck by a spent round in the center of the chest, knocking him to the ground. Fortunately for him the slug had lost much of it's killing power, having already plowed through a wall before finding its way into human flesh.

Moments after their fellow lawmen made their hasty retreat, members of the raiding party commenced to riddle the place with tear gas bombs, machinegun and shotgun fire. Suddenly Cooper burst out the back door, paused a split second, then pitched to the ground after some twenty-seven slugs had torn through his torso. Amazingly, the outlaw was still breathing and conscious.

The badman, near naked and bleeding profusely, was roughly loaded on to a gurney and rushed to Picher's American Hospital. For the next several hours he refused to speak except to ask attendants to remove his nonexistent coat due to being "hot." He died later that evening in great agony. Deputy Hodge was dead on arrival at the same hospital.

Seconds after the fight had subsided, Cooper's sister and a Howard Pew, who had both been hiding in a closet located in the rear of the house, came stumbling out of the residence, gagging on the effects of the tear gas. Both were held for questioning.

There was no sign of Clinton Cooper, who had wisely split from his reckless sibling hitchhiking out of town before the arrival of the officers. He was captured the following day by Detective Joe Anderson and extradited to Columbus, Kansas, to face an armed robbery charge.

While young Buster was getting his comeuppance, Bob Johnson, in a headlong frantic flight to nowhere, traveled to

Galena, Missouri, where he released his hostage before moving on to Joplin. There he quickly abandoned the car after stealing another from L.A. Corlis of Topeka, Kansas. The fugitive forced Mr. Corlis to accompany him for several miles before releasing him unharmed.

In the early morning hours, Night Patrolman Robert Zinn spotted Johnson twenty odd miles west of Joplin speeding through the town of Sarcoxie. When Zinn turned on his red light the outlaw responded by firing several rounds at the officer before punching the accelerator. The lawman began a high-speed pursuit while riddling the fleeing car's back window forcing the badman to abandon his vehicle and flee on foot. When the car was searched officer's discovered a sweater covered in blood, convincing them Johnson was currently suffering from a wound inflicted at either the gunfight in Picher or the more recent shoot-em-up.

Some hours later, a man described as disheveled and dirty, approached a car containing a school teacher named Darrell Young, which was parked on the main drag of Pierce City, Missouri. According to Young, the individual pulled a pistol on him, jumped into the passenger seat and ordered him to "stomp on it!" The teacher reacted by leaping out of the vehicle and fleeing in terror. The fugitive was soon spotted by Barry County Sheriff Evans Shore, driving the stolen rig through the square in Cassville, Missouri. Shore drew his pistol firing three rounds at the outlaw who returned fire, none of the bullets taking effect. Shore hopped into his cruiser and gave chase. He was joined just outside of town by a car containing two of his deputies, Troy Wilson and Gladden Daughtery.

After a thirty-five mile chase, the deputies caught sight of Johnson parked at a filling station in the Stone County village of Abesville. The officers leaped from their car, leveling a machinegun directly at the bandit who was stooped over putting fuel in his car. When ordered to "Give up or else," Johnson meekly surrendered.

Sheriff Shore, accompanied by Stone County Deputy Seth Tuttle, quickly arrived on the scene and took custody of the prisoner who was found to be in possession of $20 in cash, two revolvers and a leather bag of ammunition. Johnson was described by officers as heavily intoxicated, dressed in dirty overalls and severely fatigued.

Speaking to newsmen later that day Sheriff Shore stated, "I had hoped he would resist arrest so we could shoot him." The lawman also announced Johnson would be auctioned off to the highest bidder. "He is wanted in many places and whoever wants him the most can offer the highest reward." The badman was finally relinquished to Jasper County authorities after a payment of $65 in "good faith" money. Once officials there got their hands on the outlaw, he quickly turned "snitch," informing inquisitive investigators what he knew about the inner workings of Leonard Short's Ozark Mountain Boys.

Several days after the deadly incident the mortal remains of thirty-year-old Deputy Gerald Hodge, a five-year law enforcement veteran, was laid to rest at Miami's GAR Cemetery. Oddly, the departed officers burial and funeral was under the direction of the Cooper Undertaking Co. Area businesses closed up shop for the day in honor of the fallen officer. Hodge was survived by his wife and two children ages four and two. A fund was quickly set up to fi-

Top right: A young Jack Miller.

nancially assist the widow. Although several hundred dollars were collected in the humane effort, including a $100 gift from the Kansas Highway Patrol, times would assuredly be hard for a widow and two small children caught financially short during the midst of America's great depression.

Back in Picher when the last of 1700 morbidly curious citizens finished viewing the propped-up corpse of Deputy Hodge's assassin, William Ernest "Buster" Cooper, at the Todd Mortuary, his mortal remains were unceremoniously dumped in a soon to be forgotten hole in the ground.

On the evening of January 11, 1935, at a location thirty miles south of Picher, Jack Miller and six other local thugs sautéed into Joe Lewis's filling station and café in Salina, Oklahoma, with a belly full of homemade hooch. Young Percy Bolinger was the sole individual manning the counter. After losing at the pin-ball machine Miller, in a burst of anger began tilting the machine. Bolinger asked the men to leave the premises.

A couple of hours later the hoodlums returned. One of the men grabbed the clerk and pistol whipped him while the others harvested $23 from the till. They then hauled the arcade machines to a waiting truck and sped from the scene. The machines were later found in Lake Cherokee minus an estimated $200 in coin. About a week after the incident Miller and the whole of the raiders were arrested and charged with robbery. Miller was held in the Mayes County Jail awaiting trial. The authorities had not yet connected the thug with the Okemah or Fayetteville robberies.

Independence, Kansas - January 1935

In the meantime, Johnny Langan, Volney Davis and Jess Doyle were summoned to South Coffeyville by underworld middleman Alvin Sherwood, who informed them he had lined up a sweet job for the boys.

Through the grapevine Sherwood had garnered information indicating the Montgomery County treasurer in nearby Independence, Kansas, was presently holding a great deal of cash on hand in the office safe located at the county courthouse on the square. The plan was to kidnap the treasurer and transport him to his office under the cover of darkness before forcing him to let them into the building and open the safe. Sherwood assured the lads that unlike the previous postal heist this job would pay off handsomely.

The dastardly trio certainly hadn't been sitting on their duffs since pulling off the Drexal bank job in December. In early January 1935, the three thugs along with Preston Paden robbed two elderly brothers named Blankenship at their swank home located in the Winwood Beach section of Kansas City.

Posing as police detectives the quartet burst into the home flashing badges. The frightened brothers were shoved to the floor of the den, their hands bound with baling wire. While Paden and Doyle guarded the hostages Langan and Davis ransacked the home. Lifting up a mattress in one of the numerous bedrooms Langan discovered $2300 in bills in a cloth bag pinned closed with a safety pin. The thugs also stole several gold coins and silver dollars as well as a Spanish-made .38 cal. pistol, a gold watch and a shotgun.

Volney Davis

At just after sunset on the evening of January 30, 1935, Montgomery

County Treasurer Ike Graves and his wife were just sitting down to a supper of beans and franks when the doorbell rang. Upon answering the door, Graves was confronted by Johnny Langan and Volney Davis, both armed with pistols. The pair quickly forced their way into the home's parlor. The hijackers then tied-up the couple with ropes before crowding them outside into the back seat of a waiting Oldsmobile Sedan, which was being driven by Jess Doyle.

After motoring to the courthouse, the driver pulled the rig over to the curb on the building's north side and parked. Davis and Langan escorted Mr. Graves to the courthouse steps ordering him to open the door with his key, which he did. The poor man was then strong-armed into giving the bandits access to his office, which was located on the first floor directly below the second story Sheriff's office. He was then ordered to open the safe, which they looted for $1938.

Meanwhile, back in the car, Mrs. Graves was informed by Doyle, "If I hear a shot I have orders to shoot you." As could be expected, the lady spent the next half-hour literally quivering in fear. Returning to the car with Mr. Graves in tow, the outlaws drove their victims to the Sunnyside schoolhouse located twelve miles East of town where their victims were left bound, gagged, and coatless in the freezing night. The couple managed to back up to each other and untie their hands. After gaining their freedom the pair ran to the nearest farmhouse for assistance.

The following day the bandit's Oldsmobile was discovered abandoned near Louisburg, Kansas, overturned and still smoldering. The bandits had set it on fire before flagging down the first oncoming rig, stealing it from its owner. They then leisurely made their way back to Kansas City leaving the car's occupants standing on the side of the road with their hats in their hands.

Back at the scene of the crime Deputy Treasurer E. W. Rauch arrived at his courthouse office for a prearranged meeting with Treasurer Graves. (the pair intended on counting the funds on hand in the safe). On entering the office Rauch discovered the open safe and immediately contacted the police who rushed to Grave's residence where they discovered his car parked in front with the keys in it along with a dark and empty home. At approximately 10 p.m., Mr. Graves phoned the Montgomery County Sheriff's Office informing them of the robbery/kidnapping.

As was the case with the earlier Coffeyville robbery, the Independence job was a financial disappointment to the bandits. Area newspapers called the robbery a brazen act due to the proximity of both the sheriff's office and police headquarters to the crime scene. A clerk at the Booth Hotel soon came forward identifying police sketches of two of the still unnamed hijackers as being guests at the hotel the night before the heist.

Several days after the robbery, Doyle traveled to Parsons, Kansas, in order to pay Alvin Sherwood his ten percent commission. Back in Kansas City, his girlfriend, Vinita Stacey, being left unsupervised, set off a comedy of errors by getting roaring drunk and shooting John Langan's girlfriend, Francis Taylor, in a cat-fight that got out of hand. Although Miss Taylor, a physician's widow who had been engaged in a lengthy affair with Langon long before her husband's demise, survived the incident, the cops were alerted. Miss Stacey was arrested and vigorously questioned. While Stacey was unwilling to share even a scintilla of information with her inquisitors Taylor told all to investigators "Me and Vinita or whatever her real name is, had been drinking the previous night and quarrelling about something. The following afternoon I left my apartment and was walking down the sidewalk when I encountered Vinita. Suddenly she pulled out a gun from under her fur coat and shot me three times in the stomach, once in the hand and in the mouth. I fell to the ground and a man came and asked if I needed an ambulance."

Arriving back in K.C., Doyle was infuriated to hear the

news of the shooting. He soon joined his pal Davis and Edna Murray at their nearby apartment. The trio decided to take a powder just in case either woman spilled the beans on the gang. While Doyle and "Rabbit" stayed behind at the apartment house Davis visited a local garage intending to retrieve his car, a stolen Pontiac, which had been stored at the facility for over a month.

Unfortunately for Davis, the garage had been under surveillance by the laws for several days. On arriving at his destination, he was immediately captured by a squad of heavily armed G-men and Kansas City Police officers. In his possession at the time of his arrest was a counterfeit $100 bill he admitted came from Irish O'Malley. When questioned, Davis would turn "rat." Just hours after Davis's arrest, a posse of agents swooped down on Spike Lane's Three Little Pigs saloon bar, arresting the hood and charging him with harboring Davis. Ultimately, the charge failed to stick and Lane was released from custody.

Edna Murray and Vinita Stacey

Meanwhile, when Davis failed to return to the apartment in a reasonable time Doyle and Ms Murray gathered up their possessions and fled to her brother's residence in Pittsburg, Kansas, in Doyle's late model Chevy. Unfortunately for them, the cops had beaten them to the punch. The place had been under surveillance for weeks.

On their arrival, Doyle and company were immediately surrounded by a horde of feds and local lawmen. The moment the car pulled into the driveway a trigger-happy G-man fired a burst of thirteen rounds into the rig's door from a "Tommy-gun." While Doyle returned fire with a high-powered rifle, Edna ran into the waiting arms of a federal agent.

Miraculously Doyle was somehow able to flee the scene unharmed, speeding into the night. He didn't get far. Only thirteen miles from the scene of the gunfight the outlaw's car become mired in a mud hole near the town of Girard, Kansas. He was quickly surrounded by an army of frustrated officers. Naturally, the outlaw, realizing he was bested, threw his hands into the sky, shouting his submission.

When Doyle's car and Kansas City apartment located at Warner Plaza, were searched, officers discovered a pile of traveler's checks that were traced back to the Okemah bank robberies as well as a single bond, hidden in an Ovaltine can in the apartment, coming from the 1934 Coffeyville mail heist.

Lawmen began a vigorous questioning of the suspects concerning the whereabouts of Irish O'Malley and company. FBI reports suggest Edna Murray may have assisted the authorities in this vein but only after she informed officers "I'm a good girl and a victim of circumstances….Adding " I don't know what they want from me…I haven't done nothing but live a good life." Her boyfriend, Volney Davis, soon escaped FBI custody, remaining on the loose until June when a squad of G-men personally led by Agent Melvin Purvis retook him while he was in the act of sparking a lewd woman in Chicago. Volney Davis would sing like a yellow canary, informing the feds of anything and everything in hopes of garnering a lighter sentence and or better treatment from the feds.

Francis Taylor, recovering in the county jail's hospital

ward, told agents, "While with John (Langan) I met Irish O"Malley many times at various nightclubs here in town including the one owned by Spike Lane. He and Johnny seemed to be pals."

Jess Doyle was transported back to Nebraska where he faced charges of robbing the Fairbury bank. Like Volney Davis, Doyle would turn informant, snitching on his partners regarding the Coffeyville mail caper as well as the Independence county treasurer heist. Exactly what he told the investigators about the whereabouts of Irish O'Malley and company is unknown, but FBI documents suggest the subject did come up repeatedly during questioning. Doyle would later tell Investigator Joe Anderson of the Kansas Highway Patrol, "I've had a lot of time to reconsider my life and I have changed my mind as to how to make a living. I would rather live in a piano box and make a nickel a day than steal again."

Federal indictments for mail theft were soon issued for Jack Richards, Clarence Sparger, John Langan, and Tommy Hill. Richards, Sparger, and Langan were named federal fugitives from justice while Hill was arrested at his residence in South Coffeyville. In the coming days state charges of highway robbery regarding the Independence job were filed against Doyle, Sherwood, Langan and Volney Davis.

Neosho, Missouri - March 2, 1935

In the interim, Irish O'Malley and the boys were not sitting around on their backsides picking their teeth while their contemporaries were playing hide-and-seek with the laws back in Kansas.

At approximately 5 A.M. on March 2nd, with the temperature holding at a chilly 53 degrees and a light morning fog hanging over the silent streets, janitor Les Cooper reported for work at the First National Bank of Neosho. When he approached the side door he was abruptly confronted by a large masked man (*later identified as Fred Reese) armed with a pistol roughly forcing him to unlock the door. Moments later, Leonard Short and Clarence Sparger, their faces partially covered with ski masks and wearing gloves, rushed into the bank. The trio instructed Cooper to go about his daily routine, including the placing of the blue and white NRA sign in the window which was a pre-planned signal to the other employees indicating all was well. How the bandits knew about the signal is a mystery. After completing his morning chores Cooper was bound, gagged, and forced to lie on the floor. The bandits then laid in wait for the arrival of the other bank employees.

While the raiders were sweating it out in the bank, less than a block away secreted in a dark alley, Jack Richards sat patiently behind the wheel of a parked late model black Ford V8. Situated just few feet away Harry Blee fidgeted in the seat of a similarly black Chevy Coach. On the street Red Melton and Irish O'Malley took up stations across the street from the victim bank acting as spotters. By 8 o'clock the bandits inside the financial institution had overpowered nine bank employees as they showed up for work.

The employees were identified as J.K. Morris, E. C. Coulter, Delmar Harus, Mary Miller, Ralph Duncan, Dorothy Giltner, E. S. Cornish, Mary Jo Bastian, and Assistant Cashier Ruth Barnett. Barnett and Bastian were later untied and forced to assist the bandits in gathering up the cash from various locations in the bank. According to witnesses, the bandits communicated with each other through whispers and hand signals. At 8:40 the time lock on the main safe was sprung and the thieves gathered up several heavy bags of silver along with some $16,689 in cash and $2883 in negotiable Arkansas State Bonds.

Meanwhile, a trio of citizens, R. E. Armstrong, Henry Metcalf and W. A. Ford, noticing the queer goings-on at the bank, assembled across the street on the courthouse lawn and began eye-balling Virgil Melton, who was standing on the sidewalk a few feet from the front door of the financial institution. Puffing on a Lucky, his hand was firmly placed on the butt of a Colt .45 automatic stuffed in his overcoat pocket. After observing the rubber-neckers for a few minutes Red slid the gun out of his pocket and began nervously fiddling with the weapon, switching the safety on and off. Suddenly he lost his grip on the pistol causing it to fall to the pavement producing a loud metallic clank. Melton quickly scooped up the gun and attempted to act as if nothing had happened.

Thinking the young man was having some sort of fit, Mr. Ford brazenly approached the bandit in hopes of discovering what was behind his odd behavior. Melton reacted by casually leaning toward the inquiring fellow, asking for the time of day before whipping out his pistol telling him, "We are robbing this berg and your coming with us you nosey 'Son of a Bitch!'" He then ordered him into the alley and instructed the poor man to mount the running board of one of the getaway cars.

Just as Melton entered the rig, his hostage, standing behind him, abruptly jumped off the running board, fleeing across the street to safety, shouting to the spectators to, "Watch out boys it's a robbery!" Seconds later, the rest of the hijackers spilled out of the bank's side door sprinting toward the cars.

Moments after the bandits piled into the rigs, the Ford sped out of town in an easterly direction while the operator of the Chevy headed in the opposite direction. The robbers had spent a total of four hours in the bank.

The only casualty of the hold-up seems to have been arthritic bank employee, E. C. Coulter, who suffered a great deal of pain over the next few weeks due to his being bound hand and foot inside the bank for several hours.

A posse was hastily formed and gave pursuit but came up with an empty sack. The following day the black Ford was discovered abandoned a few miles south of town on Highway #13 in Stone County. The car was wiped clean of fingerprints.

In the immediate aftermath of the robbery, bank officers quickly informed their jittery depositors the stolen loot was fully insured. According to Newton County Sheriff Paul Liles, a man and a woman matching the descriptions of Irish O'Malley and Vivian Chase, were observed "casing" the bank the day before the heist. He added, "These guys were real pros." The robbery marked the first time a bank had been robbed in Neosho history.

It later came to light the Neosho heist was planned at the rural Jasper County residence of "Kate" Melton. As for the most recent addition to the gang and participant in the Neosho heist, Harry Blee, alias Harry O'Brian, he was the son of an elevator operator employed at the Jackson County Courthouse in Independence, Missouri. Tragically, the father committed suicide in 1927 by cutting his own throat with a straight razor upon receiving news of his wife's death.

While living with his grandparents in nearby Kansas City, Blee graduated from pharmacy school. Working as a druggist in the mid-1920s he became involved in the liquor and possibly the illicit morphine trade, a pharmacist being able to legally possess a reasonable amount of alcohol during the prohibition era. No doubt young Mr. Blee abused this privilege. In 1929 the youth was arrested for his suspected involvement in an arson/insurance plot which resulted in the death of three firemen. He was ultimately convicted of three separate counts of perjury in the case. Blee was a long-time associate of both Spike Lane and Johnny Langan.

Chapter 8
Tulsa Town and a Visit to Arkansas

On the morning of March 27, 1935, a dark late-model sedan slid into an alley located on West Fourth Street in downtown Tulsa. Dan Heady, Leonard Short and Art Austin exited the rig. walking across the street. While Austin and Heady stopped at a shoe-shine parlor to have their dogs buffed Short took up a position on a nearby street corner dobbing an eye with a handkerchief. Witnesses would later claim he appeared to have a bad eye infection or sty. After having their shoes shined, Austin and Dapper Dan entered the nearby Ritz Café partaking of a hearty breakfast.

In the interim Short began pacing the sidewalk in front of Goldberg's Jewelry Store. After wearing out the pavement for approximately twenty minutes he entered nearby Nelson's Buffet where he quietly sat at the counter swigging a mug of beer. Joe Holloway and R. M. Barnes, the proprietors' of a local barbershop located across the street from the jewelry store, observed the strange goings on but came to the conclusion the trio were plainclothes cops planning a liquor raid.

At 8:30, two watch repairmen, M. N. Coe and W. T. Lushbaugh, reported for duty at Goldbergs, unlocking and entering the front door of the jewelry store preparing themselves for business. Moments later the two thugs sitting in the café departed the eatery and strolled into the shop. Art Austin approached Mr. Coe requesting to see a small diamond ring, which lie in a locked glass cabinet. The clerk informed the men they would have to await the arrival of the owner since he did not possess a key.

Suddenly, Heady pulled a Colt .45 automatic pistol declaring, "You're held up, mister." The pair of watchmakers were then escorted at gunpoint to the backroom where they were bound, gagged and forced to lie on the floor. Mr. Coe would later state being gagged put him in a terrible spot since he had just placed a large plug of tobacco into his mouth and the hijackers refused to allow him to spit, causing him to nearly gag on the foul juices.

After securing and silencing the witnesses the smaller of the bandits, Heady, informed them, "This is just an ordinary stick-up so just lie still and no one will get hurt." The bandits then patiently sat back and waited for the arrival of Ben Goldberg, the shop's proprietor.

According to Goldberg, when he entered the store, a large man, Austin, thrust a heavy revolver into his ribs stating, "This is a hold-up, open the safe!" The frightened jeweler complied with the order, feverishly working the combination to the box as well as unlocking all the glass cases with a key. Upon completing his assigned task, Goldberg joined his workforce in the backroom. Goldberg added, "The smaller of the men appeared to be an expert at binding. He wrapped my hands, feet, and mouth with adhesive tape all in a matter of seconds."

After gathering up some 250 diamond rings valued at $25,000 as well as $15,000 in gold watches along with $10,000 in negotiable bonds and several gold bars, the two began to make preparations to exit the store. Suddenly a pair of unsuspecting watch salesmen, Troy Rowe and L. P. Hofstetler, entered the business. The bandits reacted by getting the drop on the men, forcing them to join the other hostages in the back

---

room. Hofststler was relieved of $35 in cash while Rowe had a watch worth $100 plucked from his wrist.

The pair of unexpected guests were tied up and the thieves exited the store's side door heading to their getaway car being driven by Leonard Short, carrying two suitcases crammed full of loot, which according to witnesses were so heavy it caused little Dan Heady to almost sink to his knees.

Soon after the robbery, a plainclothes cop, A. W. "Lefty" Strader, came forward claiming he had stopped and peered in the shop's front window in order to calibrate his pocket watch against a large clock mounted in the front display case as he did every morning. While doing so, the cop noticed a large man standing in the lobby smoking a cigarette who tipped his hat when their eyes met. The officer, not realizing anything was amiss, returned the nod and went about his appointed rounds. Strader stated, "He seemed right to me." Adding, "If I had been in my uniform I bet there would have been some fireworks."

In the aftermath of the heist, the visibly shaken proprietor of the store informed the press, "I am ruined! They cleaned me out. I have no insurance to cover this." His employee, Mr. Coe, told reporters, "These guys were pros. Very cool and collected. They knew what they were doing every step of the way."

The lead investigator on the case, Tulsa Detective Lt. Earl Gardner, stated he believed the robbery was the work of an out-of-town gang. Adding, "It wasn't done by home talent. These guys were too good." Incidentally, the Goldberg heist was the second largest jewelry robbery in Tulsa history. The biggest being the still unsolved hijacking of the Boswell Jewelry Store, located at Fifth and Main, on September 27, 1931. On that occasion $103,000 worth of precious gems were taken.

At noon, a sixteen-year-old boy observed a large sedan parked on the side of a rural dirt road at a location some ten miles east of Tulsa. Moments later the rig plunged into a hay field. Suddenly, the car came to a halt and two men exited the car. The pair commenced to dig a small hole in the ground and buried an object before departing.

The lad, identified by the media as simply, "Howard," immediately reported the odd happening to a local lawman, who upon realizing the car matched that of the one used in the Goldberg robbery, phoned the Tulsa cops. When a squad of detectives arrived they discovered the field's owner, "Shorty" Keller, had only moments before plowed under the area where the item was hidden. After digging around in the dirt for two hours investigators discovered a 1934 Kansas license plate #3-7233.

A "BOLO" (*Be on the Lookout) was issued for the car in question and its occupants to various policing agencies across the Midwest. Investigators were initially sent on a "red herring" when one of the witnesses to the robbery identified a mug shot of Barker-Karpis gangster Volney Davis as being a good visual representation of one of the hijackers.

The following day, one of the victims in the heist, Troy Rowe, received a phone call instructing him to keep his mouth shut and, "If you identify anyone you won't live long." Rowe would soon tell reporters his memory was getting a bit shaky these days.

It was later learned that after hiding the license plate the hijackers had motored north to Art Austin's Galena, Kansas, residence where they split up the loot. A few days later, Leonard Short, Dewey Gilmore, and Dan Heady departed Claremore, relocating their hideout to the residence of a bootlegger in Fayetteville, Arkansas, while Irish O'Malley returned to his haunts in Kansas City. Dewy Gilmore split from the gang as well, motoring to Texas.

According to underworld sources, most of the stolen jewelry was fenced by Russell Cooper through his gangland contacts in both Fort Smith and Little Rock.

Fort Smith, Arkansas - May 3, 1935

A little over a month after the Goldberg heist three masked men clad in "Union" overalls, wearing leather gloves along with ladies nylons placed over their faces and armed with automatic pistols, used a fire escape to gain access to a second-story window connected to the City National Bank of Fort Smith, Arkansas.

The trio, later identified as Dan Heady, Floyd Henderson and Dewey Gilmore, made use of a crowbar to gain entrance to the bank, which was scheduled to open for business in a matter of moments. The trio silently slipped down the stairs to the ground floor where they quickly burst into the bank's lobby and with surprise on their side overpowered a bevy of employees as they showed up for work.

While this was going on Russell Cooper drove the group's getaway car, a late model blue Chevy, into a parking stall located a short distance from the bank. A fifth member of the group, Otto Jackson, acting as a lookout, began circling the bank driving a 1933 blue Pontiac sedan.

At 8:30 a.m. the main vault door mechanism released the time-lock exposing the inner vault door. Moments later Chief Teller Gerald Miller was forced to open the inner vault by combination.

Amazingly, in an awesome display of courage under fire, while the heist was ongoing, bank telephone switchboard operator Carroll Cole answered an incoming phone call and preceded to ask the caller to ring the police and inform them of the robbery, even though one of the bandits threatened her with a revolver demanding she put down the phone or face death.

After looting the bank's coffers of some $22,000 in folding money (*$2000 in heavy coin was quickly abandoned by the bandits while the paper money was stuffed into an overnight bag and a smaller handbag), the freebooters raced back to the second floor where they departed the building the same way they had entered, out the window down the fire escape and into the alley.

In the meantime, police responded to the incident by dispatching a half-dozen patrol cars to the scene. Just as the cops were arriving the bandits tore off their silk-stocking masks and overalls and began casually strolled into the street while the police were crashing through the bank's front door.

Meanwhile, when the trio attempted to find their getaway car, they were joined by Russell Cooper, who anxiously explained the Chevy was blocked in by a police cruiser whose occupants were dining at a nearby cafe. After assessing the situation Dan Heady responded by leaping into the street in front of a car being driven by a sixty-four-year-old brick salesman named J. D. Morgan. The robbers forced Morgan to drive them several blocks before they abandoned his car and forced him into the Pontiac driven by Otto Jackson.

Morgan was released fifty-odd miles north of Ft. Smith near the small community of Goshen, Arkansas, located just east of Springdale. Morgan informed investigators; "Along the way they kidded me saying they were going to release me in Chicago." Adding, "The outlaws informed him they were part of Al Capone's Chicago outfit." The brink peddler continued, "We traveled up Highway #71 at a fast pace to Winslow where they turned onto a gravel road that wound through the mountains, ending up in Goshen."

Morgan also stated, "They took my spectacles so I would have a tough time identifying anyone but never threatened me. One of the bandits asked me if I had ever been in a rig traveling a hundred miles per hour? I replied, 'I have now.'" Adding, "I had to sit on the floorboard the whole way. Six grown men in a single car is pushing it ya know." He ended his statement saying, "When I was freed they opened a satchel full of money and told me to take what I wanted. I took ten dollars, it cost me eight to get home. Back in Fort Smith bank officials informed their jittery depositors, "The entire loss is covered by insurance."

The Pontiac was last spotted by Rogers County Sheriff Charley Henderson speeding through Bentonville, Arkansas. Henderson gave chase into Oklahoma, catching up to the rig near Colcord. When the lawman attempted to run the car off the road he ended up in a ditch with a bump on his head.

For all its lurid nineteenth century wild-west history involving "Hanging" Judge Isaac Parker, who once ordered eight men to be simultaneously hanged on the gallows located just outside his office, the heist represented only the first bank robbery in the city's history.

The following morning one of the victims of the robbery, Hiram Nakdimen, discovered the abandoned black Chevrolet Sedan sporting Oklahoma plates and containing two shotguns as well as a high-powered rifle concealed in a golf bag in the back seat along with several box's of buckshot lying on the floorboard. Nakidimen explained, "I walked past the car ten times before I peered in the window and saw the guns." The vehicle turned out to be stolen.

When Morgan's rig was found later that afternoon Detectives correctly theorized the Chevrolet represented the original getaway car that was abandoned when the cops unexpectedly showed up during the robbery forcing the robbers to hijack Morgan's vehicle to drive them to the location of another confederate driving a second escape car.

Since the bandits had used the same mode of operation in both the recent Neosho and Okemah bank raids, the authorities correctly assumed the robbers were the same band of thieves. Since the crime of robbery of a national bank affiliated with the newly created Federal Reserve System had recently been declared a federal offense (Dillinger Law), the FBI was immediately brought into the case. In the meantime the gang split to the four winds.

Shortly after the heist, city detectives arrested Russell

Land Cooper in a downtown Ft. Smith apartment. Newspaper reports claimed his arrest was the result of a general police sweep in which the law was picking up all the usual suspects. FBI Agent E.E. Conroy would later assert a witness standing in front of the bank during the robbery had identified Cooper as a one of the robbers. Nonetheless, his capture represented a lucky break for the authorities.

On the same day that Cooper was arrested Harry Blee was apprehended in Springfield, Missouri. The outlaw was duly transported to Stone County where he faced an attempted murder charge. Blee was released from custody after posting a cash bond. Naturally the bandit failed to show up for his own trial. Fact is, had the authorities kept him in jail another week they would have received information concerning his participation in the Neosho bank job through the questioning of Russell Cooper. As it worked out the slippery hoodlum was half way to California by that time.

Russell Cooper

Chapter 9

The Jig is Up

Upon being vigorously questioned, a jittery Russell Cooper soon folded up like a cheap suit, admitting his participation in the Ft. Smith bank heist. Emulating Bob Johnson, the crook turned snitch, spilling the beans on much of the O'Malley-Short Gang's operations. He informed the laws the Ft. Smith job had been planned in his rented downtown apartment, as was the Neosho raid. He also told his interrogators that the loot from the Ft. Smith heist had been divided at the gang's new hideout in Fayetteville, Arkansas. He stated the Ft. Smith robbery crew was made up of himself, "Dapper" Dan Heady, Floyd "Slim" Henderson, Dewey Gilmore and Otto Jackson. Strangely, he refused to talk about the Okemah robberies.

As for the witness's from the Ft. Smith robbery, several identified a mug-shot of Dewey Gilmore as being one of the bandits. Apparently Gilmore had for some reason twice taken off his silk stocking mask during the robbery.

Agents of the FBI immediately conducted a raid on the group's Fayetteville headquarters but drew a blank. Not a soul was in residence. The owner of the home was picked up, questioned and released.

Dallas, Texas - May 22, 1935

The mighty O'Malley-Short combination was about to fall. Using information provided by Cooper a fast moving posse of officers, which included FBI agents as well as Burns Detective operatives raced to San Antonio, Texas, where the informant claimed Dewey Gilmore was currently in hiding. They discovered the outlaw had just departed town, heading to Oklahoma driving a spanking new car he had recently purchased with his buxom peroxide blonde wife hanging on his arm.

The posse motored north hooking up with Dallas Detective Lt. Will Fitz (*lead investigator in the murder of President John F. Kennedy in 1963), and began scouring the roads along the Texas-Oklahoma border. Fitz, accompanied by a carload of agents, spotted Gilmore's car speeding past them just outside Lancaster, Texas. The agents caught up with the fugitive forcing his automobile off the road into a ditch.

While his terrified female companion quickly surrendered, Gilmore turned rabbit, bailing out of the car running into a field. Lawmen, in an unusual example of self-discipline rarely seen in those days, had the courtesy to fire a warning shot while preparing to fill the badman full of more holes than a fully equipped minnow-bucket. Gilmore, realizing the jig was up, wisely stopped running, fell to his knees and began begging for mercy. A search of the fugitive's car turned up a satchel containing $3572 in cash as well as a loaded pistol.

Gilmore was taken into federal custody and transported directly to the federal lockup in Oklahoma City. His curvy companion, described as dressed in fashionable riding britches and expensive knee-high leather boots, was questioned and eventually released.

After a vigorous evening of rubber hose therapy Gilmore decided to save his own bacon or at least save himself a beating and turn informant. When asked where his pals were hiding he stated, "Kansas City." As for the whereabouts of rest of the loot the gang had stolen, he initially stalled the officers but later admitted he had buried $2900 in a tree-stump in Texas. The thug also informed investigators of the details behind bank robberies in Neosho, Fort Smith, Fayetteville and Okemah,

As of late, Gilmore's luck had turned from bad to worse. Two weeks before his capture the badman's judicial appeal in abstention concerning the robbery of the Greystone filling station and his accompanying twelve-year sentence had been affirmed by the Missouri Supreme Court. A few days later the $5000 appeal bond put up by his married sister was deemed forfeited. A pretty tough financial blow during the midst of the depression.

On hearing news of Gilmore's arrest and observing his mug shot in the newspapers, numerous residents of Claremore, Oklahoma, came forward stating they had known the bandit as Dave Grant, gentleman gambler. He was described by shocked townsfolk as always well-dressed, well mannered, and well-heeled. His winning personality had endeared him to many of the town's residents.

Besides giving the authorities information concerning the whereabouts of his crime partners, Gilmore informed G-Men of a plot to burglarize the Bank of Commerce in Claremore. When a party of officers, which included Rogers County Sheriff W. A .Carson, as well as several federal agents, investigated the story they discovered a tunnel ,which was in reality an abandoned storm sewer, leading from beneath the Sequoyah Hotel to the bank. The tunnel ended beneath the vault floor that was constructed of reinforced concrete. An assortment of drill bits, sledgehammers, and pry bars were discovered at the site.

Officers concluded the gang had abandoned their plans at the conclusion of the Goldberg jewel heist due to conditions being too hot to proceed with the plot. Leonard Short, and perhaps Irish O'Malley, had resided at the Sequoyah Hotel the last few weeks of their stays in Claremore while Gilmore had remained at the Eleventh Street address.

Kansas City - May 26, 1935

Just days after Gilmore's arrest, acting on information provided by their newly found canary, officers conducted a raid on the fashionable Stonewall Court apartment complex located at the corner of Independence and Prospect Avenues in Kansas City, Missouri, capturing Dan Heady and his wife Lucille. Heady had a Colt .45 tucked in his waistband and $1277.34 in cash stuffed in his pockets.

After escorting the pair to lockup, the lawmen set up a surveillance of the luxurious digs in hopes of apprehending other gang members. Sure as shooting, a few hours later a well-dressed man in the company of a sharply attired young lady knocked on the door. A federal agent flung open the door thrusting the cold blue barrel of a Thompson machinegun into the face of none other than 'Irish' O'Malley, who responded by calmly saying, "Oh, excuse me, I must have the wrong address." The agent retorted, "No, you're in the right place pal, now put up your hands. " When asked his name O'Malley informed agents, "Leo LaRue." O'Malley's female companion turned out to be a lady-for-hire working out of one of Kansas City's more stylish "Sporting Houses."

Later that day a Kansas City hood named James Maroon was arrested and charged with harboring the pair when it was discovered he had actually rented the apartment for the pair. A search of the residence turned up an automatic rifle and a pistol stashed in a closet. Agents discovered a revolver and three counterfeit $100 bills on O'Malley's person.

Heady, who refused to make a statement, was whisked to the federal detention center in Muskogee, Oklahoma, where he faced bank robbery charges concerning the Okemah robberies.

His wife, identified as twenty-year-old Lucille Hopkins Heady, was noted in news accounts as being the ex-wife (divorced) of a Springfield, Missouri, bootlegger by the name of Bert Hasty, who was currently residing in the Missouri pen. Officials stated she was a woman with a record, being arrested in 1925 on a charge of conspiracy to commit armed robbery in Kansas City and again in 1933 for lewd conduct on the streets of Springfield. When asked by investigators exactly how she had made the acquaintance of Dapper Dan, she claimed "In a bar, but I didn't know he was a bandit when I married him. I thought he was just a bootlegger." Officers nodded their heads as if that made all the difference. Once released by the feds she quickly followed her husband by train to Muskogee where she checked into a local hotel under the name of Betty Johnson in order to be near her sweetheart.

"Irish" O'Malley was transported to Edwardsville, Illinois, and placed in the Madison County Jail to await trial on state kidnapping charges. On his arrival back in Illinois, the outlaw was promptly identified as being one of the Luer kidnappers by one of his crime partners, Lillian Chessen. Mrs. August Luer, followed up saying, "The room was well lit and I have good eyesight. He is the one who dragged Mr. Luer out of the house." Mr. Luer commented to the press, "I'm glad they got another of the gang. You remember he is the one who snatched me."

A brief trial was held in which Mrs. Chessen was the chief witness for the prosecution. Hearing the evidence presented against him O'Malley finally informed his attorneys he desired to end the ordeal and plead guilty, stating, "Although I am in fact innocent of this particular crime I would rather serve my term in Illinois than Alcatraz."

O'Malley was sentenced to life imprisonment to be served in the Illinois prison system. After sentencing the local laws allowed the gangster to be interviewed by the press. The journalists described him as a self-educated "dandy" who spoke in a dry impersonal voice and was very careful in his choice of words.

His physical appearance was noted by the newsies as 5'10", weighing about 150 pounds, large and very alert hazel eyes, brown slicked back hair, with a lower jaw that jutted out. The gangster informed the assemblage of journalists, "I had nothing to do with the old man's abduction. What the kidnappers put him through was shameful. I have no sympathy with the men who committed the crime. If I did it, I'd die of shame." He expanded on his statement adding, "As for stealing, I have never seen anything wrong with it, especially if the fellow you take the money from has plenty of it. I know that's the wrong viewpoint but I suppose I have a warped mind." Discussing the kidnapping he said, "As for Norvell, I knew him closely, to my regret. I am sorry I did not know him well enough to cast my lot with a decent thief. He is a complete louse. That is all I care to say about Randol." As for the counterfeit bills found on his person the gentleman bandit sniffed, "They were poor specimens and could only be used in a pinch."

When asked if he visited Madison County after the kidnapping O'Malley replied with a smirk, "No, and that's the only answer you can expect from that question." When a reporter inquired if he had committed any of the bank robberies he was accused of since the kidnapping, the outlaw preened, "Naturally, one must live." Asked if he had tried to go straight after his last prison term he replied, "Of course not." When a reporter inquired if he ever felt at ease while being hunted for the kidnapping? He stated, "Hardly, It's a miserable life, always on the watch, always uneasy."

When asked, "How did you walk into that trap in Kansas City?" He calmly retorted, "I got careless. When I stepped in that door and a man with a machinegun answered it I did not know what to think. I knew I could never make it to the car outside. I have a leaky heart valve and could not have ran ten feet." When solicited how he felt about a life sentence, he responded, "I have only five or six years to live. I now have heart trouble worse than Mr. Luer." When a reporter commented his latest alias "Leo LaRue" sounded like that of a burlesque queen, the badman grinned before remarking, "It is a bit florid isn't it."

On the subject of Vivian Chase, the outlaw stated flatly, "I tried to make a deal with the feds for Vivian but they rejected the offer. She had nothing to do with the kidnapping, the woman in question was a girlfriend of Norvell's."

After his interview, officers applied handcuffs and leg shackles as well as a heavy padlocked chain to his waist in preparation for his transport. According to witnesses, he winced then gave a sly grin to the reporters before shuffling out the door, armed guards taking up positions on both his flanks.

A few days after the capture of O'Malley and Heady, federal and city officers manning a surveillance of Floyd Henderson's Joplin residence, located at the corner of 12th and Murphy Streets, spotted the badman as he pulled into his driveway at approximately 11 PM. When officers ordered Henderson to surrender the outlaw rapidly shifted into reverse. Joplin Detectives Tom DeGraff and William Gibson responded by firing a volley of rounds into the car's tires forcing him to halt. Realizing the cops meant business, Henderson flung his hands in the air in submission. When searched the bandit had in his possession a short-barreled .44 caliber pistol and $600 in cash. Henderson was transported to the city jail where he was held for suspicion of robbing the City National Bank of Fort Smith, Arkansas.

Detective DeGraff had previously been involved in a 1933 Joplin shootout with members of the Barrow Gang of Bonnie and Clyde fame in which two officers were brutally slain.

The following morning Art Austin was arrested by a squad of heavily-armed FBI agents and eventually indicted along with Leonard Short and Dan Heady with robbing Goldberg's Jewelry Store in Tulsa. Austin turned informant just moments after the store's proprietor, Ben Goldberg, identified him as one of the hijackers. He pled guilty to the Goldberg jewelry heist while pleading for leniency in a federal courtroom in Tulsa, Oklahoma. As a reward for his cooperation, Austin was given a light sentence.

On June 1, 1935, a federal grand jury in Muskogee, Oklahoma, indicted Dan Heady, Irish O'Malley, Leonard Short, Red Melton, Fred Reese, Dewey Gilmore, Jack Miller, and Russell Cooper for the Okemah bank jobs under the Dillinger Law statutes.

Ten days later a small army of G-Men raided the Short residence in Galena capturing the badman while he was taking a nap. Even though a nickel-plated Colt .45 automatic pistol was discovered on a table located next to his bed the outlaw offered no resistance. Short was immediately transported to the federal lockup in Oklahoma City for questioning.

A Short family friend and neighbor later commented sarcastically, "I watched those government men gather around Leonard's home making preparations to raid the place. They were all shaking like leaves."

Ironically, the day after Short's arrest, two bookkeepers from the Okemah National Bank were charged with embezzlement. It appears in the days following the bank's robbery by Short and company the pair had siphoned a combined $3000 from the tills, believing it would never be missed in the confusion. Both men admitted to the crime saying they needed the cash to pay some gambling debts. Apparently the bank had been robbed both inside and out. The two bankers were later sentenced to a year in the El Reno Federal Reformatory. Ironically, the pair was initially held at the Muskogee City/Federal Jail lodged near the cells of several of the Okemah bank bandits.

Meanwhile, back in Springfield, Missouri, one of Leonard Short's associates, Elmer "Coody" Johnson, pled guilty to the recent robbery of the Bank of Strafford, Missouri, while Frank

Simmons held out for a few months before admitting his part in the affair. He would later turn states evidence. Simmons was given a heavy sentence but released after serving only a year in jail. A third suspect in the Strafford heist, Pretty Boy Floyd associate Wesley "Shine" Rush, was not indicted since he was already serving a 25 year sentence in the Oklahoma pen for another bank robbery.

Seneca, Missouri - July 2, 1935

At high noon, a late model Chevy Sedan driven by Fred Reese parked in front of the State Bank of Seneca located in the extreme southwest corner of Missouri very near the Oklahoma line. Two armed and masked men later identified as Red Melton and Jack Richards, exited the car and entered the bank. Melton strolled up to the counter being manned by Cashier R. L. Hughes announcing, "Hey Slick, it's a stickup" as Richards stood in the lobby covering a farmer named Charles Lofland with an automatic pistol at the ready.

While Melton gathered up the loot that amounted to

Fred Reese under arrest in Kansas city.

roughly $741, Richards forced the hostages to the floor in a rough fashion, pistol-whipping both men in order to gain their submission. As the robbers were finishing their business, Imogene Patton entered the bank's front door but the moment she realized the place was being hijacked, abruptly turned on her heels and fled into the street, screaming at the top of her lungs. Moments later, the bandits fled to their running getaway car.

Strangely, the robbers paid no attention to the bank's safe or its contents, which were currently being protected by a security system dubbed the "Bandit Barrier Method." The bank's insurance provider had required the system be installed soon after the financial institution was robbed the previous year. In that incident, Banker Hughes was taken for a ride by the bandits and released a few miles outside town unharmed. In both instances, the loss was covered by insurance.

When the robbers departed, Hughes ran to his office. He grabbed a high-powered rifle and sprinted into the street in time to spot the robber's fleeing car kicking up dust on the way out of town heading east on Highway #60. "Sons of bitches." he spat as he angrily fired four evenly spaced shots at the speeding rig.

That evening, officers discovered the getaway car smoldering on the side of the road near the small community of Hornet located a few miles north of Seneca (the bandits had set fire to the interior). The car, which had a pair of bullet holes in the rear panel, was later traced to R. G Horner of Miami, Oklahoma, who stated it had been stolen in Joplin a few days past while parked in front of Freeman Hospital.

A couple days after the bank heist, Newton County Deputy Sheriff John Brock along with Constable John Box, who had been scouring area roads looking for clues to the crime, spotted a suspicious vehicle speeding through the village of Racine located a few miles northeast of Seneca. A man sitting in

Red Melton under arrest in Kansas City.

the car's backseat matched the physical description of one of hijackers.

The officers followed the automobile to the farm of Epp Melton (Red's half-brother). When questioned, one of the suspects, suffering from a bullet wound to the shoulder, claimed his name was George Ralston. When asked about his wound he stated he had accidentally shot himself. Observing how the entry hole to the wound was in the rear of his shoulder, the cops inquired how he managed such a feat. He replied, "That's for others to find out." When questioned as to the whereabouts of the gun, the suspect stated, "I threw it in the brush alongside the road somewhere." When lawmen accused him of bearing false witness the accused calmly replied, "Prove it cop"

The hard-boiled suspect was initially identified as "Blackie" Doyle, but fingerprints taken corresponded to those of Jack Richards. He was hauled before the witnesses from the robbery who identified him as one of the Seneca looters.

Epp Melton along with his wife, Grace, were charged with conspiracy to rob the Seneca bank and harboring criminals. After a few days in custody Epp decided to cut himself a break and put the snitch on his brothers, Red as well as Kate, who apparently had helped plan the bank heist. No honor among thieves or kinfolk on this occasion. A warrant was quickly issued for the arrest of both siblings.

In the case of Kate, he was easy to locate. When a party of officers attempted to apprehend him at his home in nearby Spurgeon, he bolted out the back door and lunged bodily into a nearby forest, dashing from rock to brush pile for cover. One of the pursuers claimed the big man's run to freedom reminded him of " a dog looking for a hole in the fence." Even though he had suffered for years with bad lungs, Kate somehow managed to evade the posse on foot for nearly a mile, ultimately seeking sanctuary in a isolated cave where lawmen discovered him curled into a ball shivering from fear and exhaustion.

After questioning, Kate was released on a $2000 bond.

At the time of his capture he was already under a $5000 bond concerning federal bootlegging charges. On the evening of April 12, 1935, he had been arrested near New Orleans driving a truck bound for Kansas City loaded down with illegal bonded bourbon.

Kansas City

On the evening of August 2, Kansas City police received a call concerning an obviously inebriated individual armed with a pistol, directing traffic on busy Troost Avenue. When police arrived the suspect leaped into a running car and sped south at a high rate of speed. At the conclusion of a perilous chase that covered some thirty-five blocks officers manhandled the thug out of his vehicle, which had suffered two flat tires from police gunfire.

Although the man initially identified himself as Leslie Johnson of Topeka, Kansas, he changed his tune after a few hours of rough-house questioning being applied by skeptical detectives and admitted he was in truth Otto Jackson. It appears the outlaw had been residing with an unnamed barfly in a decrepit boardinghouse located in the downtown area for several weeks. Prior to the police call that instigated his arrest Otto had been drinking heavily at a clip-joint when according to witnesses, he and a fellow hoodlum had heated words before stepping into an alley and engaging in a bit of fisticuffs. Something about a gambling debt. After coming out on the losing end of the knuckle-duel Jackson chased his antagonist into the street armed with a revolver and blood in his eye. The bar's owner promptly called the cops and the rest is history.

After investigators established his identity Jackson was transferred to a holding facility in Fort Smith where he was charged with robbing the First National Bank.

Mincy, Missouri - August 7, 1935

The day after Kate Melton's apprehension, Epp led a party of officers to a "shotgun" style shack located deep in the Stone County woods where he had last seen his younger brother. The place was deserted. A week later Epp received word his notorious sibling had "Gone Fishing."

An hour before dawn on August 7 a large group of federal, local, and state officers began a surveillance of an isolated fishing camp located where Bee Creek flows into the White River in southern Taney County Missouri, situated hard on the Missouri/Arkansas border (*area is now part of the Drury-Mincy Wildlife Refuge). The posse, led by FBI Agent E. E. Conroy, settled in for a lengthy wait. According to sources the laws had high hopes they could not only apprehend Red and his buddy Reese at the camp but Blackie Doyle as well.

Agents manning the stakeout felt a wave of encouragement when at just past dawn they observed a man and a woman matching the descriptions of Red and his wife strolling about the camp. At midday, Epp Melton, accompanied by undercover officer Roy Hanse, posing as a recent escapee from the Missouri pen named Jack Monahan, arrived at the compound. After introductions were made Red warily offered the spy a cup of coffee.

According to Officer Hanse the ensuing conversation went something like this; "Red took Epp aside and the two had a serious conversation. Afterwards Red asked if I knew Leonard Short. I replied 'ya.' After asking a few more questions I asked why the tough-guy routine? He retorted, 'You know how it is when a man is hot. Epp comes dragging you in here and I want to know a few things.' 'Not from me you don't,' I replied. Things got a little heated for a minute or two. I really started sweating bullets when I noticed Fred Reese out of the corner of my eye standing in the door of the fishing shack fingering a rifle. Pretty soon things quieted down and we sat quietly and drank some java. Then I asked 'You got any grub?' To which he replied, 'No, why don't you and Epp go into town on a grocery run?' I gladly agreed."

Moments later, Hanse and his stool-pigeon departed the camp heading to town for groceries. Instead of driving into nearby Forsyth for chuck, Hanse, the car's driver, hightailed it back to the posse headquarters located at a hunting lodge situated near the small backwater community of Mincy, where he placed his companion into a set of handcuffs.

The following morning the heavily armed posse, mounted in a five car caravan, motored down a narrow dirt road to the junction of Bee and Fox Creeks. They dismounted and made their way on foot, clawing though the hilly glades dominated by a legion of scraggly post oaks and scrub cedar until coming to a thick cane break located near the banks of the White River.

After traversing through the cane field, they burst into the camp swooping down on the bandits, who were caught totally unaware and offered no resistance. Arrested in the raid was Melton, Fred Reese, his female companion, identified as Lucille Davis, and Melton's better half, Maxine (aka Juanita).

While both men were transported to a federal holding facility in Kansas City, their

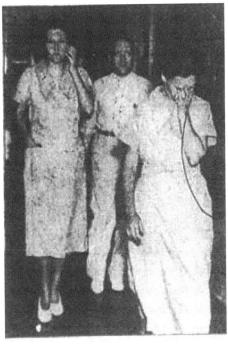

Molls under arrest after Mincy raid.

women were held in the Taney County Jail in Forsyth facing federal charges of harboring wanted fugitives.

Reese and Melton faced federal charges of robbing both the Neosho and Okemah banks as well as state charges concerning the hijacking of banks in Webb City, Reed Springs, Billings and Seneca, Missouri. The powers that be in Fayetteville, Arkansas, also expressed interest in questioning the pair concerning the 1934 robbery of the McElroy bank. Both men were held on a $50,000 cash bond.

The day after the arrest, A spokesman for the US Department of Justice made a public statement saying, "These men are members of the O'Malley combination and are responsible for thirty major robberies in five states which yielded loot totaling nearly $2,000,000." A slight exaggeration to say the least.

On August 30, a Kansas City federal grand jury representing the Western District of Missouri officially indicted Red Melton, Fred Reese, Leonard Short, Irish O'Malley, Harry Blee, and Clarence Sparger for the Neosho bank robbery. Epp and Kate Melton were indicted in state court for harboring while Jack Richards, Fred Reese and Red Melton were indicted on state charges of robbing the Seneca bank.

Although gang members Clarence Sparger and his pal John Langan were still on the loose as was Blackie Doyle, Dave Sherman, and Harry Blee, the authorities considered the O'Malley organization splintered.

But, like a Phoenix, the slippery outlaw combination would rise from the ashes once more.

Chapter 10

A Shocking turn of Events and Two Redheads Dead

While the questioning of various members of the mammoth criminal enterprise was underway in Kansas City, Clarence Sparger and his pals John Langan, Blackie Doyle, and Russell 'Spike' Lane were plotting a raid on a St. Joseph, Missouri, bottling company in hopes of stealing its payroll. On the afternoon of August 7, 1935, a vehicle parked just down from the Hund and Eger Bottling Company. Three individuals, Doyle, Langan, and Lane, unloaded from a car and approached the business on foot while Sparger remained at the wheel. The trio entered the company's office and began gathering up various employees at gunpoint herding them into a room located just behind the office. Unluckily for the hijackers a pair of colored men lounging on a nearby street corner observed the three and reacted by dashing into an adjacent creamery calling the cops.

Meanwhile, back at the bottling works, Doyle ordered the hostages to drop their valuables into a hat. When Louis Hund, one of the company's owners, was slow in responding due to his believing the affair was a hoax or a practical joke, Doyle smashed him upside the head with a pistol butt screaming, "Take that, you police lover. Well, we got you now. The cops can't do a thing for you." Doyle also roughed up a female employee who started loudly weeping in response to witnessing the pistol whipping.

After gathering up approximately $150 in cash and a horde of watches, rings, and other valuables, the trio ordered their captives to hit the floor face-first and began backing out of the building. On reaching a side door, they were met by a pair of city detectives named Swepston and Swope. The bandits and the coppers immediately began trading shots. One round struck Doyle grazing his head. Another slug tore into Langan's shoulder producing a painful flesh wound. The pair made a mad dash down an alley while Lane ran the opposite direction.

Sparger, sitting in the getaway car, fled the scene on hearing the gunfire. The detectives, now joined by an armed gas company worker named Reynolds, who held a special policeman's commission, took out after the wounded pair while ignoring the third suspect who eventually made a successful escape. The cops cornered the two fleeing bandits in the alley and a lead-filled slugfest broke out.

Area residents reported bullets whizzing and whining up and down the street, ricocheting off the pavement. Windows of local business's were shattered and wood splintered off a dozen storefronts. After a few moments of exchanging rounds with the cops, the bandits cried "calf-rope," retreating over a nearby wooden fence before disappearing through a backyard to an adjacent street. They then rushed into a drug store flourishing pistols demanding the proprietor fork over the keys to his car that was parked out front of his shop. Jumping into the vehicle, the bandit's floor-boarded the rig, motoring west toward the bridge over the Missouri River.

Making it safely across the waterway, the pair abandoned the vehicle at a prearranged rendezvous point located in Elwood, Kansas, where they reconnected with Clarence Sparger, who was driving the original getaway car. The trio quickly escaped into the night.

Back in St. Joe, officers recovered the stolen loot as well

as a leather satchel filled with spare ammunition, which had been dropped by the brigands when they climbed over the wood fence. The druggist' car was discovered the following morning, the interior covered in bloodstains. Although an intensive search was conducted well into the day and following night throughout Eastern Kansas, there was no sign of the desperadoes.

On the evening of September 1, 1935, Sparger and Langan stole a 1935 V8 Ford Tudor Sedan from the front yard of Lyle Cleveland in Sioux City, Iowa. The pair then motored in their pirated rig to a hide-out in Kansas City.

Blythedale, Missouri - September 5, 1935, 8 AM

When Truman White, the cashier for the Citizens Bank of Blythedale, Missouri, a small crossroads village located some sixty miles east of St. Joe, unlocked the front door of his place of business he was rudely greeted by three armed men standing behind the counter. When ordered to raise his hands the cashier turned on his heels, fleeing into the street shouting "Robbery."

Within minutes, a large crowd of vigilantes armed with every conceivable type of weapon had formed in the road directly in front of the financial institution. Suddenly, the hapless bandits made a break for it, dashing into a nearby cornfield. The posse responded by unleashing a volley of lead toward the departing robbers.

A block away from the action, twenty-four-year-old Robert Jones, hearing the commotion, borrowed a high-powered rifle loaded with only two rounds from a neighbor and joined the other citizens who were in the process of surrounding the cornfield. Jones, spotting one of the thugs hightailing it through the corn stalks, fired a single round at the running target, hitting the fleeing suspect in the back and inflicted a serious wound. The posse immediately surrounded the injured bandit, placing him under arrest. Moments later a second subject came into sight and the youth shot him as well. He was also easily captured.

Out of the blue, a gray Ford Sedan with red wheels driven by Clarence Sparger pulled into view, racing to the far end of the cornfield where it stopped. Seconds later, John Langan came crashing out of the field and leapt into the car's backseat. The pose fired a withering but ineffective volley toward the vehicle. Sparger stomped on the gas, leaving a dense trail of dust as the getaway car raced out of view.

Upon questioning the wounded bandits in custody, one admitted he was thirty-six-year-old St. Joe thug Charles "Bad Eye" Arbogast. The other identified himself as Raymond Fletcher, also of St. Joe. While Fletcher soon expired from his

wounds Arbogast recovered and turned informant, claiming the two missing robbers were indeed Clarence Sparger and John Langan. Young Bob Jones was the hero for the day and the talk of the town for the next several months.

Citizens Bank of Blythedale, MO.

White Church, Kansas - September 13, 1935

At approximately 1 a.m. Wyandotte County Kansas Deputy Sheriff Ellsworth "Red" Edwards was patrolling a section on US 40 located just west of Kansas City, Kansas, searching for a Ford Sedan, which had been stolen earlier that evening from a Kansas City parking lot. Riding shotgun at the time was a young friend named Arthur Ashley. Suddenly, a vehicle matching the description of the hot rig, passed them a mile west of the community of White Church. The pair followed the suspicious automobile into the inky dark night for several miles until it pulled off the road into the driveway of a farmhouse owned by G. H. Meredith. Edwards pulled in behind the rig exiting the cruiser and approached the open window on the driver's side in order to question the subject behind the wheel. Just when the deputy came abreast of the vehicle the driver punched the accelerator, the car spun gravel lurching forward, leaving the officer standing in the drive with his hat in his hand. The vehicle then pulled in behind the farmhouse where the occupants leaped out and ran into the shadows. Edwards pulled his pistol and walked toward the parked car while his partner began patrolling the opposite side of the house. In due time, a shot rang out in the night.

Ashley reacted by running back to where he had last seen Deputy Edwards. He discovered the officer sprawled out on the ground. Ashley then observed an individual running across the lawn. Edwards, in a superhuman effort, gained his feet staggering back to the patrol car where he stopped just long enough to reach in and withdraw a riot shotgun. The deputy, swaying on the balls of his feet, pressed the gun to his shoulder and after shouting, "Halt" fired before falling into a bloody heap next to the cruiser.

According to Ashley, the fleeing subject made a jerking motion in reaction to being hit by the shotgun blast then emitted an unearthly moaning noise before pitching to the earth.

Ashley placed the wounded officer into the car and drove to a commercial garage located a few blocks to the west in search of a assistance. Although the business was closed he was able to use the outside pay-phone to call the sheriff's dispatch who sent a bevy of officers as well as an ambulance to their assistance.

On the lawmen's arrival, they discovered a red-haired woman lying in the grass dead from the impact of eighteen rounds of buckshot. Next to her lay a .45 cal. revolver and a roll of bills amounting to $35. When officers questioned the terrified occupants of the farm, who turned out to be innocent of any wrongdoing, they claimed to have heard the deceased lady's companion scream "Margie, Margie" several times before driving off the property.

Officer Edwards, who was reportedly hit by a single 45 cal. slug that entered his chest near the collarbone, piercing his windpipe before exiting his back, was transported to a local hospital where he lingered between life and death for several days.

Red Edwards

Even though Edwards was unable to speak for over a year, he would eventually recover from his wounds and return to duty. Ironically, the gunfight was not the first time Edwards had traded shots with associates of the O'Malley combination. In early July 1933, he had been one of a half-dozen Kansas Troopers involved in a gun-battle that occurred with a band of robber's connected with O'Malley and Blackie Doyle at the conclusion of a Leavenworth, Kansas, bank robbery.

Around dawn, the vehicle being driven by Edward's assailant crashed into a newspaper delivery truck near the community of Paola, Kansas, located some thirty miles south of the of scene of the gun-duel. The driver of the truck gave first-aide to the subject, who appeared to be heavily intoxicated.

After regaining his composure, the suspect pulled a rifle from his wrecked rig and calmly stepped into the gravel road forcing a truck, occupied by three farmers, into the ditch. Two of the farmers refused to surrender, instead choosing to run into a nearby cornfield, while the third man was taken hostage.

Upon ascertaining the truck was no longer roadworthy, the assailant forced his hostage to accompany him to a nearby farmhouse. Unable to arouse the occupants the pair then walked back to the road where the hijacker was able to halt a second vehicle. Leaping into the front passenger seat he ordered the driver to, "Step on it, pal!" Upon being granted his freedom the farmer from the initial truck hijacking fled into a cornfield where he remained silently hidden for over an hour.

After motoring several miles down the road the fugitive bailed out of the rig, making his way on foot to the nearby Kansas State Hospital for the Insane, where he phoned a taxi that picked him up and delivered him to a bar located in nearby Osawatomie. The hack-driver would later state the man in question was very inebriated and bleeding profusely from a cut on the head

Directly, officers arrived at the Paola crash site and while searching the fugitive's wrecked car discovered a half-dozen stolen license plates and a postcard addressed to Margaret Cooper bearing a Kansas City address. Following up on the

---

postcard, agents visited the address in question where they interviewed an elderly lady who turned out to be the mother of thirty-five-year-old Margaret Cooper Langan, the wife of outlaw John Langan. On being shown a photograph of the slain woman she began sobbing hysterically, "I knew it. I just knew it when I read about the incident in the newspapers this morning."

The woman later identified the body of her child lying on a mortuary slab at a Kansas City funeral home. Tragically, the results of Langan's misbehavior included leaving a ten-year-old child without a mother and a father on the run from the law.

According to the slain woman's sister-in-law, Margaret had departed home several days ago with a unidentified man who came to their door. "The man told Margie that her husband's brother Lee wanted to talk to her. She grabbed her hat and coat and left with the man in a waiting taxicab. That's the last we saw of her."

Officers later identified the wrecked Ford V8 as being recently stolen from a residence in Sioux City, Iowa. The rig also perfectly matched that of the one used in the recent Blythedale bank robbery attempt. The taxi-driver as well as the hijacked farmer involved in the affair would both positively identify John Langan as the assailant through mug shots.

While there was no sign of Officer Edwards's assailant, lawmen discovered that Langan had been observed visiting the residence of a gambler and bootlegger named John Rose in Paola in the past. Officers, suspecting Langan had been heading to Rose's residence when the accident occurred, picked-up Rose whose brother Tony had recently been convicted of a $22,000 postal robbery. After questioning, Rose was charged with harboring a fugitive from justice.

For the next two weeks, investigators throughout Eastern Kansas and Northwest Missouri conducted a series of raids of Langan's hideouts. Unfortunately, nothing was seen of the outlaw who had been officially charged with assault with intent to kill. According to the underworld grapevine the fugitive had fled to Texas seeking medical assistance for injuries sustained in the wreck and a nagging gunshot wound he had received in the raid on the St. Joe bottling works. Evidently, he was treated by a well-known defrocked physician noted for caring for criminals on the run. Some investigators were certain Langan was now traveling with a female companion whose physical characteristics perfectly matched those of the long missing Vivian Chase.

On September 30, 1935, a man and a red-haired woman dressed in crimson entered the Silverfob Pharmacy located at 220 East Thirty-First Street in Kansas City both brandishing pistols. The clerk was forced into the rear of the store and forced to open a safe containing $200 in cash and coin. While the robbery was in progress the female waited on several customers who had entered the store. She put on her best smile and gladly took their money as well as the proceeds from the day's sales from the register before departing the establishment.

The drug store was the seventh pharmacy robbed in the past few weeks in the Kansas City area by the same team of hijackers. A total of $1700 was stolen in these raids. In due time the female involved in the various heists was identified as Vivian Chase and her male counterpart, Johnny Langan. As quick as the raids began, they abruptly ceased.

Vivian Chase mug shot.

Kansas City- November 3, 1935, 8 AM

A driving rain pelted the cars parked in the lot located in the rear of Kansas City's St. Luke's Hospital as nurses and other medical personnel darted under umbrellas, reporting for work in the medical center. A few minutes past eleven the rain ceased and the city's Sabbath morning church bells began chiming in the distance.

Moments later, Mrs. Roy Shackelford, on her way to visit a sick friend, noticed a late model black Ford V8 Sedan parked at a strange angle. On one of the car's running boards, she observed a pool of dried red substance, which appeared to be blood. As she leaned toward the rig, pressing her nose against a closed rear window, she saw what looked like a female manikin stuffed into the rear floorboard. Suddenly, she gasped as she realized the red-haired figure was not a dummy but a human-being crammed headfirst into the car's carpeted floor its arms sprawled about at grotesque angles. Most noticeable was

St. Luke's Hospital, Kansas City.

a large hole covered in blood located just above the body's upper right shoulder blade near the spine. She immediately rushed into the hospital reporting her find to personnel, who after calling the police, quickly walked to the car where Dr. Murray Ballenger pronounced the female dead, She had been deceased for roughly two hours.

Within minutes of the grisly find detectives arrived on the scene. Under the body they discovered a .38 caliber Spanish-made pistol (possibly stolen by John in the earlier Blankenship bros. robbery), a bloody five-dollar bill, a handbag containing a dozen .45 caliber bullets, and the spent slug that had directly caused her demise. But no identifying papers.

According to a reporter on the scene, the woman's body was attired in a "cheap blood soaked green dress, an imitation Persian lamb coat, an inexpensive vanilla felt hat and rather common black pumps."

The car's grill was covered in weeds and mud stained the

Vivian Chase's death car.

frame. Inside, on the backseat was a collection of a dozen or more crumpled bloodstained roadmaps and a man's brown felt fedora hat. The detective's ascertained the car's engine bloc was cold. Workers from the hospital come forward, stating the vehicle had not been there as early as 7 a. m. and no one had heard a shot or noticed the arrival of the rig.

A cursory inspection at the scene told investigators that a large caliber bullet had entered the right base of the neck, plowed a downward spiral and exited from the chest.

The victim was moved to the morgue where fingerprints were taken and the bullet that had done the damage was confirmed as .45 caliber. The body was then sent by ambulance to the Bergman Funeral Home then later that night moved to St. Mary's Hospital where an autopsy was performed.

Through fingerprints the victim was positively identified as that of Vivian Chase. She had been the victim of a classic gangland "One way ride."

Kansas City's Director of Police Otto P. Higgins announced her identity. "Miss Chase was a known associate of many well known criminals including members of the O'Malley Gang as well as Egan's Rats." he stated. "She was the ranking female criminal in the United States."

Immediately after positive identification, the FBI entered the case, due to Miss Chase's suspected involvement in the Luer kidnapping, which was a federal crime. A dozen agents soon arrived at the crime scene before fanning out, to chase down a host of leads. Agents also turned their attention to the vehicle in which Chase was discovered, going over it with a fine-tooth-comb. The car was identified as a spanking new Ford V8 stolen on the night of September 25 from a car lot in Lamoni, Iowa. The odometer had 5262 miles on it. The vehicle was equipped with stolen license plates.

The feds did find several promising leads. A man's felt hat, which was found in the murder car, was tracked to a burglar named Ray Lacy though a series of dry cleaner numbers.

Lacy was presently residing in a Savannah, Missouri, jail. Turns out, he was an associate of both Clarence Sparger and John Langan. When interviewed he clammed up and refused to make a peep. Lacy did have an ironclad alibi. He was sitting in the can at the time of Miss Chase's murder.

A dry cleaners stamp discovered on the silk dress worn by Chase at the time of her demise led investigators to the Criterion Cleaners located on 3216 Wyandotte Street, Kansas City. Lawmen were able to ascertain the garment had been pressed and cleaned twice at the facility and registered to a C. Dalton, residing at 31st and Euclid Streets. Photographs of Chase and Langan were shown to the apartment manager. While she failed to recognize the photo of Langan, she positively identified the picture of Vivian Chase as a previous resident using the name of Mrs. Charles H. Walker, stating she had known her as Doris Walker.

The couple had vacated the apartment in early September. During the next few weeks, agents were able to discover two other locals where Miss Chase and an unnamed gentleman had resided in the past, but on both occasions, the trail was cold.

Shortly after the murder, Lulu Hickey, the mother of Clarence Sparger, was interviewed by agents as to her knowledge of the case. She denied knowing any pertinent information but stated she wished her son would turn himself into the feds. She feared in the event he was arrested by the Kansas City Police they would beat him to death. She then offered to make a deal with the agents suggesting she could talk Clarence into surrendering if promised he would not serve over five years in the can. The offer was forwarded to the US Attorney who turned her down flat.

Mrs. Hickey did turn the agents on to a confidential female informant who under questioning admitted she had seen Vivian Chase in the company of Clarence Sparger and Johnny Langan as recently as a few weeks before her death. She had been shooting craps in the back room of the Belt Tavern located in Kansas City's industrial East Bottoms District. A second informant verified her statement.

While several detectives pushed the theory Chase was executed in the parking lot, others suggested she was slain by one of her many lovers or accomplices on a country road due to the collection of weeds attached to the radiator grill. They believed the car was subsequently driven to St. Luke's and abandoned.

Another theory implied whoever dumped her thought she was merely wounded and left her at the hospital in hopes she would be discovered and treated for her wounds. Police Detective Phil Hoyt claimed the chief suspect in her murder was John Langan since several witnesses had placed Vivian in his company over the past month. Langan was also known to pack a .45 pistol, the same caliber weapon that caused Chase's untimely demise.

A few days after the grisly slaying, which made national headlines, the funeral director handling her arrangements received a call from a man, who wished to remain anonymous, inquiring how much it would cost to give Miss Chase a decent funeral, coffin, and gravesite. The undertaker, who had already arranged for her burial in a pauper's grave, informed the individual of the cost. The following morning a box containing a blue dress and some undergarments, along with an envelope containing a cashier's check drawn from the Columbia National Bank of Kansas City bank for the entire amount arrived in the mail. That afternoon three bouquets of roses along with a wreath saying "From the Boys" was delivered to the funeral home with envelopes containing cards signed, "A Friend."

When bank officers were interviewed by agents, they claimed the person who purchased the draft gave her name as Mary Ellen Bradley. They described the woman as 5"3", 140 pounds, about 38 years old, dark hair, black eyes, and hard looking. She was well dressed, wearing a black dress and fur coat. The lady paid for the draft from a thick roll of bills. When investigators interviewed the florist, he stated the bouquets were purchased by a female matching the banker's description.

That same night the funeral director received a call from a woman identifying herself as Jackie Bondurant, inquiring of the funeral arrangements. She asked if officers would be present at the services. Mr. Bergman assured her they would not. He also heard from Rev. A.J. Haggett, a local Baptist minister, who offered to say a few words over the departed at the burial. The funeral home was immediately placed under heavy police surveillance. Agents hoped either Messer's Langan or Sparger would make an appearance.

On the morning of November 8, the redheaded femme fatale was buried at a somber ceremony at Kansas City's Greenlawn Cemetery. Witnesses included a half-dozen female and one male mourner accompanied by a crowd of reporters along with a small army of wide-eyed detectives. According to news reports, none of the mourners would give their names to the press or sign the funeral home registry. All arrived in a four car caravan. One vehicle was described as a shiny red Reo Coupe being driven by Miss Bondurant, a second as a 1929 Ford Sedan occupied by two ladies, and a third, a 1935 Chevy Sedan containing three women and a bulldog. The fourth car was described as a 1928 Chevrolet Sedan occupied by a man and a woman. Several FBI Agents were recruited at the gravesite to assist funeral home and cemetery workers to lower the coffin into the grave. (*oddly, although Vivian Chase would go down in history as was one of America's most notorious female criminal figures, she is basically unknown today.)

While none of the bereaved matched the descriptions of Langan, Sparger or their close associates, the bulldog riding in the new Chevy certainly attracted the officers attention since Langan was known to possess a pet bulldog, which often times accompanied him on his travels. Although agents put a tail on the Chevy they soon lost the rig in traffic.

When lawmen ran the registration for the vehicle it came back to a H.J. Carney of 1833 E. 59th Street. When the residence was raided they discovered the home unoccupied. The property owner told investigators the tenants had moved the previous week. When shown a photo of John Langan he stated the gentleman looked familiar. The name H.J. Carney turned out to be bogus.

On the day of the burial, thirty-year-old habitual criminal Joe Spano, presently being held on a carrying a concealed weapons charge at the Jackson County Jail, contacted FBI Agents, offering information concerning the death of Ms. Chase and the activities of her hoodlum companions. Spano had ended up in the can due to his making a disturbance at a Kansas City whorehouse ran by Freda Ash, the attractive platinum-haired wheelchair-bound daughter of the infamous Kansas City madam Sadie Ash.

One of Sadie's regulars in the early 1930s was Charles "Pretty Boy" Floyd, who would one day receive top billing on J. Edger Hoover's "Public Enemies" list. Apparently, Floyd and his sidekick, Bill "The Killer" Miller, had taken a liking to Sadie's daughter–in-law Rose and her sister Beulah. On the morning of March 25, 1931, the lifeless bodies of Sadie's sons, Wallace and William, were discovered in a ditch just south of Kansas City minus most of their skulls. Floyd and Miller soon became the chief suspects in the case since Wallace was married to Rose and naturally his departure made things easier for Mr. Floyd in the romance department.)

As for Spano, when the cops arrived at Freda's joint in answer to the disturbance call, he was searched and found to be carrying a Lugar automatic pistol. It appears there had been trouble brewing between Spano and Ms. Ash for some time. The young thug was married to Freda's sister, Mary Jo, who had recently committed suicide by leaping off the top of the Pickwick Hotel. Evidently, Freda blamed Spano for her sister's death and along with her surviving brothers, Leo and Delmar, the madam and her mother had publicly sworn revenge. On this particular night Spano, who had received a parole from the Missouri State Penitentiary on February 1, 1934, had gotten a bellyful of liquid courage and decided to confront the whoremaster at her establishment. Problem was, the Ash family operated under the protection and full blessings of Johnny Lazia and the Pendergast machine.

When questioned by FBI Special Agent B. P. Cruise, Spano informed the investigator he was the friend of O'Malley associate Bill Newman, who happened to be locked up in an adjoining cell on a charge of robbery. According to Spano, Newman had informed him that he and Blackie Doyle along with Clarence Sparger, John Langan, and Vivian Chase had recently pulled a stickup in Iowa. On their return to Kansas City Sparger and Chase, who was in her cups, had gotten in a fierce quarrel resulting in Sparger's putting a .45 slug into the leggy moll's lovely neck . In an attempt to find her medical assistance, the carload of thugs had dumped her in a second car outside the hospital.

On another subject, Spano laughingly informed the G-Man Blackie Doyle had been hiding out at his residence at the time of his own arrest and had quietly slipped out the back door unnoticed during the raid. He further informed the lawman Vivian Chase and Newman's wife had once roomed together in Omaha. The snitch also told Agent Cruise, Doyle had sworn to bump-off James Maroon believing he had a hand in the recent apprehension of Heady and O'Malley, calling him a "Two-bit snitch." Spano then made a pitch to the agent requesting he be given his freedom in return for his assisting the feds in their pursuit of O'Malley gang members. It appears J. Edger Hoover was duly impressed with his new stoolie. A deal was struck.

Over the next few months Sparger, Langan, and Doyle were spotted on several occasions but in each instance the feds arrived just moments too late. A tail was place on Sparger's wife, Juanita, but led nowhere. Lulu's home and tavern was raided as well but produced no results.

Credible witnesses identified Sparger and Langan as the same two individuals who stole a 1935 Ford Sedan from a parking lot in Falls City, Nebraska, on the evening of November 16. The automobile was eventually recovered, abandoned on the side of the road near Martin City, Missouri.

In late November of 1935 FBI agents spotted the pair motoring down a road near the home of one of Langan's siblings located in a Denver suburb. Later that same day the owner of a downtown Denver nightclub, who was also an FBI informant, phoned the feds reporting the pairs appearance but by the time a squad of agents arrived at the bar the dangerous duo was nowhere to be found. By all indications, when the head G-Man back in Washington received news of the pairs' escape he was not amused.

In the meantime, Spano connected investigators with the owner of the New Deal Tavern located in the small berg of Winthrop, situated hard on the banks of the Missouri River just south of St Joseph. The proprietor informed agents Sparger often visited his joint in order to take part in the never-ending crap game taking place in the back room. He offered to turn in the outlaw if the feds could convince the local laws to stop raiding his establishment due to his numerous liquor violations. While the agent in charge declined the deal, he ordered two agents to watch the honky-tonk for the next few weeks. In nearby St Jo, a dozen agents were ordered to fan out and set up a dawn to dusk surveillance of five different roadhouses where the pair was known to partake in their favorite hobbies of drinking, gambling, and skirt-chasing.

Chapter 11
Escape and Murder Most Foul

While Ms Chase was meeting her fate in Kansas City, the rest of the gang was undergoing legal troubles to the extreme. The state of Missouri refused to turn over Red Melton and Fred Reese to their fellow prosecutors until they were tried for the Seneca bank job. Illinois got dibs on O'Malley and Heady was extradited to Muskogee's federal court while Short, Gilmore, and Cooper, all caged at the federal lockup in OKC, were transported to Muskogee as well for trial on federal bank robbery charges (*Okemah bank robberies).

On October 22, 1935, Jack Richards was sentenced in a state circuit court in Neosho, Missouri, to a fifty-year sentence for robbing the Seneca bank while Epp Melton received a two-year term for the same offence.

Muskogee, Oklahoma - October-December 1935

Federal investigators had been working on Jack Miller ever since his indictment for participating in the Okemah heists in hopes he would testify against his crime partners. Their strategy was beginning to work. Miller, who had been sitting in a cell in the Mayes County Jail since January on a separate robbery charge, was weakening.

Actually, the prosecution was initially blessed with informants in the case. But, Dewey Gilmore, who had told all to detectives and the Grand Jury, refused to testify in open court against Dan Heady or Irish O'Malley and although Russell Cooper initially cooperated with investigators he had since clammed up as well. That left Miller and since the big Indian appeared to have less blood on his hands, the federal prosecutor picked him to be the golden-boy in the case. Federal Judge Robert L. Williams, the ex-Oklahoma Governor who had been appointed judge in the Okemah case, agreed to grant the Chelsea, Oklahoma, native full immunity for his testimony if he was willing to fully cooperate. Miller eventually agreed to the testify against gang-members concerning bank robberies occurring in Okemah as well as Fayetteville, Arkansas.

In the meantime, Leonard Short was doing hard time. He complained to his jailors incessantly about the food saying, "All we eat is potatoes and a concoction they call 'apple-core soup.' Disgusting fare."

Shortly after his arrival at the Muskogee jail, a letter written by Short to his ex-crime partner Ralph Wilson, who was currently being held at the Greene County Jail in Springfield, Missouri, under a charge of robbing the Strafford, Missouri, bank, was intercepted by censors. It read in part: "Dear Friend Ralph, Would like to see you and Red (Melton).... Talk about a kangaroo court, this district has one...That G-man Frank Smith and Burns dick Cooper sure win the prize. Smith is hauling people in here and really showing us up...They got me for a double bank robbery in Okemah. I've also been indicted with Dan Heady and Art Austin for a $50,000 jewel robbery in Tulsa. Austin told all. I am standing trial on every charge and not afraid of getting stuck on any of them. Dewey Gilmore went before the grand jury and told them everything he ever did and that's plenty... This is a good jail but tighter than hell. We are locked in heavies and only out of the cage once a week for a bath…Well, Ralph I know they will turn you loose at your trial…Your Friend, Leonard."

Okemah bank robbery victims from 174, okemah robbers & victims of FNB of Okemah from 175)

Wilson, along with his side-kick Floyd Maples, would ultimately be convicted of bank robbery. Wilson was sentenced to a twenty-year term while Maples was given a ten-year jolt. At the time of their trials the pair were also under indictment for June 22, 1935, robbery of the Nafziger Bakery in Kansas City as well as a 1934 jewelry heist which had occurred in Springfield.

The combined trials of the Okemah robbery suspects began on the morning of November 26, 1935. The defendants were led into the courtroom en-mass chained and shackled hand and foot. Short's attorney requested a separate trial but the motion was denied. All the defendants were charged with two felony counts. Count one, which carried a twenty-year term, read, "Robbery by force and violence by putting the victims in fear." Count two; requiring twenty-five years imprisonment, stated a defendant had committed "Robbery with firearms, putting in jeopardy the lives of victims."

Jack Miller, who was kept in protective custody at the Oklahoma State Penitentiary in McAlester throughout the trial, was the prosecutions star witness. He testified he was initially approached in Claremore by Dan Heady with a proposal to rob all three Okemah banks (in fact, only two were robbed). He went on to identify the Okemah raiders by name before admitting he had received a $2100 cut for his part in the affair. In order to bolster Miller's testimony various individuals were called to the stand stating they had observed Miller in the company of Leonard Short, Dewey Gilmore, and Dan Heady at various locations in Claremore over the past few months. The Okemah bankers also gave testimony as did G-Man Frank Smith and several others before the prosecution rested. The following morning the defense took over.

While the attorneys representing Gilmore (whose hair had turned completely gray since his arrest), Cooper and Heady offered only a half-hearted effort, Short's mouthpiece argued his defense with great vigor, claiming he was in Galena, Missouri, when the robbery occurred. While the shyster tried mightily to shake Jack Miller's testimony in cross-examination, the plump informant stuck to his story.

Aggravating his situation Okemah restaurant owner Mrs. Rosa Pope testified Short had eaten breakfast in her café, located a few doors down from the Okemah National Bank, an hour prior to the double bank robbery. Pope's fourteen-year-old son, Leroy, confirmed the sighting. Both witnesses claimed the bandit was dressed in bib-overalls and a plaid hunting cap at the time. The description perfectly matched one of the robbers of the Okemah National.

During the proceedings, Short's wife and several other family members sat in the courtroom in stern silence. In his

Robbery victims of First National Bank of Okemah.

Okemah robbers on trial in Muskogee.

Okemah Bank robbery victims.

summation US Attorney Cleon Summers plead with the jurors to find "This vermin guilty and give them the maximum punishment prescribed by law." While listening to the prosecutor Short wiggled uncomfortably in his seat. Except for Russell Cooper, who raised up and loudly cursed jack Miller when he took the stand, the other defendants showed little or no emotion throughout the proceedings.

The cases were handed over to the jury at midday. Within two hours, the jury came back with guilty verdicts on both counts for all the defendants but Leonard Short. It appears they were deadlocked in his case. Judge Williams briskly sent them back for further deliberations instructing them to "try harder." At midnight jury foreman Woodie Hunt contacted the judge, announcing they had reached a verdict in Short's case. Apparently, the jurors, who were identified as mostly farmers, had come to a compromise finding the little man guilty of count one but acquitting him on the second count. Hearing the news, Leonard turned pale and was visibly shaken while his wife broke into loud sobs. His attorney immediately announced he would appeal the sentence, calling it, "unjustified and unfair." Sentencing was set for December 9 and the prisoners sent back to their cells.

Around this time, Heady's young wife, Lucille "Betty" Heady, breezed into town taking lodging at a local boarding house. For the next week, the redheaded moll spent her days bending the ear of any policeman, newspaper reporter, bailiff, or lawyer pleading her husband's cause. In a fatal mistake of judgment County Sheriff Tom Jordan agreed to allow her generous visitation rights with her husband.

At 11:30 in the morning of December 3, 1935, Jailor Elmer Bernard patiently stood guard over Dan Heady in the dayroom of the newly constructed Muskogee City/Federal Jail while he visited with his attractive wife. Bernard, ready for his lunch, urged Heady to wrap up his visit. The outlaw leaned through the bars kissing his life's love farewell, the pair cooing like a pair of school kids. "Come on pal, let's go" demanded the keeper. Heady abruptly turned and began strolling down the hallway toward his cell. Suddenly, the thug whirled about, thrusting a small pearl-handled .25 caliber semi-automatic pistol into Bernard's ribs.

After taking possession of the jailor's keys, he ordered him to move down the corridor to a door, which led to the main police station. In the meantime, the pair was joined by Leonard Short, who was taking a bath at the time in an unsecured area. Short had up to that point been characterized by the authorities as a meek prisoner. The group was soon joined by two trustees, Donnie Garrett and John Blackburn, The pair was engaged in mopping the cell house floor when the incident occurred.

Garrett, a twenty-five-year-old drifter incarcerated for violating the Mann Act (White Slavery) was a Claremore native with an IQ of 55 (near moron). He had quit school upon failing to complete the fourth grade. After being arrested a dozen times on minor charges over the years, the dull-witted hoodlum was convicted of auto theft and served two years at the Kansas State Reformatory. He then joined the Civilian Conservation Corps but was promptly drummed out of the program for stealing a fellow workers wallet. For the next couple of years Garrett resided in a small broken-down camper-trailer located in a relative's auto junkyard in Claremore. In October 1935 the young hoodlum kidnapped a fourteen-year-old girl off the streets of Lexington, Missouri, transporting her to Wagoner, Oklahoma, where he put her on the street, selling her favors to the highest bidder.

Blackburn, a West Virginia native, was being held under a federal indictment for mail theft.

Believing he had tentative control of the situation, Heady ordered Short upstairs with the jailor's keys to the arsenal in hopes of garnering some weapons. The pudgy bandit quickly returned with two sawed-off .12 gauge pump shotguns as well as a pistol and ammunition. Finding themselves with enough firepower to take over a small town, the mutineers slowly moved toward the main exit.

Hearing the commotion, Police Sergeant Norman Cobalt cautiously stuck his head around the doorway but was promptly confronted by the escapees and loudly ordered to, "Stand aside." Cobalt quickly retreated into the police station breathlessly informing Desk Sergeant Claude Wood of the jailbreak. Wood, still feeling the effects of various infirmities suffered in a 1931 gun battle, hobbled to the office of Chief of Detectives Ben Bolton seeking assistance.

Meanwhile, Blackburn began opening the cell doors of Dewey Gilmore and Russell Cooper.

The moment Bolton received news of the breakout he grabbed a machinegun and opened his office door to take a peek. He was met by a blast of buckshot emitting from a riot shotgun fired by either Leonard Short or Dan Heady. The detective hit the floor with a thud lying in a rapidly expanding pool of blood, half his face shot off. Blackburn approached the downed officer and cautiously leaned down taking possession of the "chopper" before joining his companions.

Pretty Betty Heady

On hearing the explosion, Chief of Police Marsh Corgan, who was reading a newspaper in his office at the time, sprang into action. The lawman, armed with a machinegun, rushed into the hallway and observed Dan Heady sitting in the desk officer's chair giving his companions and their hostage marching orders. Heady, noticing the big cop, raised a shotgun to his shoulder and cut loose, the blast shearing a doorframe with several wood splinters striking Corgan directly in the face. The Chief reacted by retreating deeper into the bowels of the hall while "Dapper Dan," in an act of bravado, began taunting the officer shouting, "Come out and fight, you yellow Son of a Bitch."

Anticipating the arrival of police reinforcements, the group of escapees withdrew toward the jail's side door that exited into the facilities' garage using their hostage as a human shield. Corgan, seeing his chance, sprinted to the doorway and squeezed the Tommy-gun's trigger unleashing a deadly volley into the fleeing group. Several rounds struck Blackburn, the last man in line, in the back. The fugitive hit the concrete moaning and withering in pain. One round grazed another of the escapees, described by Corgan as "The cocky little fellow," (Heady was the shortest of the group) who whirled about cursing and firing several shotgun blasts at the angry cop before continuing his run for freedom.

Officer Bernard, taking advantage of the ensuing chaos, slipped away diving under a parked police cruiser. Dashing on to Court Street, the thugs flagged down a bright yellow late model Chevy Coach being driven by a Reverend N. R. Hickman, pastor of the local Seventh Day Adventist Church. The padre, believing the men were officers in need of assistance, promptly pulled over and upon exiting the car was brutally shoved to the street suffering a split lip and the loss of a tooth in the process. Gaining control of the vehicle, the killers, with Dewey Gilmore at the wheel, motored east to Highway #64 where they turned south.

Reacting to the news of gunfire emitting from the jail, a horde of lawmen poured out of the city police station, as well as the nearby sheriff's office, descending on the scene. Officers immediately secured the jail and locked the loose prisoners into their cells while summoning an ambulance for the victims.

On arrival of the medics, Detective Bolton, barely clinging to life, was given first aide before being loaded onto a gurney and rushed to Muskogee General Hospital. Little hope was held-out for his survival. Doctors informed reporters the lawman was missing most his face and the top of his skull. Blackburn, also judged to have life threatening injuries, was taken to the same medical facility.

When questioned by officers at the hospital Blackburn inquired of Sheriff Tom Jordan if he would die. The lawmen bluntly responded, "Yes, you are going to die and I hope you do, but you can go with a clear conscience if you tell us the truth while you are still living." Within minutes of this conversation the thug went into shock and expired later that afternoon in agony to the end.

In the meantime, Sheriff Jordan began forming a massive posse numbering nearly one hundred officers and assorted armed vigilantes, giving them orders to "Don't take any chances. Shoot to kill if that vermin is encountered!"

Within hours of the escape, a large contingent of federal officers headed by FBI Special Agent Frank Smith also took the field. Smith was a survivor of the so-called Kansas City Massacre, an event that took place on the steps of Kansas City's Union Station in June of 1933 in which a group of assassins, possibly led by Charlie "Pretty Boy" Floyd, slaughtered four law officers and the prisoner they were guarding.

FBI Special Agent in Charge Dwight Brantley, headquartered in faraway Oklahoma City, informed newsmen "They were our prisoners and it will be our job to put them back where they belong."

Intelligence soon arrived at the sheriff's office implying the getaway car had been spotted in the communities of Keefeton and Warner. An all-points bulletin was issued to law enforcement agencies throughout Oklahoma, Arkansas, and Texas. Two small planes were sent into the skies from Muskogee's Hat Box Field in an effort to spot the fugitive's car.

A bevy of federal officers sprinted to Claremore in an effort to provide protection to their chief stool pigeon, Jack Miller. Officers suspected the gang might head that way in an effort to extract revenge on the big Indian for his damaging testimony. Miller was nowhere to be found. Evidently the oversized thug had heard the news and swiftly went into deep hiding.

An hour after the jail delivery, Heady's spouse, soon to be dubbed "Pretty Betty Heady" by the press, was arrested at her hotel room and charged with complicity in the escape. Ironically, according to Chief Corgan, Bolton had shown her many kindnesses over the past weeks. Just prior to her fateful visit where she passed the pistol to her husband she and Bolton had been joking back and forth in his office.

At four in the afternoon a guard at a prison work camp spotted the convicts fleeing car on Highway #2 just south of Wilburton. The guard gave chase and was soon joined by Pushmataha County Sheriff John Helm. Unfortunately, the officers lost sight of the vehicle shortly after the suspect's rig turned west on a graveled county road heading toward the community of Higgins. Several hours later, the getaway car was discovered abandoned on a blind lumber road near the crossroads settlement of Ti, located deep in the sparsely populated, rugged Kiamichi Mountains of Southeast Oklahoma.

The fugitives had fled the car on foot, coatless and scantily dressed, moving into the thick forest while the temperature plunged into the upper twenties and a sharp icy rain began to come down in sheets as darkness fell.

The following morning Governor E.W. Marland ordered thirty-two heavily armed National Guardsmen from K Company 180th Infantry out of McAlester commanded by Captain

Hiram Impson to join the already oversized posse, which had swelled overnight to nearly two-hundred man-hunters.

A pack of bloodhounds led by the legendary K-9 Old Boston, soon arrived on the scene from the Oklahoma State Penitentiary in nearby McAlester. Spotter planes out of Oklahoma City, Claremore and Rogers soon joined those from Muskogee to keep an aerial watch over the area of operations. Pittsburg County Sheriff H. H. Sherrill took to the radio airways declaring, "We have 'em bottled up. They can't get through the net."

Meanwhile, mountain residents and their wide-eyed children, who rarely observed a car a day pass by their primitive cabins, stood watching the long procession of guardsmen and law enforcement personnel pass by with a mixture of awe and suspicion.

The heavily timbered area, dubbed the soft-pine district, was dotted with silent sawmills, small run down tenant farms and sagging "fork in the road" villages. Stark evidence presenting the ravages of the ongoing economic depression was visually apparent at every turn. Farms had turned nonproductive due to recent severe droughts, livestock prices had slipped to nil and the sale of lumber was almost nonexistent. Unemployment spiked throughout the region causing twenty percent of the population of Pittsburg and Pushmataha Counties to flee west in search of jobs during the past few years.

The region's rarely visited deep hollers, carpeted with thick tangled underbrush, wait-a-minute vines, and sharp thorny bushes the size of a man's thumb that savaged ones limbs, offered a perfect hiding place for anyone scouting from the law. Warnings were issued to local residents over the radio requesting all but essential vehicles stay off the roads.

While the bulk of the posse, accompanied by a bevy of reporters, began filtering into the area, a smaller group of lawmen led by Deputy U. S. Marshals Alan Stanfield and George Hall started tracking the escapee's footprints emitting from the abandoned car into the woods. Due to the ongoing rains washing away the majority of tracks the effort proved to be tough sledding. While most of the group returned to Hartshorne for hot food and coffee just a few hours after the advent of darkness, Stanfield, accompanied by a pair of guards from the nearby prison camp, remained in the field.

Stanfield, nicknamed "The Bloodhound" by Judge Robert Williams, had forged a formidable reputation as a manhunter during his two years serving the federal court. Born in 1894 at Wild Horse, Indian Territory, he was the son of a pioneer storekeeper. In 1915, he attended East Central Collage in Ada but the academic life proved too tame for the spirited youth. He soon left school gaining employment with the Ada Police Department as a patrolman. He later served several years as a Pontotoc County Deputy Sheriff before being appointed a Deputy US Marshal. Over the years Stanfield had been involved in the pursuit of various noted badmen such as "Pretty

Marshal Alan Stanfield

Boy" Floyd, Wilbur Underhill, and others. The lawman proved to be an extraordinarily skilled tracker of men.

Back in Springfield, Missouri, the aged mother of Dan Heady sobbingly told newsmen, "He broke out cause he knew the least time he would serve would be 45 years." Adding "I wish Dan would give himself up before he gets killed but he won't. He's too stubborn." When asked about the outlaw's wife, Mother Heady stated, "She's been good to me. Why, all the furniture in this house belongs to her."

On the afternoon of December 4 Marshal Stanfield was contacted by a farmer who stated Cooper had approached him only hours earlier asking for directions. A young Native American girl also informed Stanfield an individual matching the fugitives description had offered her a quarter for directions to Talihina.

It was now becoming obvious to lawmen Cooper had split from the others. An hour after receiving the tip from the girl Stanfield and company spotted Cooper attempting to scamper across an isolated dirt lumber road located on the side of New State Mountain. When the officers warned the outlaw to halt he stopped dead in his tracks and immediately dropped to his knees begging the lawmen to, "Please don't kill me!" Stanfield later informed reporters, "He was yellow to the core."

After transporting the prisoner to the state pen in McAlester for safekeeping, Stanfield and Hall joined up with a group of posseman led by Sheriff Tom Jordan, it's members included Muskogee County Deputies Paul Hinson, R. M. Pickins, and Treve Weimer as well as Okfuskee Deputies Ernest Neeley, Millard Fisher, and Roy Mogridge.

By nightfall many members of the main posse had played-out, returning home from twenty-four tough hours of tramping many miles through rough forested mountainous country in freezing rain without the benefit of hot food or dry clothes. On arrival at his Fort Smith, Arkansas, residence Chief of Police Mike Gordan told reporters, "Those boys undoubtedly found aid. That's why they headed straight into the heart of mountain country. It's the 'Code of the Hills' in those parts to help fugitives from justice."

At roughly 11:30 on the evening of December 5, Jordan was approached at a location eight miles south of Hartshorne by a local man named Ben Standifer. He informed officers he had received word the fugitives were hiding at a secluded cabin owned by Perry Walker located deep in the woods on the side of Jackfork Mountain near the small village of Weathers. According to the informant, the fugitives were holding Walker and his family hostage. He explained, "Walker and his wife, Babe, approached me earlier this evening telling me three rough looking men had come to their home asking for shelter and a meal, stating they had been trapped in the storm while out squirrel hunting. After eating, the men asked Walker and his wife to carry food, blankets, and medicine three miles up the mountain to one of their companions who was sick and had to be abandoned on the trailside. The pair, led by one of the interlopers, who the Walkers described as silent and glossy-eyed, hiked up the hill discovering a desperately ill man lying in the mud and freezing rain next to a roughly constructed slab-board hog-house suffering from pneumonia. The Walkers dragged and pushed the sick man into the small shelter, wrapped him in blankets, put some Vicks vapo-rub on his chest and left him some porridge made of milk and raw eggs.

While the injured man's companion decided to remain with his pal the Walkers departed the scene convinced the men were prison escapees. "The Walkers quickly hiked to my place seeking advice as to what to do next." said Standifer. "I told them to go back home and keep the outlaws there until I could lead a posse to their position."

After his encounter with the couple Standifer jumped into his truck and sought out the posse. At approximately midnight the posse received news of the death of Ben Bolton. Since many of the officers had known Bolton intimately for years, they took the news badly.

Just outside of Weathers, the posse's vehicles became mired in the mud, forcing the man-hunters to continue the chase on foot. With hardened hearts, they plunged through the thick timber hoping for the opportunity to revenge the murder of their fellow officer.

After fording the overflowing North Jackfork Creek in a steady freezing rain, members of the posse, in a bloodthirsty mood, cursed while slipping and sliding up the rough ice covered path leading to the cabin site with Standifer taking the lead.

Observing smoke curling out of the structure's chimney, Jordan and Stanfield decided to pull off a bit of subterfuge sending Standifer to the cabin's door to ask Walker and his wife if they could come to his home and assist him in caring for his sick wife. Thus clearing the noncombatants from the battlefield.

According to Standifer, "I was scared on approaching the cabin figuring I'd get shot for sure but luckily when I called out the outlaws paid no mind." Walker and his terrified spouse slipped out of the cabin most likely not even noticed by the fugitives who were curled up next to the fireplace covered in heavy blankets in a severe state of exhaustion.

With the Walker's now safely out of the line of fire, Stanfield, accompanied by Deputies Mogridge and Wiemer, slipped behind the house covering a rear door while Jordan and his companions covered the front entrance to the cabin. Mogridge claimed it was raining so hard at the time, "You couldn't see your hand in front of your face." Incidentally, Deputy Mogridge was armed at the time with a high-powered rifle he claimed could fire a round which was capable of penetrating an engine block. Ironically, it was one of two such weapons that had recently been purchased for the Okfuskee

County Sheriff's Department by the two Okemah banks, which the O'Malley Gang had robbed in December 1934. Marshal Stanfield carried the second donated rifle.

On gaining their positions the battle commenced. What happened next is still hotly debated to this day. Statements later given by Marshal Stanfield were in complete opposition to those given by Ben Standifer and Deputy Mogridge. In this case, both versions will be given and the reader can make up his own mind as to the truth of the matter.

According to Stanfield, he fired a warning shot in the air before calling out to the escapees, "Come out boys we have ya covered." Hearing no response he kicked in the side door and spotting Dan Heady ordered him to drop his weapon. "Dapper" Dan responded by leaping to his feet shouting, "Piss on 'em. Let's fight the bastards" before swinging his shotgun toward Stanfield. The lawman reacted to the threatening move by ordering his brother officers to, "Let 'em have it" before shooting half of Heady's skull into the next county with his high-powered rifle. He and his fellow officers then raked Gilmore's hide with a volley of shot before ceasing fire. Stanfield estimated fifty shots were fired in the melee.

A different version of events was given to the press via the mouths of Ben Standifer as well as the Walkers and Deputy Mogridge, who stated all the officers involved simply began firing away on Stanfield's orders without warning before the marshal kicked in the door and finished off the groggy-headed outlaws. The officers then withdrew from the cabin and called on the fugitives to surrender. Gilmore cried out his submission and was ordered to come out the front door, which he did.

According to Deputy Mogridge when Gilmore exited the cabin, dressed only in a blood drenched T-shirt and boxer shorts, he began slowly walking toward the posse as if in a trance. When the deputy ordered him to halt, he continued to approach their position until an officer "Busted a cap at his feet." The badman then fell to his knees and began loudly sobbing. Stanfield ordered the outlaw to shut up and to drag Heady out of the cabin. Gilmore, his ears ringing and suffering from a slug in the chest along with a dozen birdshot pellets to the legs, followed orders dragging Heady's corpse out the front door feet-first his fractured bleeding skull bouncing roughly off the door jam and porch steps.

Whatever version is correct, the result was the same. Dan Heady was dead and Gilmore wounded and captured.

The interior of Walker's cabin was destroyed beyond recognition. Furniture was shredded, lamps and glassware shattered, the walls splintered and blood-stained. Most of the couples canned food, eggs, and other foodstuffs were destroyed. To top it off, what food remained, a ham and two-dozen eggs, was consumed by the posse in the aftermath of the gun-battle.

Mr. Walker would later remark, "How will we make it through the winter with no rations?" He added, "I'll tell ya, the outlaws were a sight more decent to us then the laws." Walker would later request the state reimburse him for his losses. His request was denied. A search of the cabin turned up the two stolen shotguns.

When questioned by the cops about the whereabouts of the remaining escapees, Gilmore, turned talkative saying, "Short is sick. We left him in a hog house up on the mountain and Garrett is wandering around the woods." He added, "Heady forced me to take part in the escape. He threatened my life if I didn't assist him!"

While Stanfield and company manacled and transported Gilmore to the prison hospital in McAlester, Jordan and his fellow officers followed Perry Walker up the mountainside in search of the missing fugitives leaving several lawmen to guard the Walker cabin.

After traversing the mountain the posse came across Leonard Short lying near naked in a mud hole next to a scorched hog shelter delirious with fever and shivering uncontrollably while holding his hands stiffly clasped in prayer. The chubby outlaw was suffering from pneumonia as well as severe burns covering much of his legs and backside. Evidently, since the Walkers had visited the poor man leaving him some food and a blanket Garrett had built him a fire for warmth before he departed trying to make his way back to civilization. Apparently, during the night, the rotund bandit had rolled into the flames catching his clothes and the blanket on fire.

When officers attempted to revive the emancipated outlaw, he suddenly leaped to his feet making a mad dash toward the top of a nearby knoll. On reaching the top of the incline he came to a sudden halt before collapsing in a dead heap. Strangely, instead of gunning down the badman, lawmen observing Short's surreal dash to nowhere merely stood shaking their heads in dismay at his bizarre behavior.

Officers, unable to locate Garrett, hauled the badman's lifeless body down the mountain roped to the back of a surefooted plow horse. On their arrival at the Walker residence, the corpse was placed on the ground in the cabin's front yard and covered with a blanket.

At midmorning, a confused, hungry, and freezing Donnie Garrett silently stumbled into the front yard of the Walker cabin and directly into the waiting arms of the law. He was immedi-

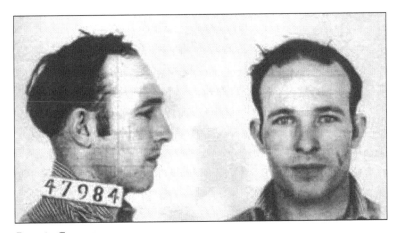

Donnie Garrett

ately handcuffed to a tree. When searched the fugitive was found in possession of the pistol believed to be the weapon that had been smuggled into the jail by Betty Heady to her husband.

That afternoon officers attempted to transport Heady's body across the creek flowing past the cabin, which was now swollen and out of it's banks, in a rickety raft they had found tied to a tree. While in midstream, the craft, operated by Sheriff Jordan capsized dumping the lawman and his motionless baggage into the cold drink. Nearly a half-hour later, a thoroughly soaked and chilled Jordan was fished out of the water. Sometime later officers discovered Heady's stiffened corpse hung up on a snag near the creek-bank a ways downstream.

In the meantime, Sheriff Jordan was sent back to Muskogee in order to seek medical attention for his condition. On his way back to civilization, Jordan stopped at the store in Weathers to phone his wife as well as fill in reporters as to the dramatic developments in the case.

At midday, a local man pulled a proper boat to the scene on a trailer and the craft was used to successfully transport the bodies of Short and Heady across the raging stream. By late afternoon, the rest of the posse had successfully forded the creek and was joined by a bevy of newspaper reporters and photographers.

After posing for a series of gruesome photographs the officers transported Garrett by car to the Muskogee jail while the corpses of Heady and Short were moved by mule to the main road where they were shifted to the bed of Ben Standifer's truck and hauled to a McAlester funeral home for embalming.

Back in Muskogee, reporters interviewed Marshal Stanfield who informed the newsies: "According to Gilmore, Leonard Short was in a state of panic since the escape. He was terrified of the consequences of shooting Bolton. Since he physically out of shape foraging through the rough timber and cold weather was too much for the flabby outlaw. He soon contracted pneumonia and could not continue, his friends dumped him in a pigpen and departed. Evidently, Garrett built him a fire. He rolled into the flames in the middle of the night and caught fire. When we found him his clothes were burned off as was most his hide." He added, "The escapees were depending on Cooper to lead them to freedom since he had done some bootlegging in the district in the past. But he quickly left the group due to his fear Heady intended on killing him for being too talkative to the authorities after his arrest."

On another subject Stanfield mused, "Although they didn't give Ben Bolton a break, we gave them boys every opportunity to surrender, but Heady who was the only one of that bunch with guts and knew the score, refused. He was determined to die rather than surrender so we accommodated him."

According to witnesses, when Dan Heady's widow was informed of her husband's death she just smirked and said, "Well, that's his tough luck." Further informing reporters, "Boys, I don't shed tears."

At her arraignment on a charge of aiding prisoners to escape Betty was informed by Judge Williams, "If you are guilty of this charge you can see what it means. Your husband is dead, killed while resisting arrest and you are his murderer. Madam, your final kiss in the jail that fateful morning was the kiss of death"

After pleading not guilty to the charges, Mrs. Heady was escorted past a flock of aggressive photographers from the federal building to a police cruiser for her trip back to jail. When a reporter shouted if she would comment on the jailbreak she spat some profanities his way before flinging a sporty fur coat over her head in an effort to hide her face.

That afternoon US Attorney Cleon Summers informed reporters, " If we can prove Mrs. Heady handed her husband the pistol that 'engineered' the escape and Bolton's murder she will be charged with murder and face the death penalty and I will prosecute her as vigorously as a man."

Ben Bolton was buried at Muskogee's Greenhill Cemetery as a crowd of 3500 somber citizens, friends and family looked on. There were reportedly so many cars in the funeral procession, streets leading to the cemetery had to be blocked off for over an hour to enable the entire motorcade to make its way to the burial grounds.

The lawmen had served in law enforcement for nearly twenty-five years beginning in 1912 when he spent six years as a Dallas County deputy sheriff in Texas. From 1919 to 1922 he served as a security officer for Swift and Co. before being hired as a special agent for the KATY Railroad. Bolton moved to Muskogee in 1927 taking a job with the police department as a plainclothes officer. He was elevated to detective in 1930 and appointed Chief of Police in 1932. During is time as chief he was credited with modernizing the force installing two-way radios in patrol cars as well as issuing officers steel vests and buying several "Tommyguns" for departmental use. In 1932, Bolton was appointed Chief of Detectives. He was survived by is wife and a son, Jack.

Meanwhile, just hours after Bolton's interment the body of John Blackburn was unceremoniously lowered into the dirt. He lies just a few dozen yards from Bolton's final resting place in an unmarked paupers grave. Since the authorities were unable to make contact with his family, Blackburn was buried at the county's expense with no flourishes save a cheap pine box. The earthly remains of Leonard Short and Dan Heady were claimed by their next of kin and transported by rail back to their hometowns in Missouri.

Short's corpse, which was unclothed and wrapped in a white linen sheet, arrived in a crude shipping crate at the Missouri Pacific Rail Depot in Crane, Missouri, under the watchful eyes of several dozen silent tearful witnesses. The body was unloaded and taken to the Hilton Funeral Home where it was washed and dressed in a suit and tie before being placed in an expensive coffin and transported by hearse to the Short family home in nearby Galena.

Although Oklahoma officers insisted Short had not been wounded in the affair, undertaker Ernest Hilton declared when he prepared the body for burial he discovered several buck-

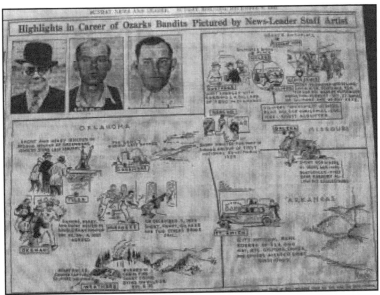

O'Malley Gang exsploits: top left-Ben Bolton, center-Leonard Short, right-Dan Heady.

O'Malley mobsters at the back door of the Muskogee jail.

shot wounds on his body. He also stated the badman was not marked by nearly as many burns as implied in statements made by Oklahoma officers. He added, "It looks to me he has lost about thirty-five pounds since I last saw him." Adding, "I believe he died of either lead poisoning, exposure or fright, not burning." Adding, "He had a bad heart for years ya know." Oklahoma lawmen promptly dismissed the report calling it nonsense. The outlaw's carcass lay-in-state in an open coffin in the front parlor of the Short residence for twenty-four-hours while hundreds of residents passed by to pay their respects.

A massive crowd overflowed a local church where the funeral was conducted. The Reverend John Crockett, the so-called "Bishop of the Ozarks" preached the funeral. He began his remarks by saying: "When I looked upon his face of death it was the first time my old friend "Shock" did not meet me with a smile." He also informed the crowd, "If Leonard were alive today he would say, "Let not your heart be troubled, neither be afraid." Adding, "A great friend and patriot has come to journeys end."

The possession then moved to the town's muddy hilltop cemetery where a horde of grief stricken family members and friends shed a multitude of tears to the strains of "*The Old Rugged Cross*" and "*In the Sweet Bye and Bye.*" The flag-draped coffin was then lowered into the earth while members of the local VFW fired a twenty-one-gun-salute to the memory

Dan Heady in death.

of a charismatic war veteran (*Short served in the Navy during WWI) and patriot, misunderstood social misfit, kindhearted patron of the area's poor or murderous bank-robbing hoodlum...Take your pick.

Over 1000 persons attended Leonard's burial at the Galena Cemetery. According to local news reports, most were in an ugly mood, accusing the cops of cold bloodily murdering the badman. Evidently, "Shock" Short, as he was locally known, had established a Robin Hood-like reputation of taking from the rich in order to give to the area's poor and underprivileged.

Such comments as, 'Sure, he did a little bootlegging during prohibition. So what?" abounded. Others waxed "Yea, he had a little money but he gave it all away to the less fortunate. He used to take a whole gang of kids to the picture show on Saturday mornings, springing for not just the price of admission but popcorn and candy to boot."

One elderly lady, touched by a previous act of kindness, reportedly walked seven miles through the hills to the cemetery in order to lay a wreath of flowers on the outlaw's grave. A Short family friend informed writer Vance Randolph at the time, "They sent Dewey Short to Congress and Leonard to the pen. Some folks think it should have been the other way around."

Just forty odd miles north of Galena the sixty-seven year

Grave of Ben Bolton

old mother of Dan Heady, standing on the front porch of the modest frame home her son had purchased for her the previous year, addressed reporters with tears in her eyes. "Dan was my favorite. Mothers are always fondest of their black sheep." Adding, "He was not a bad boy at heart."

According to a local mortician, Heady's corpse had arrived in a rough shipping coffin dressed only in a dirty T-shirt

Grave of Dan Heady

Grave of Shock Short

and silk underwear with the top of his head missing. Heady's sister informed reporters, "The funeral and burying will be private. I know how the public acts when a thing like this happens. They want to see the body." Services were held at the Lohmeyer Funeral Home. Rev. Scars Riepma read Psalms 39 and 90 before ending the ritual with a brief prayer and the singing of *"I know he cares."* The outlaw was outfitted in a dark gray suit and an expensive coffin of the same shade.

Daniel Turner Heady, the offspring of noble trailblazing pioneers turned bad was laid to rest on a hillside overlooking a clear spring-fed stream just south of the small community of Turners Station located a few miles east of Springfield. According to news reports, due to the recent rains his kin was forced to haul his coffin up the hill to the graveyard in a mule-pulled wagon since the hearse had gotten hopelessly mired in the mud. Nearly fifty persons, mostly relatives, were present at the burial. His wife, who was being held in the Muskogee County Jail charged with conspiracy to murder and assisting a jailbreak, was not allowed to attend the somber ceremony.

On the morning of December 9, Russell Cooper and Dewey Gilmore were whisked into federal court under heavy guard. Judge Williams summarily sentenced the pair to forty-five years each for the Okemah robberies and a promise of future prosecution concerning the mass escape and Chief Bolton's murder. When asked if he had any recommendations for mercy concerning the defendants, his honor firmly stated, "No, I hope they serve every day of their sentences."

(uncle same shows his long reach from pg 198)

The prisoners were hurriedly transported by rail to Leavenworth Federal Penitentiary for safekeeping where they joined Donnie Garrett, who had been sent there the day after his capture at the Walker farm. Prosecutors had decided not to charge him with escape, instead choosing to simply allow him to serve out his seven-year term for the Mann Act.

On the day of Leonard Short's funeral, his old pal turned informant, Bob Johnson was sentenced to a ten-year term at the Missouri State Penitentiary for the Dillard diamond robbery. When informed of Short's death he shrugged his shoulders in silence. When a reporter asked if there was any love lost between him and Short, the bandit quipped, "Not much."

Chapter 12
The Last Gasp and a Day at the Races

In the intervening time, Blackie Doyle, Dave Sherman, Spike Lane, Clarence Sparger, and Johnny Langan moved their operations to Omaha, Nebraska, where they were involved in a lengthy crime spree in an effort to drum up a little cash.

Sitting squat on the banks of the Missouri River adjacent to Council Bluffs, Iowa, Omaha's cultural ties were part old west but mostly agricultural being surrounded by the vast Midwest corn belt. The town ranked third behind Kansas City and Chicago for being the nations largest meatpacking center as well. Like most major cities located in the Middle America, Omaha, population 229,000 in 1930, was going through hard times because of the ongoing depression. Due to the collapse of the worlds major feed markets, corn and soybean prices had hit rock bottom thus plunging the area into economic chaos. The big mills as well as a horde of slaughter houses closed their doors and the railroads laid off an army of workers. The big berg was also noted as the site of Father Flannigan's Boys Town, and the headquarters of the giant Union Pacific Railroad.

Since the turn of the century the city had been held hostage by a Pendergast-style political machine headed by boss Tom Dennison and his cronies. Dennison, a gambler by trade, located to Omaha in the 1890s before starting a very successful lottery in the third ward. Around the turn of the century he turned to politics. Over the years his power and influence increased until he held virtual sway over the city's Democratic party machine as well as the police department and legal machinery.

In the latter 1920s he organized the Omaha Bootlegging Syndicate, which controlled the manufacturing and sales of illegal liquor throughout the city. For the next decade dozens of honky-tonks and nightclubs offering liquor, prostitutes and gambling operated openly throughout the city protected from police raids by the Liquor Syndicate. When competing sources challenged his control over the thriving booze trade Dennison and his associates imported several out of town professional killers including Mike "Shifty" Regan and Larry "The Chopper" DeVol as muscle, directing them to silence the competition. During 1930-31 the deadly crew flexed their muscles, shot-gunning a half-dozen competitors in a series of drive-by shootings. The cry and hue from shocked citizens groups forced the town council to order a cleanup, which was the beginning of the end of boss Dennison.

In 1932 Dennison and several of his associates were indicted on prohibition charges. With Dennison's fall from power the legion of gambling/liquor joints that had previously operated unhampered by the law were forced to go underground or move outside the city limits into the county to locations such as Carter Lake. One of those thriving nightclubs was *The Races,* located at on the city's southwest side at 6311 Center Street. Nearby, was the AK-SAR-BEN horse-racing track. The nightclub was owned and operated by Jimmy Corcoran, a longtime Omaha gambling figure.

The racing track offered legal betting on harness, pace, and running races since 1921. It had recently reopened after a four year hiatus due to the economic hard times. A horde of illegal mob controlled betting parlors were located nearby disguised as honky-tonks, dance halls, and pool parlors. .

At three in the afternoon of December 18, 1935, the janitor at *The Races*, which was closed at the time, received a mysterious phone call from a man who insisted he had left his expensive camel-hair coat in the cloakroom the previous night. When the custodian, who was later identified as eighteen-year-old Melin Rogert, checked the closet, he indeed found the coat and informed the caller of this fact. The man on the phone then insisted he would be right over to retrieve the garment. Three hours later, Blackie Doyle showed up at the club's door inquiring about the garment. When young Rogert let Doyle into the establishment the thug quickly drew a pistol and ordered him and another man to, "Hit the floor, face down!" Suddenly, Dave Sherman burst into the business and began setting a series of nitro charges on the door of the club's large safe while witnesses claim a third and four individual, later identified as Clarence Sparger and Johnny Langan sat at the wheels of two getaway cars positioned in the club's parking lot waiting on their crime partners to finish their work.

Shortly after the hijackers entered the establishment, two workers strolled into the business and were forced to join the other witnesses on the floor. After giving the safe three shots of explosive juice the steel box sprang open and the yeggs were able to gather up the cash inside which amounted to a disappointing $200. After cutting the telephone line, the pair of hooligans exited the business, hopped into the two rigs and made a clean getaway.

A week after the nightclub incident, Doyle, Sherman and Langan bullied their way into the Western Auto store located at Farnam Avenue at opening time ordering several customers and employees to lie the floor and, "Keep your biscuit-hole shut." While one of the men covered the hostages, the other two rifled the safe and cash drawers before exiting the establishment with a goodly sum of cash as well as $650 in merchandise. The bandits jumped into a running car manned by Clarence Sparger and made a successful departure.

According to news reports a group of thieves had attempted to loot the store several months earlier. On that occasion a gun-battle erupted, which resulted in the deaths of Patrolman Reynold Wolfe and one of the robbers. A second officer was wounded in the affair while the dead bandits companion was shot and captured.

On January 11, 1936, at 8:30 a.m. Doyle, Sherman and Spike Lane rushed into Louis Cantoni's beer tavern located at 723 South 16,[th] herding a dozen patrons and employees into a back room. While Doyle kept herd over the hostages with a shotgun, the other two blew the tavern's safe with nitro stealing $2850. Apparently, the tavern's owner had the large amount of cash on hand in order to cash checks for railroad workers. On departing the business Doyle turned and warned the frightened hostages, "If any of you stick your heads out that door I'll blow your brains out." While the robbery was in progress, Canotni attempted to take a peek at the hijackers but when the bandits noticed his stare one of them kicked him in the shin saying, "Keep your eyes to yourself." He later described two of the hijackers as, "One was taller and mustached while the other needed a shave." Witnesses on the street observed the bandit trio hop into a light colored sedan manned by Clarence Sparger.

On the afternoon of February 11, "Spike" Lane took time out to travel across the river to Council Bluffs ,Iowa, where he and thirty-year-old Josephine Church were wed by a local Justice of the Peace. Dave Sherman and his attractive girlfriend were witnesses to the event. Instead of using an alias Lane signed his true name on the license and listed his occupation as "Salesman."

On February 13, the same quartet that had looted Cantoni's joint raided the headquarters of the Yellow Cab and Baggage Company of Omaha located at 619 South Twentieth Street. According to Sam Hilmes, General manager of the business, three armed men entered the establishment at 3:45 in the afternoon just as he was distributing pay checks to a line of employees. When Himes protested the money they were stealing was meant for the benefit of working men, Lane struck him in the head with a gun butt while Doyle menacingly ordered the line of witnesses to, "Hold still or I'll kill every G-ddamn one of ya." After fleecing the joint for a little over two grand, the trio entered a light colored sedan parked in an alley that was manned by Clarence Sparger.

Within days of the taxicab robbery, a heavily armed posse of G-men and police raided the gang's hideout, located in a swanky apartment building situated at 28th and Dewey Streets in Omaha (just south of present–day Turner Park on the westside of the downtown area, now a run down area occupied by warehouses and a few dilapidated houses). Unfortunately, the hooligans had fled to parts unknown. Frustrated federal agents suspected a double-cross. It soon came to light the hoodlums had been tipped-off by cohesive elements inside the Omaha Police Department.

Although news reports claimed federal officers had ascertained the gang's whereabouts from Spike Lane's marriage license, a copy of the document shows no such address was given by either the happy couple nor the witnesses, save "Omaha, Nebraska." It is more likely the feds garnered their information from an underworld snitch. It seems ironic that while the FBI had its informants, so did the men they were pursuing.

Neighbors stated gang members had lived a lavish lifestyle, drove fancy cars, and patronized area nightclubs in the evenings. At the conclusion of the Omaha crime spree Doyle, Sherman, and Lane, accompanied by their molls, retreated to Dallas, Texas. Sparger, and Langan relocated to their familiar haunts in and around Kansas City.

Fort Smith, Arkansas - January 1936

On January 14, 1936, Art Austin and Dewey Gilmore pled guilty to the illegal interstate transportation of stolen funds concerning the 1934 robbery of the McIlroy Bank and Trust in Fayetteville. Austin, who had turned states evidence in the case, received three years probation while Gilmore was sentenced to ten years in prison. Bank robbery charges in the same case brought against Red Melton and Fred Reese were not further pursued.

The following day, Gilmore, Russell Cooper and Floyd Henderson along with Otto Jackson pled guilty to robbing the City National Bank of Ft. Smith. Judge Ragon sentenced Gilmore and Cooper to a twenty-five year jolt, Jackson to the same and Henderson was issued a twelve year term.

Back in Oklahoma, the chickens were coming home to roost. On January 28, 1936, Dewey Gilmore and Russell Cooper arrived in Muskogee from Fort Smith by train under the watchful eye of Federal Marshal Joe Wilson and four others, all armed with automatic weapons. The Muskogee court had plans to try the pair for the murder of Ben Bolton. The following day Red Melton and Fred Reese arrived from Leavenworth at Muskogee's KATY depot also under heavy guard. An accord had been reached between the federal courts in Kansas City and Muskogee allowing the Muskogee court to prosecute Melton and Reese for the Okemah robberies before their being tried for the Neosho heist. The state of Missouri also decided to delay trying the pair for the Seneca and Webb City bank jobs.

Two days later, Irish O'Malley blew into town fresh from the Illinois State Penitentiary at Joliet where he was currently doing life without parole. Illinois authorities had temporarily released the sophisticated bandit to federal officers with the agreement that whatever happened in federal court the badman would serve his sentence in Illinois before doing federal time.

On his arrival at the jail O'Malley asked guards for a smoke and inquired, "When do they ring the dinner bell around this joint? I haven't ate a single bean since we left Illinois." He was given a ham sandwich and a lukewarm cup of coffee once he was lodged securely in his cell.

Within days of the gang's being collected under one roof, rumors began to fly indicating the defendants were making plans for another bust-out from Muskogee's City/Federal Jail. Reacting to these reports, extra guards were brought in and visiting privileges temporarily suspended for all prisoners. Chief of Police Corgan ordered the O'Malley prisoners chained to their cell bars and handcuffed unless on bathroom call. Under no circumstances were they be allowed to speak to each other. He further instructed jailors to never allow any of the gang outside of their cells unless he was personally present, saying, " That means if I go out and get myself drowned they are in for the rest of their lives. If one of them tries to escape I want the honor of killing 'em."

Sheriff Tom Jordan informed reporters gathered at the federal courthouse awaiting the trial if any of them approached within thirty feet of the prisoners when they made their appearance, the interlopers would be shot. As for photographers, he warned them to also keep a respectable distance or else. Sharp-shooting Deputy Ray Crinklaw, the survivor of a 1932 Cherokee County gun battle in which two officers and a badman was slain, was ordered to cover the cellblock with a fully-automatic Browning Automatic Rifle with orders to "Shoot to Kill" if the notorious inmates so much as loudly snored. He was soon joined by Muskogee PD Night Captain Jess Adair, armed with a Thompson Machinegun.

On February 12, O'Malley, Melton, and Reese appeared before Judge Williams where they pled guilty to bank robbery charges, and each sentenced to forty-five year terms. None uttered a word at the proceeding except "Guilty." All three were dressed in moth-worn clothing and aging overcoats to break the cold winter wind. When the trio was led out the courthouse steps, an ingenious reporter, positioned across the street, shouted through a bullhorn asking Melton why he pled guilty. The hoodlum shouted, "Why not? They were going to get me sooner or later."

The murder trials for Russell Cooper and Dewey Gilmore began on February 14. The pair pled not guilty, vigorously insisting Bolton had been slain by Dan Heady without their assistance. Cooper claimed in the immediate aftermath of the escape Heady had remarked Bolton was a, "Tough guy. I had to shoot him loose from that gun!" Although Gilmore had previously told investigators Short had killed Bolton, he suddenly did a one-eighty asserting he had also overheard Heady make the damning remark.

Both men further reiterated their past claims suggesting they had joined the escape due to their fear of Dan Heady. According to Cooper, "Heady put us on the spot judge." On hearing the claim, the prosecutor leaped to his feet proclaiming "Balderdash!" A red-faced Judge Williams reacted to the interruption by instructing the prosecutor to, "Calm yourself sir. I will not tolerate such outbursts." Throughout the proceeding the widow of Ben Bolton sat in the courtroom tears flowing from her eyes.

At the conclusion of a very short trial the jury promptly found both men guilty as charged. Although Assistant US Attorney Charles W. Miller demanded the death penalty, saying, "Hanging instead of electrocution is better for fellows like these," the jury refused his request due to the myriad of conflicting testimony concerning who exactly had pulled the trigger. In passing sentence, Judge Williams instructed the pair they could expect no clemency from him, "As long as I live and of sound mind." The pair was sentenced to 99 years each to run concurrently with the 45 years they had already been sentenced to serve in the Okemah robbery case.

To the consternation of all involved, Betty Heady was

eventually granted temporary freedom after posting a $500 appearance bond. She returned to Missouri where she lived with her elderly mother-in-law for the next year. Federal charges of harboring and conspiracy to aid in an escape were finally dismissed against her by Judge A. P. Murrah in July 1937. (*the Murrah building in Oklahoma City, which was demolished by domestic terrorist Tim McVey was named after Judge Murrah) According to a statement made by US Attorney Cleon Summers, "There exists insufficient evidence to proceed with the indictment."

Jack Miller swept back into town in order to testify and collect his witness fees. Upon granting Miller his freedom, His Honor chastised the squealer, "You were lucky this time to escape prosecution. I would advise you to find an honest line of work and quit this gambling business." Miller responded by meekly mumbling, "Thank you judge." before high-tailing it back to Claremore with his thirty pieces of silver where he was presently engaged as the proprietor of a bar/gambling hall located just off Route 66 in downtown Claremore

Soon after the multiple trials and sentencing were completed, the prisoners were marched through Muskogee's downtown streets in handcuffs and leg irons from the steps of the jail to the nearby KATY rail depot guarded by a dozen shotgun and machinegun toting federal marshals in an early morning bizarre public spectacle, which was observed by a crowd made up of several hundred curious citizens. Walking down the courthouse steps Russell Cooper paused long enough to spit at a bevy of reporters. Just before boarding the train, Gilmore boldly turned to the crowd and produced an obscene gesture causing some of the young girls in the crowd to audibly squeal with excitement. Some older folks openly cursed the convict for his contemptible act.

The group was then placed in a special passenger car and shipped to various destinations. O'Malley returned to Illinois while Gilmore, Cooper, Melton and Reese returned to Leavenworth Federal Penitentiary.

On April, 27, Red Melton pled guilty in federal court in Kansas City for the robbery of the bank in Neosho. Melton was handed a twenty-five year sentence to be served concurrently with his previously issued prison terms. Fred Reese stubbornly maintained his innocence in the Neosho affair. Prosecutors eventually threw in the towel and dropped the charges against him.

Within a short time after their arrivals at Leavenworth, Melton, Reese, Cooper, and Dewey Gilmore were processed and each declared extreme escape risks and transferred to Alcatraz Island, California, the federal systems premiere maximum facility. The old military prison had been turned over to the US Bureau of Prisons in 1933 to be used as a receptacle for the worst of the worst now serving time in the federal corrections facilities nationwide. All the bad eggs in one basket so to speak. Others serving time at the facility at the time were "Machinegun" Kelly, Al Capone and "Doc" Barker.

Dallas, Texas - March-April 1936

On March 9, 1936, Blackie Doyle, Dave Sherman, and 'Spike' Lane looted the Progress Wholesale Drug Company of Dallas, Texas, of $1200 at gunpoint. Three nights later, the trio robbed the desk clerk at the Ambassador Hotel of $400 as well as stealing a car from the parking lot.

On the morning of April 6, Spike Lane entered the Borden Milk Plant, approached the switchboard operator and thrust a pistol in her face demanding she, "Unplug that damn thing." When the terrified operator just stood in silence with her mouth wide open the bandit reached out and tore the headphones off her head then jerked the cord from the wall before forcing her to stand up and walk into the lobby where he encountered a dozen employees.

Lane informed the crowd, "This is a holdup. Put your faces against the wall." While this was going on, Doyle and Sherman forced their way into the business's money cage and robbed Cashier Robert Carmichael of $1513 in cash and $4225 in payroll checks before making their escape.

Five days later Blackie Doyle and his moll, Doris Adams, were driving down a Dallas street in a car stolen in Omaha, Nebraska, when a group of fast moving detectives pulled them over and placed them under arrest. Doyle reportedly offered no resistance and when patted down was found to be holding $1500 in cash and an automatic pistol. When the lovebird's North Dallas apartment was searched, lawmen discovered another pistol as well as a great deal of ammunition including a fully loaded drum for a Thompson machine gun but no "chopper."

Although Doyle gave his name as Charles Miller, officers were fully aware of his true identity. For the past month FBI agents had been in town making a nuisance of themselves plastering the place with wanted posters of Doyle and Sherman.

The attorney general of the state of Illinois immediately demanded Doyle's return to that state saying; "Although Doyle did not participate in the actual Luer kidnapping, he did help guard Mr. Luer while he was held in that cellar."

Omaha detectives also expressed interest in the fugitive's future since not only was the car he was driving at the time of his capture stolen in their fair city but numerous victims in the recent Omaha crime spree had already identified photos of Doyle, Sherman, Lane, Sparger and Langan as being involved in those deprivations. Kansas City officers also wanted to question the thug concerning the heinous slaying of Vivian Chase. Doyle's female companion was described as an ex-waitress and sometime call-girl hailing from Kansas City.

The day after Doyle's capture the $4225 in payroll checks stolen from Borden's Dairy was discovered in a canvas bag hidden in a storm drain by a pair of curious boys searching for crawdads to use as fishing bait. Hoping to get a line on the whereabouts of Sherman and Lane, officers placed their photos in the Dallas Morning News. They hit pay dirt.

On the morning of the fifteenth a relative of a county jailer phoned police stating she had rented an apartment to a man who closely resembled Dave Sherman. Dallas officers immediately raided the residence capturing Sherman and his newly acquired wife, Lucille Norse Sherman.

While both Sherman and Doyle were charged with the Dallas drugstore and dairy robberies, their female companions were charged with harboring felons. The two ladies were soon dubbed "The know-nothing girls" since they at first refused to discuss anything about their men-folk. They later reconsidered and began singing like a night at the opera.

Miss Adams admitted meeting Doyle at a Kansas City restaurant where she was employed as a waitress. The eatery was located only a block from police headquarters. She stated, "We thought they were gamblers." Adding, "I don't like the lives our boyfriends led but they treated us swell." Mrs. Sherman told reporters, "We always saw the best side of Dave. I still love him and will be waiting for him when he gets out of the penitentiary."

On receipt of news of the duos' capture, agents from the FBI again flooded Dallas in search of the much-wanted Alvin Karpis, who was reputably a one-time crime-partner of Doyle's.

Although Nebraska authorities demanded the pair's extradition to the "Cornhusker" State for their suspected participation in the Omaha robberies, Texas authorities denied their demands, Instead choosing to prosecute them for their Dallas crimes. Perhaps they figured possession was nine-tenths of the law, so to speak. Even though the pair at first pled not guilty to charges of robbing both the Progress Wholesale Drug Co and the Borden Milk Co. they changed their tune when a combined thirteen witnesses from both robberies came forward to identify them.

Top to Bottom: Dave Sherman, Blackie Doyle, and no-nothing girls under arrest.

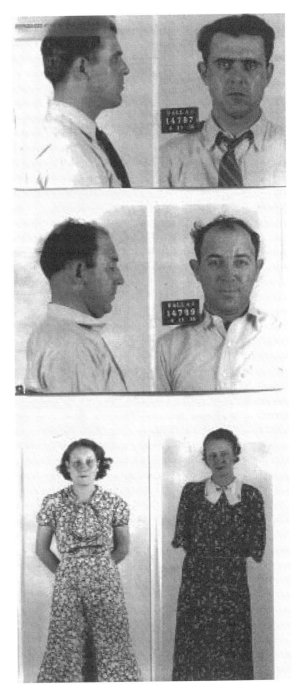

On May 25, 1936, Judge Noland Williams sentenced the pair to fifty-years each (25 yrs each for both robberies) in the Texas big house for their crimes. Several months after their sentencing Doyle's lawyer filed suit in an effort to regain possession of the $1500 in cash his client had been holding when arrested, saying the money was not part of the loot stolen from the two robberies of which they were convicted. The request was quickly denied.

In December 1936, Russell 'Spike' Lane was apprehended in Des Moines, Iowa, and immediately extradited back to Texas. En route from Iowa, Dallas officers were informed Lane was in possession of a hacksaw blade hidden on his person. After contacting several police departments on the trip route, Pittsburg, Kansas, cops were able to flag down the car carrying Lane and his captors. Although the prisoner was searched, nothing was found until he reached Dallas. There he was re-searched and a pair of hacksaw blades was found sewn into the heels of his

Spkie Lane

shoes. Shortly after his arrival in Texas, he was tried as being Doyle and Sherman's accomplice in the two Dallas robberies. As was the case with his companions, numerous witnesses from both hijackings came forward positively identifying Lane as one of the bandits. After a brief trial Lane was convicted and sentenced to twenty years in stir on a charge of robbery with firearms for the dairy heist. Several weeks later, he was convicted of the drug warehouse job and sentenced to an additional 99 years. On hearing this sentence, his wife, who was attending the sentencing, loudly and sarcastically remarked, "Well, that's something to look forward to!"

Upon his parole from the Texas pen in 1950 Lane was transported to Oklahoma where he pled guilty to a charge of grand theft dating from 1934. While serving time at McAlester "Spike" was suspected of trafficking in narcotics. He was paroled in 1953.

Hickman Mills, Missouri - April 1936

In early 1936, an inmate of the Missouri State pen named Ray Marks contacted the FBI offering to exchange information in the case of Langan and Sparger for his freedom. Marks was the cellmate of Charles Arbogast, who was doing a ten year hitch for assisting the outlaw pair in the attempted robbery of the Blytheville, Missouri, bank. The prisoner also inferred he was a pal of Sparger associate Ted Rogers.

Due to Mr. Hoover's disgust concerning the failure to garner results from their previous dealings with informant Joe Spano, the feds demurred. Col. Marvin Casteel, Director of the Missouri Highway Patrol, was curious as to what Marks had to say. The following day, a Sergeant Poage of the Highway Patrol arrived at the prison to question Marks.

Although the con had little of substance to share, he turned the investigator on to the wife of Ted Rogers, who was presently wanted on a charge of armed robbery. Lawmen were able to convince Mrs. Rogers into talking her husband into turning himself into the authorities and telling all. Rogers was a fountain of information giving investigators the locations of the bandit's hideouts and current associates. Officers initially put a tail on gang associate "Shorty" Cramer who led them to a bootlegger hangout located in Lamoni, Iowa. A large party of lawmen made up of two St. Jo detectives as well as Col. Casteel and Sgt. Poage were joined by three Iowa and two other Missouri State Troopers along with FBI Special Agents Farland, Hopton, Franklin, Brandt, and Egan immediately raided the joint armed with automatic weapons and tear gas. Unfortunately lawmen missed Sparger and Langan by just a few hours.

In the aftermath of the failed Iowa raid. the dangerous duo had taken refuge at Fay's Roadhouse and Tourist Court, located one half mile south of the small rural community of Hickman Mills, just off Highway #71, ten miles south of Kansas City proper.

The proprietor of the place, forty-six-year-old Fay Fulbright, described by officers as "heavy set and wears smoked glasses," was apparently an old friend of Langan's from his bootlegging days. Prior to relocating to the suburbs, Mrs. Fulbright, twice widowed, had operated a series of underworld connected "sporting" houses located in the downtown area of Kansas City.

Records show she was arrested in early 1933 for operating a public nuisance and selling illegal spirits. Although she pleaded guilty, was fined and placed on one years probation, Fay failed to mend her ways. She was re-arrested on November 7, 1934, for manufacturing home brew. Her case was still pending and she remained free on $2000 bond.

While staying at the establishment, the pair was joined by Clarence's wife, Juanita. The Spargers took quarters in a one-room wood frame cabin situated just behind the main roadhouse. Langan, who had been drinking heavily as of late, slept wherever his ass hit the floor.

On the evening of April 14, the pair of desperadoes attempted to hijack a filling station located on Wilson Road in Independence. The operator of the station, J. D. McCall, refused to hand over the loot instead choosing to grab a pistol he had stashed in the cash register. The gutsy clerk sprayed the pair with a half-dozen rounds, one projectile striking Langan in the right forearm. The bandits hastily departed the scene with their tails tucked between their legs, empty handed.

In the early morning hours of April 21, ten FBI agents under SAG W. A. Smith accompanied by a contingent of six Missouri Highway Patrolmen led by Colonel Casteel, and three Jackson County Deputy Sheriff's, lay in wait for several hours in the predawn darkness within spitting distance of Fay's Roadhouse. The big posse was armed to the teeth and jumpy since receiving a tip that Johnny Langan and Clarence Sparger were staying in one of the establishment's outlying tourist court cabins.

At 4:30 AM Colonel Casteel grabbed a bullhorn shouting, "Come out, the place is surrounded." Not a sound emitted from the tiny wooden frame structure except the squeak of the front door. Sparger, dressed in his underwear, stuck his head out to survey the area. Spotting the good Colonel and his trusty bullhorn, the badman raised his automatic pistol and loosed a couple of rounds of "by your leave" his way. The Colonel reacted by quickly taking refuge behind a steel car body.

In an act of either incredible courage or a demonstration of gullibility seldom seen in humans past the age of consent, FBI Agent George Franklin was singled out and somehow convinced to approach the rear of the cabin on foot in order to toss a tear gas bomb into the structure. Franklin got into position, put down his bullet-proof shield and raring back, threw a beer-can sized gas canister through the closed glass pane into the room. After tossing the grenade Franklin whirled about and began sprinting back to the posse's position. He suddenly felt something rip into his left thigh knocking him to the ground.

Hearing the shot, the itchy-fingered posse opened up with an incredible deafening crescendo of fire involving machinegun, shotgun, pistol, and rifle fire as well as a dozen tear gas canisters. Round after round smashed into the cabin.

Reacting to the disturbance, electric lights and oil lamps began to brightly apear across the nearby prairie emanating from the homes of frightened farmers. (future President Harry Truman's mother lived on a farm just a mile distant). A quar-

---

ter mile from the scene, at Lee Erb's chicken diner, his wife, Mrs. Mary Erb, was jolted out of bed hearing an, "ungodly racket." She later told reporters, "Sure I heard the shooting. I figured the law had finally caught up with that pack of thieves who had been stealing dairy cattle in these parts recently."

In a small cottage located several hundred feet to the west of the scene, an unidentified woman not only heard the sound of gunfire but felt the whir of rounds passing just inches above her head. She later stated, "I grabbed my little daughter and fled to the far side of the room hiding under a wood table where we remained until the shooting stopped. I thought it would never cease."

Thinking a bunch of drunks were setting off firecrackers, the owner of the roadhouse and her mother angrily rushed outside dressed in their flimsy nightgowns. They suddenly halted like a deer in the headlights when they observed the assembly of lawmen pointing evil looking guns their way. The pair promptly retreated back into their abode, letting the officers get on with their business.

After a short lull in the battle, Sparger, realizing resistance was useless, tossed his .45 semi-auto Colt pistol out the door and flopped outside the cabin's front door. He crawled on his hands and knees, bleeding like a stuck hog and screaming for mercy. A pair of FBI agents immediately ran to the suspect handcuffing him while a score of other officers burst into the shack pumping a couple of drums of .45 caliber slugs from a pair of "Tommy Guns" into the room just in case Clarence had any pals inside.

Almost blinded by the tear gas the agents stopped firing long enough to hear a whimper. Amazingly their flashlights uncovered an unarmed woman dressed in a skimpy nightgown and wearing no underclothes cowering in a corner of the bullet-riddled room. Tears visually streamed down her face from the effects of tear gas as she begged the officers to spare her. Miraculously, although she was suffering from a few minor bruises and glass cuts, not one of the several hundred rounds fired into the cabin had as much as scratched her. The lady, who turned out to be Clarence's wife, Juniata, was cuffed and taken into custody.

When officers searched the cabin's interior they discovered nearly every square foot of all four walls punctured with bullet holes, windows blasted out, woodwork splintered and the metal bed frame mangled. Lawmen then moved on to the main building of the court that housed a restaurant and bar. Entering the building's attic, officers discovered Johnny Langan lying on a cot passed out from the effects of strong drink seemingly without a care in the world. Lawmen noticed he was suffered from a partially healed wound to the shoulder. The wound had obviously not been inflicted in the present shootout. He was promptly shackled and placed into a police cruiser. A crowd of over 100 persons began to assemble in the resort's parking lot. Witnesses stateed once the sun came up

FBI agent WA Smith and Col. Marvin Casteel.

nearly 400 bullet holes were counted in the resort's walls. The crowd began gathering souvenirs of the event, such as spent rifle and shotgun shell casings as well as bits of broken glass and empty tear gas canisters.

On questioning, the properties' proprietor stated she had no idea of the identities of the two badmen but admitted the trio had been staying at her establishment for over a week, saying, "All I know is they paid by the day. Sometimes they hung around all day and other times they were gone all day. The man and wife registered as Mr. and Mrs. Davis. As for the other fellow, he was drunk every time I seen him."

Clarence Sparger was transported to St. Joseph's Hospital in nearby Kansas City. He was x-rayed and treated for flesh wounds to the left hip and shoulder before being moved to the infirmary at the Jackson County Jail.

Juanita Sparger

Both Juanita Sparger and Fay Fulbright were taken to the Jackson County Jail in Kansas City where they were both charged with harboring a fugitive from justice (*Mrs. Sparger would later plead guilty to the charge while Fay Fulbright demanded a trial by jury).

When questioned, Langan admitted his participation in both the Blythedale and Drexal bank jobs but denied involvement in the Coffeyville mail heist as well as the robbery of the Montgomery County Kansas treasurer. He faced a plethora of charges in-

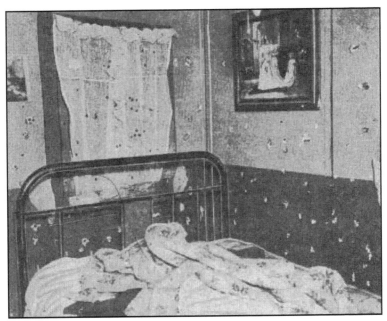

Effects of gun battle in Hickman Hills.

Resort in Hickman Hills where Sparger and Langan were captured.

Cabin where pair was captured.

Cabin after raid.

cluding two violations of the Dyer Act for stealing cars in Sioux City, Iowa, and Fall City, Nebraska, participating in a pair of Omaha robberies, the attempted murder of Deputy Red Ellsworth in Kansas as well as the Blythedale and Drexal bank robberies. His bond was set at $25,000.

Sparger was charged in several of the Omaha heists as well as the Neosho, and Blythedale bank jobs. For some reason he was never actively prosecuted for his part in the Coffeyville mail truck robbery. His bond was set at $50,000. Both men were also wanted for the attempted robbery of the bottling works in St. Joe as well as the attempted hijacking of the filling station in Independence.

Agent Franklin was moved by ambulance to Kansas City's St. Luke's Hospital where he was treated for his wound. He was given a tetanus shot by Dr. Murray Ballenger (*the same doctor who had pronounced Vivian Chase dead at the facility some time earlier). After receiving the hypo he suffered an

John Langan under arrest.

adverse reaction to the medicine going into shock. Luckily he survived the allergic reaction as well as the bullet wound.

FBI SA George Franklin.

Kansas City Star cartoon.

Resort owner Fay Fullbright under arrest for harboring

FBI wanted poster for Clarence Sparger.

Chapter 13
The Rest of the Story

Soon after Jack Miller was released from custody, the United States Fidelity Company, the insurer of the Okemah banks, sued the squealer in an effort to regain some of their missing funds, but got nowhere.

Miller managed to stay out of the limelight until early 1938. He and Frank Layton were spotted peddling illegal moonshine in the Claremore area by Federal Treasury Agents. The revenuers immediately put a tail on the pair in hopes of discovering the whereabouts of their still. On the morning of April 18, agents followed the duo to an isolated shack located in a heavily wooded area just over the Arkansas line near Siloam Springs. Later that afternoon officers raided the cabin. Although lawmen did manage to uncover a still, it had long been

Jack Miller at the time of the Okemah trials.

out of service. A hundred pounds of sugar, an essential ingredient to making illegal whiskey, was found bagged-up in the shack.

When the dejected agents searched Miller's truck, they were pleased to discover a Stevens shotgun with the barrel sawed-off to a length under eighteen-inches, a clear violation of the National Firearms Act of 1934. When arrested, the oversized hoodlum protested he was forced to carry the weapon due to his fear of reprisals from the O'Malley mob. Deaf to the defendants protests, officers lodged the pair into the Fort Smith jail.

Ironically, even though he was obviously engaged on the illegal whiskey business at the time of his arrest, Miller had long-ago given up the consumption of liquor due to diabetes.

Miller's partner, Frank Layton, was a native of Rogers County. In early life he worked as a roughneck in the Osage oil patch before turning to whiskey making as a means of support. In 1918, he and B.H. Smith were arrested in Claremore for robbing J.E. Barbara at pistol point for $3.75. Several days after their apprehension the pair was charged with hijacking A.M. Milam for "A ruby ring worth seventy-five dollars in lawful money." Layton was eventually convicted of the first robbery and sentenced to ten years in the state pen.

In early 1934 Layton was captured at a Missouri tourist court in the company of Robert Trollinger, an ex-member of the notorious bank robbing Cookson Hills Gang. Evidently the pair had as of late been engaged in robbing a series of filling stations located in Arkansas, Texas, and Oklahoma. Layton was promptly extradited back to Oklahoma.

Within days of his incarceration, Miller, in an effort to curry favor with the authorities, approached his keepers informing them of the whereabouts of Joel Carlson, who had killed a guard at the Arkansas State Penitentiary during a recent escape and was presently scouting in rural Rogers County.

Soon afterwards Miller and Layton pled guilty to the gun

charge. When counseled by Federal Judge Heartsell Ragon to withdraw their plea and plead innocent, they did, setting the stage for one of America's greatest legal disputes. Judge Ragon quickly dismissed the charges against the pair, setting them free. "The National Firearms Act is invalid since it violates the second amendment of the constitution" he stated. The pair was re-indicted on the same charge in September 1938 but made bond. Around this time, Miller's wife died of cancer and three of his five children were sent to an orphanage since Jack had no means or inclination to care for them. (One of the kids, Edward, was decorated tanker in the Korean War who wound up permanently missing in action.)

On April 2, 1939, Robert D. "Major" Taylor and two other individuals robbed the Route 66 nightclub located near Miami, Oklahoma, for approximately $100. While departing the honky-tonk a man tentatively identified as Jack Miller recklessly fired a shotgun into the crowd wounding several patrons.

The owner of the bar, Earl "Woodenfoot" Clanton, a notorious area underworld figure, one time associate of Leonard Short and the uncle of outlaw Eddy "Newt" Clanton, publicly swore vengeance on the hijackers.

The following morning, Miller was observed departing his home near Ketchum in the company of Major Taylor and a second unnamed individual. According to a witness, Taylor and his companion arrived at Miller's home in possession of a case of beer, inquiring if he wanted to go on a picnic on the banks of the Verdigris River. Jack responded in the affirmative.

At noon April 5, a farmer motoring down a gravel road near the tiny settlement of Cherokee Central, located seven miles southwest of Chelsea, spotted a large object lying in the sandy banks of Spencer Creek. On approaching the object he discovered the bullet-riddled corpse of Jack Miller. The badman had suffered five .38 caliber bullet wounds to the torso. His personal weapon, a semi-auto Colt .45 pistol, was found lying a few feet from the body. Three rounds were missing from the clip suggesting the badman had went down swinging in the final moments of his twisted life

The following day, Miller's missing 1934 Ford Sedan was discovered smoldering on an isolated dirt road in the Verdigris River bottoms just inside the Nowata County line. The automobile had been stripped of its wheels and seats before being torched. Naturally, investigators immediately suspected Miller had been executed by either "Woodenfoot" Clanton for robbing his club or remnants of the O'Malley Gang for his past damaging testimony.

After a brief service held at Claremore's Holiness church, Jack Miller's mortal remains was interred next to his recently departed wife at Woodlawn Cemetery.

When Judge Ragon requested the FBI to enter the investigation Rogers County authorities protested. In the end the Feds admitted lack of jurisdiction and backed out of the case.

Over time, the authorities became convinced Miller's killer was Major Taylor, a Chelsea native and a long time acquaintance of Jack Miller. Taylor possessed a lurid past. In 1927 he and Newt Clanton robbed the bank at Bluejacket. He was soon captured and eventually convicted of the heist and sentenced to a ten-year hitch at "Big Mac." The outlaw was paroled in 1931.

The following year he and others looted banks in Jasper and Avilla, Missouri. The authorities suspected O'Malley gangster Leonard Short played a part in at least one of those hijackings. Taylor

Grave of Jack Miller in Claremore.

was captured and convicted of both robberies. He was given a seventy-five year sentence at the Missouri pen. Just days after the trials conclusion Taylor attempted to escape custody but was thwarted when an officer shot him in the arm. In 1938 Taylor escaped from the Missouri State Penitentiary in Jeff City fleeing back to Oklahoma, hiding out with kinfolks in rural Nowata County.

Several weeks after Miller's murder, authorities captured Major Taylor in Kermit, Texas, where he was working as an oilfield roughneck. He was promptly extradited back to Oklahoma. Due to lack of hard evidence prosecutors were unable to indict him for Miller's murder. Instead, Taylor pled guilty to robbing the Route 66 Club. He was in turn sentenced to ten years at McAllister for armed robbery.

Taylor was paroled from the Oklahoma pen in the early 1940s and shipped to the Missouri Penitentiary to serve the remainder of his bank robbery term as well as an added sentence for escape. Finally given his freedom in 1954, the outlaw settled in Tulsa.

Late in life he would privately admit his complicity in the slaying of Jack Miller. According to credible sources, Taylor and the second man shot and killed the big thug in his car, dumped his body in the creek bed and after stripping his car of the tires, which they sold, set the vehicle on fire. The seats were stripped due to incriminating bloodstains.

While Taylor never admitted his motive for the killing, several theories were put forth by investigators. Some suggested Taylor killed the gambler as part of a "contract" put out by O'Malley sympathizers, while others thought the slaying sprang from either a alcohol fueled quarrel over the division of spoils from the nightclub robbery or the abrupt settling of a gambling debt. To this day, no one has ever been charged with the murder of Jack Miller.

A little over a month after Miller's death the case of *United States vs. Miller* was decided by the US Supreme Court. Their opinion amounted to a rejection of Judge Ragon's ruling. The court upheld the National Firearms Act, concluding the second amendment did not guarantee a citizens right to possess some types of firearms such as a sawed-off shotgun, automatic weapons, etc.

The landmark ruling would become settled law having a watershed impact on the nation's legal landscape and acted as a legal precedent concerning nearly all challenges to federal firearms restrictions since 1939. The case was remanded back to Fort Smith where Frank Layton was found guilty of the gun charge and given five-years probation. Layton died of natural causes in 1967 and was buried in the same cemetery in Claremore as Jack Miller, who by chance or fate will be forever remembered as a key figure in the history of American jurisprudence.

Two of Jack Miller's cousins would also leave a bloody mark on Oklahoma's criminal landscape. Henry Miller, shotgunned to death Claremore Patrolman Joseph Hause in 1954 before turning the weapon on himself after a night of drunken revelry. A second cousin, Jim Miller, fatally knifed twenty-four-year-old Jimmy Nails at a Muskogee tavern in 1962. And the beat goes on: The adventures of the Irish O'Malley-Ozark Mountain Boys Gang was chronicled in most of America's premier newspapers and crime magazines of the day. The gang received further national attention when their story was told in a December 1937 segment of the popular radio program "Gangbusters" titled "The Case of the Dan Heady Gang," But, for whatever reasons, they remain one of least known criminal enterprises of the blood-soaked depression-era Midwest Crime Wave.

The Outlaws, their Associates and Molls

As for the fates of various players involved in the narrative: John Lazia, top underworld henchman for Boss Pendergast, was shot and killed by sub-machinegun fire by his gangland competitors in mid-1934. The tough racketeer was buried at Kansas City's St. Marys Cemetery.

Robert Drake "Major" Taylor, the chief suspect in the murder of Jack Miller, took up residence in Tulsa after his 1954 parole from the Missouri State Penitentiary where died of a heart attack in 1964. He is buried near Chelsea, Oklahoma.

Fay Fulbright, the mobbed-up proprietor of the roadhouse where Sparger and Langan were arrested in the aftermath of the 1936 gun-duel with G-Men, was convicted of harboring felons and sentenced to a two-year term. In mid-1937 the verdict was overturned by the US Circuit Court of Appeals. Ms Fulbright died in 1954 of a burst gallbladder. She was buried at Kansas City's Memorial Park Cemetery.

Leonard Short associate Homer Hight was paroled from his five-year sentence in connection with the 1933 Model Bakery heist in March 1936. On the evening of April 21st Homer, along with three other men and a woman were motoring down US Highway #65 just south of Springfield when they stumbled into a roadblock manned by a dozen officers commanded by Missouri Highway Patrol Sgt. O. L. Viets. The car's occupants were later identified as Hight, Miss Pearl Good, a waitress at Wilma's Café located on Boonville Avenue in Springfield, fifty-year-old Harry Thomas, an old-time safe-cracker from Kansas City, his protégé, nineteen-year-old Robert Edward Rice, also of Kansas City, as well as an individual from Howell County named Lindsey.

Lawmen suspected the group was responsible for a dozen recent area burglaries. When the vehicle, which was stolen, was searched, investigators discovered a horde of pirated articles including several new shotguns. Also found in the vehicle's trunk was a dozen blasting caps, a bottle of nitro, and various burglary tools.

When Thomas, the gray-haired professional yeggman from Kansas City, was questioned he haughtily threw his head back, exclaiming, "Sir, I resent being called a safecracker. I am a safe expert of the first order and I want to be addressed as such." He then pointed to his young companion saying in a fatherly manner, "I am currently schooling this lad in the art of hijacking." Homer Hight informed officers in no uncertain terms, "I ain't talking. I'll just take the rap and skip the chatter."

While Hight was eventually released from custody it didn't mean he was out of the woods. A month later the incorrigible thief was arrested on a charge of burglary of a private residence. He was eventually convicted of the crime and sentenced to a term of six months in the Greene County Jail.

In June of 1941, Homer and Robert E. Rice, were charged with burglarizing a Gainesville, Missouri, bank. After a time the charges were dropped but replaced with armed robbery of a Joplin filling station. In July a Jasper County Judge sentenced both men to a term a forty years incarceration. Hight's lawyer appealed the sentence due to both defendants being forced to wear shackles in court, thus creating a bad impression to the jury. The Missouri State Supreme Court refused to overturn the ruling but did reduce the sentence from forty to ten years labeling the previous sentence "Harsh."

Harry Blee, a participant in the 1935 Neosho bank robbery, was captured on July 20, 1937, by agents of the FBI in Los Angeles, California. He had been working as a filling station attendant under an assumed name. He was transported by train to Kansas City under heavy guard where he was under indictment for the Neosho heist. The highwayman pled guilty to the bank robbery charge in 1938 and was sentenced to a twenty-five year term. Blee was paroled in 1947 and died in California in 1960.

Dave Sherman attempted to escape from a Texas prison farm in 1944 and was punished by being given 20 lashes with a whip and 27 days solitary confinement. Records indicate that during his stay at Huntsville he spent some time in the TB ward. He was given a conditional parole in 1951 and allowed to relocate to Denver, Colorado.

Soon after being granted his freedom, Sherman and an accomplice were involved in a holdup and gun-battle in Golden, Colorado, in which a deputy sheriff was wounded. Although Sherman's partner was captured the badman was somehow able to slip the net.

Shortly thereafter, he relocated to southern California where he reconnected with "Blackie" Doyle and Spike Lane. Doyle had received his parole from Texas in March 1951 and moved to Los Angeles. Lane was released from Texas custody in April 1950 and handed over to Oklahoma where he was tried and sentenced to a prison term for a 1934 larceny. Upon his release he also drifted to the "Golden State." Thus the stage was set for the final comeback of the remnants of the O'Malley gang.

Over the next eighteen months the trio was involved in the robbery of a half-dozen supermarkets in the Los Angeles area including two in Long Beach, one in Gardena, another in Santa Monica as well as two others in South L.A. They also robbed a furniture store as well as a bank messenger carrying a payroll.

The gang's M.O. usually involved following armored trucks as they made cash deliveries to various stores before raiding the business's just moments after the delivery was made. In late 1954 law enforcement personal launched a series of raids at various locations in Long Beach where the suspects were residing, capturing Lane, Sherman, Doyle, and Raymond Wagoner, a one-time member of the notorious Ralph Sheldon Gang. Apprehended with Sherman was his latest sweetheart, thirty-seven-year-old Beulla Balenti. Reports state Sherman was captured with a pistol and $1500 cash crammed in his coat pocket.

At their preliminary hearings, a spokesman for the Long Beach PD robbery detail claimed the quartet had stolen over

$100,000 in various holdups. "We have been watching and trailing these fellows for nearly a year and this investigation makes the TV and dime novel detective stunts look silly." He added, "This is the toughest band of criminals to work this area in ten years."

All three ex-O'Malley mobsters were convicted of armed robbery and spent time in various California prisons. Soon after his release, Sherman's parole was revoked and the outlaw was sent back to Texas to serve out his original fifty-year sentence. His parole was reinstated in 1961 and again revoked in 1963. He was paroled from the Texas prison system for the final time in 1969 and died of heart failure in 1970 at his home in Houston, just months after his release from prison.

Russell "Spike" Lane died from the effects of a drug overdose in 1962 while residing in Los Angeles.

Lloyd "Blackie" Doyle simply drifted into obscurity.

James Maroon, who harbored O'Malley and Dan Heady in Kansas City, was slain by persons unknown in gangland fashion on November 30, 1940.

Soon after his February 1935 capture, Jess Doyle cut a deal with prosecutors, pleading guilty to participating in the Fairbury, Nebraska, bank heist. He was sentenced to ten years imprisonment at the Nebraska State Prison at Lincoln. As a reward for his guilty plea a charge of robbing the Independence, Kansas, treasurer was dropped.

In mid-1937, after serving a little over a year of his ten-year term, Doyle was paroled to federal and Kansas authorities in order to testify at the trials of all involved in both the Independence and Coffeyville mail-hack robberies.

As a direct result of his testimony, as well as that of Edna "Rabbit" Murray's, South Coffeyville crime-boss Tommy Hill was convicted of masterminding the Coffeeville mail job. The salty middle-aged thug received a light two-year federal sentence, but unfortunately for him, the state of Kansas was not so forgiving. Since the moon-faced bandit had recently been convicted of conspiracy in the case of the January 9, 1933, robbery of the Union Gas Co. of Coffeyville, as well as numerous liquor violations in the past, Kansas authorities branded him a "habitual" criminal, which qualified him for an added bonus, a life term, as required by a new state law in regards to repeat felonious offenders.

Even though the lawyers of Alvin Sherwood put up a game court battle he was convicted of acting as the fingerman in the Independence hijacking.

On the conclusion of Jess Doyle's giving testimony against his ex-crime partners he was sentenced to a twenty-five-year federal sentence for his part in the Coffeyville mail heist. Doyle died in 1947 of natural causes while serving time at the Atlanta Federal Penitentiary.

Doyle's pal Volney Davis was sentenced to Life imprisonment for the Bremer kidnapping. He was paroled in 1959 after doing time at Alcatraz and Leavenworth and pardoned in 1966. He died in 1979 and was buried at Evergreen Cemetery in Sebestopol, California. His gal, Edna Murray was paroled in 1940 and died in 1966 in San Francisco. She is buried at the Golden Gate National Cemetery.

Clarence Sparger was convicted of the March 2, 1935, Neosho bank robbery in federal court in Kansas City on May 18, 1936. He was sentenced to a twenty-five-year jolt and promptly transported to nearby Leavenworth Federal Penitentiary. According to US Prosecutor Maurice Milligan, Sparger was arguably the worst of the O'Malley Gang.

When Sparger was processed at Leavenworth prison officials noted he was habitual criminal and a constant menace to society. They recommended his transfer to Alcatraz due to the probability of his being a disciplinary problem, stating he needed "maximum supervision." On admission to 'The Big Top' he was noted as being in poor physical shape and still suffering from the results of recent gunshot wounds. Sparger was also described as underweight, walked with a limp, possible hernia, and suffering from gonorrhea. Penal reports went on to state he was emotionally unstable, had an IQ of 82, harboring no respect for authority and openly hostile toward society.

Sparger was transferred to 'The Rock' on August 6, 1936, and returned to Leavenworth in 1945. He was finally given his freedom a few years later. Although prosecutors held a Robbery of US Mails charge hanging over his head for over a decade they ultimately chose not to press the issue, letting the matter drop. Clarence inherited his mothers estate after her death in 1952 and apparently spent his remaining years operating a bar in his hometown of St. Joseph, Missouri. He died in 1977 at the age of seventy-three.

Sparger's pal, Johnny Langan was convicted in state court in Bethany, Missouri, for the burglary of the Blythdale bank. He was sentenced to a ten-year term to be served at the Missouri State Penitentiary.

Soon after his state conviction Langan pled guilty in federal court in Kansas City to two counts of the National Motor Vehicle Act and was given dual five–year sentences to be served concurrently upon his release from Jeff City. Evidently as a reward for his guilty plea federal prosecutors dropped the Robbery of US Mails charge regarding the incident in Coffeyville. Langan was never prosecuted for his alleged participation in the 1935 Independence, Kansas, robbery.

Prison records indicate Langan was highly intelligent and cooperative in nature. He worked as a clerk in the rope factory at Jefferson City. On July 1, 1942, the outlaw was released from the Missouri pen and brought directly to Leavenworth Federal Penitentiary in order to serve his federal sentences. A detainer was immediately placed in his folder by Drexal, Missouri, authorities concerning a charge of bank robbery. The detainer was waived when the bank was reimbursed for their loss by their insurance company. Upon his conditional release from Leavenworth on November 16, 1945, Langan relocated to California where he died at the age of fifty-seven in 1957.

Floyd Henderson also moved to the "Golden State" finally settling near San Francisco where he passed on in 1950 at the age of fifty-four. His earthly remains were returned to Joplin for burial.

In 1939 Walter "Irish" O' Malley was transferred to the psychiatric division of the Illinois State Prison at Menard after complaining of mental delusions and hallucinations. Prison authorities described him as a disciplinary problem with highly schizophrenic tendencies. For the first few years of his incarceration O'Malley was involved in numerous disciplinary infractions that included fighting, stealing and disorderly conduct .

One morning he simply woke up and refused to leave his cell stating, " I do not wish to be sent to the salt mines as a slave to the Germans." He then began complaining of a buzzing in his head and spent the rest of the day babbling incoherently. The following day he was reclassified and summarily dispatched to a padded room where he spent the rest of his days until he passed away on May 1, 1944, from heart failure.

As for the other Luer kidnappers, Randol Norvell and a companion escaped from the Southern Illinois Penitentiary in Menard on the afternoon of April 26, 1934, by crawling twelve-hundred yards though a vile waste-coated sewer pipe until they spilled out on the banks of the Mississippi River. They quickly commandeered a rowboat and rowed to the Missouri side. The pair soon split up, Norvell making his way to East St. Louis. His partner was captured napping in a hobo camp two days after the escape.

Norvell remained on the lam for forty-nine days until a posse led by Madison County Sheriff Peter Fitzgerald pinched him at an East St. Louis boarding house. Five other inhabitants of the residence were charged with harboring the fugitive.

Investigators found a seventeen page handwritten letter addressed to August Luer in the fugitives possession. The correspondence amounted to a pathetic rant by the outlaw claiming he had been the victim of a "railroad job" concerning his 1933 kidnapping trial. In 1944, the badman filed suit against the state of Illinois stating he had been repeatedly tortured by guards over the years, thus suffering cruel and unusual punishment while incarcerated. The state Supreme Court found no merit in the suit. He was paroled in 1955 and relocated to a rural Pulaski County Missouri fishing village where he died in 1974 at the age of seventy-four.

Charles Chessen and Christ Gitcho, who both played minor parts in the Luer snatch, were paroled in 1937 after completing three-years and nine months of their original five-year sentences.

Lillian Chessen was released from custody on October 23, 1955, after serving twenty-two-years and twenty-one-days of her life sentence. Michael Musiala was paroled in the early 1940s.

Perry "Dice Box Kid" Fitzgerald was killed in 1964 when the car he was driving was cut in two by a speeding Wabash Railroad freight train near Illiopolis, Illinois.

August Luer, the victim in the case, passed on at the age of eighty-six in 1942 and is buried in Alton, Illinois next to his wife who died in 1939.

Muskogee escapee Donnie "D. C." Garrett was received at Alcatraz August 6, 1936, where he faced a seven-year sentence for white slavery. His classification report from Leavenworth stated Garrett had a near-moron IQ and was a sexual degenerate who enjoyed the company of questionable characters. "A classic drifter who lived most of his life in abandoned automobiles and cheap flophouses." Reports went on to claim he was in good physical condition, although he admitted suffering from venereal disease in the past.

Due to his escape history, Garrett was classified as a flight risk and it was recommended he be housed at Alcatraz. After serving some eighteen months on The Rock, he was transferred back to Leavenworth to finish out his term. A letter was attached to his prison records written by Muskogee County Sheriff Jordan that read, "As for Donnie Garrett; we will extradite on notice from your office of his release. It is not our intension to prosecute him for murder but we have four felony counts against him." In the end Oklahoma officials failed to follow through with the threat of extradition. Garrett died in Leavenworth, Kansas, in 1975.

On his initial arrival at Leavenworth, Virgil "Red" Melton was categorized as an extreme escape risk and a menace to society. Since he was judged in need of close supervision, Melton was shipped off to Alcatraz. He was transferred back to Leavenworth in October 1945, yet still categorized as a notorious offender.

In March of 1948, he was released from federal custody and turned over to the state of Missouri, which he owed a ten-year sentence for bank robbery. On being processed into the facility officials described Melton as Height-5'11"-Weight-

Red Melton at Alcatraz

163lbs.-Eyes-gray Hair-red, with a shoulder sporting a rose and scroll adorned with the name "Mother."

On the afternoon of September 17, 1950, Melton and August Overbeck, who was serving a life term for murdering a soldier with a claw hammer, along with a burglar named Charles Bales, walked away from State Prison Farm #2 located north of Jeff City across the Missouri River.

When the trio reached civilization they hijacked taxi driver George Hewitt forcing him to transport them to the community of Eldon by means of holding a handmade shiv firmly against his neck. Unfortunately for the escapees after enjoying their freedom for only a few hours they were spotted by a state highway patrol cruiser and taken into custody. The trio were charged with armed robbery and escape.

While sitting in the Cole County Jail awaiting trial on the armed robbery charge, a not so bright corrections officer allowed Melton and Overbeck outside their cells in order to wash and wax certain county owned vehicles. When the officer returned to the jail proper to retrieve a bottle of car wax the evil pair simply turned on the ignition of the car they were washing and drove into the bone-chilling night. When interviewed by the media the embarrassed officer in question, Horace Debo, stated, "It's nobody's fault but mine. I guess it's a case of being too big-hearted." His boss, Cole County Sheriff Ben Markway, disagreed calling the incident a "Simple dereliction of duty" adding, "It won't happen again." The Sherriff went on to inform the journalist, "Overbeck is a killer and one of the meanest inmates I've ever come in contact with. Melton is not much better"

In response to the escape, spotter planes were sent into the sky while dozens of officers took to the field setting up roadblocks while closely watching bridges and crossroads. Local radio station KWOS broadcast a description of the escapees, calling them both extremely dangerous. The car used in the jail delivery was discovered abandoned just south of Jefferson City the following morning. Bloodhounds were brought in but soon lost the scent.

At midnight, just nine hours after the pair had departed the jailhouse garage, Dr. E. R. Price, heard a knock on the door of his up-scale Jeff City residence. When the physician answered the door he was greeted with the sight of a bedraggled character, dressed in dirty clothes, his face scratched and his hands blue and shaking from the bitter cold. The man stated "I'm Melton. I want to turn myself in." The doctor , trying not to show fear to the interloper, calmly informed him to sit on the porch while he phoned police. Moments later the half-starved inmate was returned to his warm cell.

Eight hours after Melton's capture two officers on routine patrol spotted Overbeck ambling down an alley just blocks from where his companion had surrendered, his hands crammed in his pockets and shaking from head to toe. On seeing the lawmen, the outlaw raised his hands in submission.

Overbeck would later inform the authorities he and Melton had been living on some raw ears of corn and a few eggs they had stolen from a chicken coop. He also stated they spent the first night on the loose sleeping in a barn located less than a mile from where they had abandoned their getaway car.

Apparently the bloodhounds had circled the barn but quickly lost interest even though their quarry was slumbering just a few feet away. "We heard 'em bellering and seen 'em run right past the barn door. I thought they had us treed for sure!" claimed Overbeck.

On March 20, 1951, Judge Foster Wheartly sentenced both men to serve an extra five years for robbery and two more for escape.

Melton was paroled from Jeff City in 1959, but within a month of his release he was arrested and charged with a federal parole violation and sent back to Leavenworth. The incorrigible rouge was eventually given his final discharge and relocated to Kilgore, Texas, where he lived with his mother and brother, who owned a laundry, for many years. Melton died in 1994, the last surviving member of the Irish O'Malley Gang. The badman would go down in history as one of the most prolific, yet little known, bank robbers of the depression-era.

Fred Reese was transferred to Alcatraz shortly after his arrival at Leavenworth. A prison psychiatrist noted in a report

"Subject is of the vicious type and due to his bad nature will probably attempt to dominate his fellow inmates." In 1938, he was shipped to the Federal Prison Hospital in Springfield, Missouri where he remained in poor health well into the latter 1950s. Reese was finally released from custody around 1966.

Fred Reese

Russell Cooper at Sprinfield Medical Center for prisoners.

He relocated to Farmington, Missouri, where he died on January 1972 at the age of seventy-six. The badman's mortal remains were shipped back to the place of his youth in tiny Koshkonong and buried in a country graveyard next to his mother.

Russell Land Cooper was sent to Alcatraz as well when prison officials at Leavenworth noted he refused to admit his guilt, instead claiming he was the victim of perjured testimony and "would not hesitate to take advantage of any opportunity to escape." Cooper was transferred back to Leavenworth in 1948 and paroled some years later. President Lyndon Johnson issued Cooper an executive pardon in 1964. He died in April of 1971 in Fort Smith, Arkansas, and is buried at the Fayetteville National Cemetery.

Dewey Gilmore was sent to Alcatraz on April 26, 1936, where doctors dug a small bullet fragment out of his left side. Officials there observed he was, "a nervous, high strung individual of the viscous type who would likely resort to violent acts to evade taking responsibility for his actions."

The bandit informed officers he was in fear of his life,

since there were inmates at the facility who had knowledge of his testimony against his crime partners. He noted, "I haven't had a good nights sleep since the trial." In fact, US Marshal Allan Stanfield stated publicly Gilmore would not last a month on The Rock while Muskogee Police Chief Marsh Corgan stated, "Dewey is worried about his future as he should be. I suspect they will kill him in prison."

He fooled them all. In 1949, he was transferred to the Federal Medical Facility for prisoners in Springfield where he stayed until 1954. He sued the state of Missouri for wrongful imprisonment concerning the time he spent in jail for the 1933 filling station robbery. The Missouri State Supreme court eventually dismissed the suit. In August of the same year, Gilmore was paroled back into society taking up residence in Joplin for a time before re-marrying and relocating to Lima, Ohio. He worked as a successful clothes-tailor for many years, a trade he likely learned in prison. Gilmore died at the age of eight-five on September 1, 1983, at St. Ritas Medical Center in Lima. Rumor has it, Gilmore kept a private journal concerning his adventures with the O'Malley Gang, which disappeared upon his death.

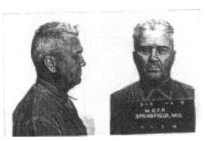

Dewey Girlmore

Grave for Russell Cooper

Arthur Glenn Austin was eventually transferred from El Reno Federal Reformatory to a similar facility in Milan, Michigan where he was paroled in January 1939. He died in the early 1960s.

Jack Richards was paroled from the Missouri State Penitentiary in the 1950s. What became of him is unknown.

After his release from prison, Epp Melton (involved in both the Neosho and Seneca bank robberies) returned to farming, or ,at least, so he claimed. He died in 1943 at the age of fifty-nine from the effects of tuberculosis, which he had contracted during his incarceration. Melton is buried at the Oronogo Cemetery located in Jasper County Missouri.

His brother "Kate" operated a successful Joplin nightclub dubbed the Chicken Inn throughout the 1940-50s. He passed on to his reward in 1962 and was buried at the Webb City Cemetery in Missouri.

The Good Guys

Okfuskee County Deputy Roy Mogridge, who was present at the Jack Fork Mountain shootout, went on to serve as a state investigator and a U.S. Treasury Agent in Alaska during WWII, as well as a special investigator for Oklahoma Governor Lee Phillips. Mogridge died in 1964.

John Marsh Corgan, the slayer of escapee John Blackburn, was forced to resign as Muskogee's Chief of Police in May 1936. He soon became mentally depressed over his misfortune. On the morning of September 4, the legendary lawman took is own life by way of shotgun to the mouth. Corgan was buried as Muskogee's Greenhill Cemetery.

Deputy US Marshal Allan Stanfield, who led the effort to capture members of the O'Malley Gang after their escape from the Muskogee County Jail, was involved in a ferocious gun battle with a seventeen-year-old subject in February 1937 in which Pontotoc County Deputy Alvis Jones was slain. Stanfield was grievously wounded in the affair. He retired from the Marshal's Service in 1962 and accepted a commission to serve as a Pontotoc County Deputy Sheriff the following year. In 1965, he retired altogether from law enforcement and passed away the following year at his daughters' home in Michigan.

Officer Ellsworth "Red" Edwards, who shot and killed the wife of John Langan and was in turn severely wounded for his troubles in a bloody gunbattle taking place at White Chapel, Kansas, went on to serve as Sheriff of Wyandotte County Kansas 1943-47 and 1951-55. He died in Kansas City, Kansas, in 1998 at the age of ninety.

Muskogee County Sheriff Tom Jordan, the leader the Jack Fork Mt. manhunt, served as sheriff until 1947. He died of a heart attack at the age of 53 in 1956 while on patrol as a Muskogee City Policeman. He is buried at Memorial Cemetery in Muskogee.

Paul Frey, the Chief of Police in Springfield, Missouri, 1932-40, who had vast dealings with members of the Ozark Mountain Boys, died at the age of eight-three in 1967. Late in life, he was appointed State Chaplain for the Missouri American Legion. Frey was a highly decorated veteran of the First World War.

William "Billy" Schmulbach, the slayer of Vivian Chase's common-law husband, Charley Mayes, continued his controversial and blood-soaked career as a lawman. During the hunt for notorious badman Wilbur Underhill in 1927, Billy shot and severely wounded a man who refused to submit to questioning. Later that same year the wayward peace officer killed a Kansas farmer named Hugh Herrill that he incorrectly suspected of being an armed prowler.

On October 4, 1930, Schmulbach was involved in a fifth killing when he gunned-down the town druggist. Apparently, the pharmacist, Frank Carlock, who owed the lawman a $1000 gambling debt, had just parked in front of his business in the company of a young lady when Billy approached him demanding immediate repayment of the debt. Carlock exited the car and started making his way to the store when the cop shot him in the back. Carlock screamed and continued running toward the store's front door while Billy pumped three more slugs into his backside. The following day Ottawa County Sheriff Dee Watters arrested Billy on a charge of murder. Several months later, Schmulbach was convicted of first-degree murder and sentenced to life imprisonment. The errant lawman was paroled on December 30, 1935, and given a full pardon in 1938. Schmulbach died in 1946 at the age of seventy-one. The outlaw/lawman was buried at Joplin's Fairview Cemetery..

As for Dewey Short, he was elected to numerous successive terms in Congress, 1935-1957, and was chairman of the powerful Armed Forces Committee and a congressional delegate to inspect Germany's concentration camps at the close of WWII. His picture once graced the cover of Time magazine. From 1957-1961, he served as the Assistant Secretary of the Army before retiring and spending the rest of his days as a lecturer and an ardent supporter of all things Republican.

Dewey S. Short died in 1979. He was justifiably eulogized as a decent and honorable man who played a key role in the stirring pageantry of twentieth century American history. The "Orator of the Ozarks" was buried at the little hilltop cemetery in Galena, Missouri, near his outlaw brother.

The O'Malley Gang was back in the news a final time in the fall of 1953 in connection with the case of six-year-old kidnap victim Bobby Greenlease.

A woman named Bonnie Brown Heady along with her alcoholic lover, Carl Austin Hall, snatched the youth from a catholic school located in St Joseph, Missouri, on September 28. After brutally murdering and burying the poor child in Heady's back yard, the lurid couple contacted the lad's father, a wealthy area Cadillac dealer, demanding a $600,000 ransom for his return. The pair was arrested in St. Louis just days after receiving the loot.

Shortly after Bonnie Heady's arrest a FBI spokesman informed the national press Miss Heady possessed a grim past, stating a check of the records indicated she was in reality the notorious Betty Heady, who was involved in the escape of a group of prisoners from a jail in Muskogee County Oklahoma in 1935. Several days after releasing this lurid bit of information the feds made a rare apology, stating a clerk in the identification section had made a terrible mistake. A check of fingerprints proved Bonnie Heady was not Betty Heady after all.

By all indications, Director J. Edger Hoover was not pleased at the snafu and the bureau was soon short one clerk. Bonnie Heady and Carl Austin Hall were promptly convicted of murder in the case and both were executed by means of cyanide gas on December 18, 1953.

As for the real Betty Heady, according to FBI records she was arrested on May 3, 1938, in Danville, Illinois on a charge of prostitution then indicted for Harboring Wanted Felons in California in 1948. What became of her after that date is unknown.

Nowadays the hills and hollers of Stone County, Missouri, are known more for their illicit methamphetamine labs than moonshine stills. The names Leonard Short and Red Melton have little meaning to its citizens, being replaced in area folklore by modern-day meth outlaws like Darrell Mease, who was given a reprieve from a death sentence for committing a triple murder by Governor Mel Carnahan in honor of Pope John Paul II's 1999 visit to St. Louis.

The county seat in Galena is still a picturesque little berg bypassed by the economic benefits provided by the country music explosion located twenty-odd miles south in Branson. The people seem not to mind very much. They are a clannish bunch. There is a museum on the square dedicated to the memory of Dewey Short, who was the most prominent citizen to ever come out of the area. It's doubtful local folks are ashamed of Leonard and his dubious doings, but figure outsiders might be, so they just stick to talking about Dewey.

In the peaceful county seat town of Okemah, Oklahoma, the scene of the O'Malley gang's most spectacular robbery, the biggest event of the year nowadays is the annual Woody Guthrie Folk Festival. Folk music enthusiasts from all over the globe congregate to hear singers such as Arlo Guthrie, Bob Dylan, Pete Seeger, Neil Young, and "Wild Bill " Elliott attempt to do justice to the "Father" of American Folk Music. For a few days, a steady stream of penniless long-haired folkees hailing from the east and west coasts, along with cadre of well-groomed conservative ranchers as well as middle-aged traditional house wives, admirers of all things Woody, congregate and ignore their vast cultural differences while sitting shoulder to shoulder in Okemah's Crystel Theatre. The same theatre was holding a production of a high school play the night before the infamous 1934 double robberies.

Downtown Okemah has changed little in the past seventy-odd years. Even today, standing next to the now vacant Okemah National Bank building on an early Winter's morn, if the light is right and there is just a bit of biting cold in the air ,one can still close their eyes and, with enough imagination, clearly envision a street full of hard men, equipped with fast cars and armed with deadly weapons, swiftly making their way out of town with a screech of tires, their pockets crammed full of evil gains as their larcenous souls enjoy every minute of it...

-The End-

Sources

Books

Hayde, Frank R.-*The Mafia and the Machine: The Story of the Kansas City Mob*- Barricade Books 2007

Butler, Ken- *More Oklahoma Renegades*- Pelican Publishing Co.-2007

Goins, Charles Robert, and Goble, Danney- *Historical Atlas of Oklahoma*-University of Oklahoma Press-Norman-2007

Helmer, William and Mattix Rick- *Public Enemies: America's Criminal Past*- Checkmark Books-1998

Neosho: A City of Springs-Newton County Historical Society-Neosho Printing Co.-1984

History of Stone County, Missouri-Stone County Historical Society-1989

Okemah Remembered- Okfuskee County Historical Society

Reddig, William- *Tom's Town: Kansas City and the Pendergast Legend*- J. B. Lippincott Company- Philadelphia 1947

Morgan, R. D. –*The Tri-State Terror-The life and Crimes of Wilbur Underhill*-New Forums Press-2005

Morgan, R.D.-*Taming the Sooner State*-New Forums Press-Stillwater, Oklahoma-2007

Montgomery, Rick and Kasper, Shirl- *Kansas City: An American Story*-Kansas City Star Books-1999

Gregory, George H.- *Alcatraz Screw*- University of Missouri Press-2002

Brown, Jack-*Monkey Off My Back*- Zondervan Publishing House-Grand Rapids, Michigan-1971

Burroughs, Bryan-Public Enemies, *Penguin Press. NY, NY 2004*

Wiley, Robert S. -*Dewey Short: Orator of the Ozarks*- Cassville, Missouri-Litho Books-1985

Oklahoma Almanac—Oklahoma Department of Libraries-2007

When the Banks Closed, We Opened Our Hearts: Memories of the Great Depression- Reiman Publications-Greendale, Wisconson-1999

Articles and Periodicals

Bates, Robert E. -*Irish O'Malley and the Okemah Caper*-Oklahombres Journal-Summer 2001

Higgins, Thomas J.-*The Flaming Career of the Red-Haired Gun Moll*-Startling Detective-June 1936

Faherty, Robert-*The Illinois Snatcher and his Daring Break*-Startling Detective-May 1935

Beerman, Brian-Life After the Barkers, *On The Spot Journal*

Butler, Ken-The Gooch Hanging, *Oklahombres Journal*

Webb, Mike-*Egan's Rats*-On the Spot Journal-Spring 2008

Beerman, Brian-*The Assassination of John Lazia*—On the Spot Journal-Spring 2008

General Sources

National Archives (NARA) Joe Sanchez -San Bruno, Cal.-Alcatraz Prison Records

Wyandotte County Sheriff's Department-Kansas

Johnson County Sheriff's Department-Kansas

Muskogee County, Oklahoma-Clerk of Court-Court records

U.S. Marshals Service- Eastern District of Oklahoma-Muskogee-Marshal Jack Lloyd

Pittsburg County Genealogy Society-Oklahoma

Greene County Achieves and Records Center-Springfield, Mo.

Greene County Historical Society-Springfield, Mo.

Pottawattamie County Genealogy Society-Council Bluffs-IA

Oregon County-Archives-Missouri

US Social Security death records

Ohio death records

Texas death records

California death records

Greenhill Cemetery records-Muskogee, Ok.

Online archives-Dewitt County Illinois Genealogy

US Census-Ancestry.com-1880-1900-1910-1920-1930

Illinois State Historical Society

Koshkonong, Mo. Historical Society -Mary Lee Pease

Oklahoma Historical Society

Federal Bureau of Prisons
Muskogee Police Department-Public Information Office-Ok.
NARA-Tim Rives- Kansas City-
Leavenworth US Penitentiary Records
NARA-Washington DC- FBI records
NARA- Vance Randolph Collection
Greene County Archives and Records Center- Bob Neuman-Springfield, Mo.
Kansas Department of Corrections
Illinois Department of Corrections
Oklahoma Department of Corrections
Missouri Department of Corrections
Texas Department of Corrections
Nebraska Department of Corrections
California Department of Corrections
California State Archives
Missouri State Archives-Death Records
Missouri Historical Society
Kansas Historical Society
Libraries and Research Facilities-

Oklahoma
Muskogee Public Library
Okemah Library
Claremore Public Library
Okmulgee Public Library
Reiger Memorial Library-Haskell
Vinita Library
McAlester Public Library
Three Rivers Museum-Roger Bell and Linda Moore-Muskogee

Missouri
Galena- Stone County Library
Kansas City Public Library-Special Collections-
Dan Coleman
Neosho Library
Joplin Public Library

Webb City Library and Historical Society
Springfield-Greene County Library System- Local History and Genealogy Department -Michael Glenn

Arkansas
Fayetteville Library
Fort Smith Library

Newspapers

Missouri
Springfield Leader Press and Daily News
Kansas City Journal-Post
Kansas City Star
Kansas City Times
Neosho Times
Webb City Sentinel
St. Joseph News Press
St. Louis Post Dispatch
St. Louis Globe
Jefferson City Post-Tribune
Joplin Globe
Leavenworth Times

Kansas
Galena Times
Coffeyville Daily Journal

Oklahoma
Ada Weekly
Muskogee Times-Democrat
Muskogee Phoenix
Tulsa Daily World
Daily Oklahoman
McAlester News Capitol

Claremore Daily Progress
Vinita Leader
Hartshorne Sun
Okemah Daily Leader

Arkansas
Fayetteville Daily Democrat
Fort Smith Southwest American

Illinois
Alton Evening Telegraph
Decatur Sunday Review
Edwardsville Intelegencer

Indiana
Indianapolis Star-Indiana

Texas
Dallas Morning News

Nebraska
Omaha Bee-News
Omaha World-Herald
Lincoln Star
Lincoln Evening Journal

California
Long Beach Independent-California
Long Beach Press Telegram-Cal.
L.A. Times

418 64 7 77 2

Made in the USA
Lexington, KY
01 October 2013